ON THE SAME PAGE

Shared Reading Beyond the Primary Grades

Janet Allen

S

Stenhouse Publishers
Portland, Maine

Stenhouse Publishers
www.stenhouse.com

Credits are on pages 306–307.

Library of Congress Cataloging-in-Publication Data
Allen, Janet, 1950–
    On the same page : shared reading beyond the primary grades / Janet Allen.
    p. cm.
    Includes bibliographical references.
    ISBN 1-57110-332-5 (alk. paper)
    1. Reading (Secondary) 2. Middle school students—Books and reading 3. High school students—Books and reading 4. Literature—Study and teaching (Secondary) I. Title.
LB1632.A555 2002
807'.1'2—dc21   2002074342

Cover design by Diana Coe
Cover photographs by Donald Mitchell and Melanie Marks

Manufactured in the United States of America on acid-free paper
08 07 06 05 04 03 02 9 8 7 6 5 4 3 2 1

To my friends, new and old, who love to share the magic of exploring a great book.

Contents

Acknowledgments

In his book *Loser*, Jerry Spinelli writes, "As with all discoveries, it is the eye and not the object that changes." For many years, my students and I reveled in the richness of shared reading. We never questioned its value because we lived with the rewards of our shared literary experiences. I am still grateful for the gift of those early teaching experiences—for the students who taught me and the principal, Aaron Nelson, who let me find my way.

I know that shared reading is still a rich approach that supports teaching and learning in schools today because my eyes have changed. I am honored to have the opportunity to learn in schools where administrators and teachers help children discover the art and craft of a literate life. During my days in these schools and classrooms, I have had the joy of seeing shared reading through new eyes. I now learn through the eyes of students who finally discover a book that will be cherished for a lifetime; the eyes of teachers who rediscover why they chose the teaching profession; and the eyes of administrators who are given the gift of watching schools reinvent themselves. I am particularly grateful to the administrators of three schools who have supported the approach of shared reading with professional development for teachers, diverse resources for the school and classrooms, and the powerful model of their own reading:

Toni Issa Lahera, Washington Intensive Learning Center, Long Beach, California
Mary Louise Martin, Wilson Middle School, San Diego, California
Don Mitchell, Gompers Secondary School, San Diego, California

I count these administrators as my colleagues and friends and have learned much from our journey together.

The examples of shared reading in action presented in this book have come from educators whose classrooms are alive with books. These teachers know the value of reading and refuse to let the challenges of teaching take them away from the real goal of helping children become confident, competent, and passionate readers and writers. This book is more practical and has greater voice because of their work.

The following teachers and administrators have shared the products of their teaching and learning experiences. I am grateful for the work they do and for sharing that work with me.

Ann Bailey, Marshall Middle School, Long Beach, California
John Bailey, Los Nietos Middle School, Whittier, California
Lori Benitiz, Washington Intensive Learning Center, Long Beach, California
Kathy Burns, Wilson Middle School, San Diego, California
Elaine Coulson, McLane Middle School, Tampa, Florida
Jennifer Economos-Green, Lake Clifton Eastern High School, Baltimore, Maryland
Lynnette Elliott, Odyssey Middle School, Orlando, Florida
Mary Giard, The Center, Auburn, Maine
Toni Issa Lahera, Washington Intensive Learning Center, Long Beach, California
Christine Landaker, Liberty Middle School, Orlando, Florida
Melanie Marks, Gompers Secondary School, San Diego, California
Mary Louise Martin, Wilson Middle School, San Diego, California
Virginia May, Washington Intensive Learning Center, Long Beach, California
Mary McDaniel, Gompers Secondary School, San Diego, California
Don Mitchell, Gompers Secondary School, San Diego, California
Bernie Nguyen, Wilson Middle School, San Diego, California
Jenny Orr, Miller Middle School, Macon, Georgia
Beth Scanlon, Timber Creek High School, Orlando, Florida
Lee Ann Spillane, University High School, Orlando, Florida
Elizabeth Trude, Gompers Secondary School, San Diego, California

As always, my friends and family have supported my writing in ways that make good days great and difficult days tolerable. They alter plans to give me writing time when necessary and make new plans so we can enjoy time together when avoiding writing is equally necessary. I am fortunate to have a circle of friends who love books as I do. Many hours are spent on the phone or e-mailing as we discuss the great books we have discovered and the students we know who will love those books. Ann Bailey, Anne Cobb, Becky Bone, Lynnette Elliott, Melanie Marks, and Toni Issa Lahera form an informal book club that is essential to my reading life.

Ideas for books are always easy—taking them from the idea stage to publication is the difficult part. Denise Beasley has supported this book from the beginning with meticulous work on permissions, the creation of book lists and resources, and careful eyes during editing stages. Anne Cobb was there with the right quote at the right time.

As always, the people at Stenhouse make it all come together. Philippa Stratton is the editor many writers dream of having. She values each word, and she values the people who write the words. She knows how to give writers room to explore and how to help them find their way back to the task. Martha Drury takes the messiness of the work and turns it all into a finished product that can be held with pride. Tom Seavey provides me with just the right combination of fried clams, friendship, and humor—who could ask for more than that?

All of these people own part of the spirit and content of this book. But, as Gary Paulsen says in *The Winter Room,* "This book needs you." I believe the world and our classrooms become safer, more productive places when we discover with our students the magic that comes from being on the same page. Unlike a scripted program, we don't all have to be in the same book for this to happen. It is my hope that this book will meet you at a time and place in your learning when you are willing to take these resources and make them your own in ways you have yet to imagine.

1

On the Same Page: Shared Reading Beyond the Primary Grades

Because words are essential in building the thought connections in the brain, the more language a child experiences—through books and through conversation with others, not passively from television—*the more advantaged socially, educationally, and in every way that child will be for the rest of his or her life.*

Mem Fox, *Reading Magic*

Recently I sat in a tenth-grade San Diego classroom listening to the teacher's animated reading of Lynne Ewing's novel *Party Girl,* and I was struck with the intensity of the students' concentration on the book. No one was sleeping, no one was whispering or writing notes, no one was applying makeup, and no one interrupted the reading for a bathroom pass. The principal leaned toward me and whispered, "They're not always like this, you know." I did know.

When I began teaching and reading young adult literature with my students thirty years ago, reading an engaging novel to my students quickly became the first survival tool in my arsenal. My students were angry and fighting and bored and tired of school. So was I, and I had been there only for a few days! As I marked time until I could resign from teaching, I found two sets of young adult novels and decided to read one of them to my students. I gave them a choice by telling them one book was about sex (Head's *Mr. and Mrs. Bo Jo Jones*) and the other was about teenage rebellion (Swarthout's *Bless the Beasts and the Children*). They chose the novel about sex, and I began reading to them as some followed along with individual copies of the book.

At the time, I had no idea I was in the process of discovering an approach to reading that would meet the needs of the students in such a powerful way. I had never heard of shared reading, and I knew no way to teach English other than the ways I had been taught as a student. I was a product of the same system that the main character in Laurie Halse Anderson's novel *Speak* describes:

Code Breaking

Hairwoman has been buying new earrings. One pair hangs all the way down to her shoulders. Another has bells in them like the pair Heather gave me at Christmas. I guess I can't wear mine anymore. There should be a law.

It's Nathaniel Hawthorne Month in English. Poor Nathaniel. Does he know what they've done to him? We are reading *The Scarlet Letter* one sentence at a time, tearing it up and chewing on its bones.

It's all about SYMBOLISM, says Hairwoman. Every word chosen by Nathaniel, every comma, every paragraph break—these were all done on purpose. To get a decent grade in class, we have to figure out what he was really trying to say. Why couldn't he just say what he meant? Would they pin scarlet letters on his chest? B for blunt, S for straightforward? (100)

As far as I was concerned at that time, Hairwoman's teaching was for important literature—required literature. *Mr. and Mrs. Bo Jo Jones* was not Hawthorne, so I felt justified in not spending our days analyzing the text. I saw reading this book as a way for us to spend our time together until I could resign, so I did very little in terms of actually "teaching" the novel. We didn't look up vocabulary words, and we didn't do study guides. I didn't given them quizzes, and I wasn't concerned about test grades. We simply read the book. We laughed and cried, and we closed our door so people in the hallways couldn't hear the potentially objectionable scenes.

But a strange thing happened on the way to that important literature I wanted to teach. My students started coming to class more often, and they brought their friends who were skipping other classes. They fought less and had little patience with students who were disruptive. I spent less time managing the class and more time reading as students magically created their own forms of discipline. As they became more involved with the characters and the events of our book, I talked less and they generated our topics.

At the time, I didn't have the educational terminology or the confidence to describe the approach I was using. In fact, I always felt as if I were doing some-

2

thing less than what I was hired to do. But I did know that the more we read, the more I felt as though I were finding a measure of success with students who had given up on school and literacy. When we finished *Mr. and Mrs. Bo Jo Jones* and my students asked me to read another book, I knew I had discovered a way of teaching that I would always use to help older students discover the magic of reading a great book. My students and I had quickly discovered the affective benefit of shared reading; it took many years of experience for us to discover the cognitive support the same approach could offer.

Many years after my initial experience with shared reading, I had the pleasure of spending two years in Mary Giard's first-grade classroom. I was able to see the kind of reading environment Mem Fox describes when several times a day Mary and her students gathered in front of her chair for a time of shared reading. She used Big Books and charts so students could follow the text as she offered them the voice support of her fluent reading. As I observed the daily shared readings, I began to truly understand both the complexity and the value of this experience for Mary and the learners in her care.

Mary read fairy tales and poems, pictures books and chapter books, and with each text her students' worlds seemed larger than the day before. When they read *Seven Chinese Brothers,* her students had a rich discussion as they teased out the meaning of the word *baptism* (which many compared to time in a Jacuzzi). Multiple readings of Sendak's book *Chicken Soup with Rice* led students to explore words and imitate Sendak's language patterns in their own writing. Mary's choices for shared reading led students to further explore related titles, authors, characters, and themes during their independent reading. Some students always chose to reread texts Mary had read that day, and others chose to read more books by that same author. A community of learners was built, and in the course of that building, those students were able to comprehend issues and discuss universal themes far beyond their chronological ages or independent reading abilities.

Research in Support of Shared Reading

Mary's students were experiencing the benefits of what Don Holdaway calls a shared book experience. With the publication of Holdaway's *The Foundations of Literacy,* educators began to examine the value of the shared book experience as an essential approach offering a range of support for emerging readers. "Teachers have always used the special power of reading to a group of children as an important but separate aspect of their language teaching," says Holdaway, "but they have seldom brought that power over into the centre of the instructional programmes in reading and written expression. Reading to a group of children in school has little instructional value simply because the print cannot be seen, shared, and discussed" (64). This statement in no way diminishes the value of read-aloud. Rather, adding the approach of shared reading as *instructional* time gives read-aloud its rightful place as a time to experience the rich language, engaging stories, intriguing information, and poetic rhythms that are firmly embedded in most readers' memories without overwhelming emerging readers with too many instructional lessons.

Holdaway highlighted three important stages of the shared book experience: discovery, exploration, and independent experience and expression. He advocated that teachers control readers' familiarity with the text by using such approaches as unison reading, language experience, oral cloze, enlarged texts, whole-group readings, and repeated readings and listening posts while cautioning teachers to "maintain such a flow of *new* material that none can be processed repetitively to the point of perfect rote memorization" (127). Students would experience the text in each of these approaches with the voice support of other fluent readers.

As a way of deciding which students need more familiarity with a text than others, Holdaway suggested that we look at the nature of reluctant reading behavior as a way to decide how much repeated exposure to each text we might use. For example, with emergent readers, we might use five or six repetitions, and with those who are early readers he recommended one or two repetitions with longer delays between each exposure. For those at the fluency stage, or with older, remedial readers, he recommended full introduction of the text with no repetition (128). In establishing the parameters for how he was using the shared book experience as a level of support to meet the literacy needs of all the learners in a classroom, Holdaway provided each of us with a goal and a model for our own classrooms.

Margaret Mooney further reinforced the goal of the shared book experience in *Reading To, With, and By Children:* "Shared reading is an approach where the teacher replicates the bedtime story situation with the class, a group of children, or an individual child to enable them to enjoy and participate in the reading of books which they cannot yet read for themselves" (10). With the shared reading approach, we are able to support students as they move beyond the range of their independent reading. It is the implementation of this definition that gives developing readers the opportunity to see and hear what fluent reading sounds like, learn new words, and understand how a reader approaches a challenging text. The summer my great-niece, Madelyn, was seven, she reminded me of the critical value of shared reading in terms of reading, language, and writing.

During the previous year, Madelyn had enjoyed several shared readings of Lewis Carroll's *The Annotated Alice.* She particularly enjoyed the following passage:

"The time has come," the walrus said,
    "To talk of many things,
Of shoes—and ships—and sealing wax—
    Of cabbages—and kings
And why the sea is boiling hot
And whether pigs have wings." (235)

As we were lying in bed reading the first of J. K. Rowling's books, *Harry Potter and the Sorcerer's Stone,* Madelyn's younger sister, Melissa, came in, jumped on top of us, and disturbed our reading time. Madelyn sat at the table that night and recorded her dismay over Melissa's interruption (see Figure 1.1).

Figure 1.1

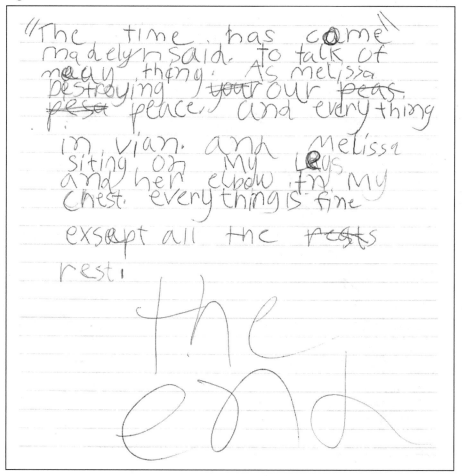

The richness of Carroll's language had become so much a part of Madelyn's thinking that she was able to use his writing as a model for her own thoughts. In *Reading in Junior Classes* (New Zealand Ministry of Education), the authors cite the primary purpose of shared reading as support for the developing reader: "This support will ensure that the children can enjoy material that they cannot as yet read for themselves, and appreciate the story as a whole, in much the same way as a completed picture in a jigsaw means more than any individual piece. Children can also be introduced to the riches of book language" (58).

Readers of all ages actually benefit from this support. Mary's classroom provided me with a model of how shared reading could provide cognitive support for reading without losing the magic of reading a good book. Even students in grades 4–12 can benefit from the additional support. Some students need the support because they are in the early stages of learning to read, and others need it because of the increasing complexity of texts they are required to read.

Shared Reading with Older Students

Those of us learning with older students always hope our students will demonstrate concrete evidence that reading is changing their literate lives. However, the reality is that many students still move from one grade to the next unable or unwilling to read. While there are certainly many students beyond the primary grades who have significant difficulty knowing how to read, one of the greatest challenges comes from students' developing the habit of not wanting to read. Smith and Elley, in *Learning to Read in New Zealand,* describe the source of this problem: "Unless children realise that reading is a source of valuable knowledge about themselves and the culture in which they live, they will never become truly literate adults. Unless they see that reading is functional, that it can help them achieve their ends, that it can produce answers to problems, and help entertain and amuse them, they will not become hooked on reading" (44). This leaves many educators still struggling with the same question: How can we effectively teach students how to read diverse texts and still ensure they will *want* to read when they leave us?

After observing Mary's first-grade classroom, I believed I had discovered a way to give high school readers the kind of support that would help them discover some of the how-to of reading without diminishing the pleasure reading can bring. I returned to my high school classroom eager to replicate the enthusiasm for reading and level of support I had witnessed in Mary's classroom. With the practical model I had witnessed there and the theoretical model I had understood by reading Holdaway's *The Foundations of Literacy,* I was able to rethink my instructional time so that shared reading could form the center of all the work my students and I did together.

My first challenge was to translate what had been a primary model of literacy into something that made sense with high school students. In most cases, shared reading had been described as unison reading or at least as an opportunity for students to join in with the reading when they chose to do so. I knew that even at the secondary level I could accomplish this aspect of shared reading with choral reading or repeated readings of poetry. However, those types of reading would account for only a small part of the reading we would do. I felt shared reading was too significant a method not to extend the instructional value of the time to longer texts. Holdaway states, "There should be many occasions every day when, at the moment they hear a flow of language, their eyes should see and their brains should perceive the visual detail which conventionally embodies the language ringing in their ears" (130).

If my students were going to have many occasions every day for this experience, I knew I would have to extend the shared reading experience to longer works of literature and informational texts. It only made sense that older students' reading fluency, language acquisition, and writing would improve if I used the voice support aspect of shared reading and extended that to short stories, nonfiction, drama, and novels. With the high level of support offered by the approach, I was able to outline the skills I hoped my older students would gain from shared reading:

- Demonstrate reading fluency.
- Derive enjoyment and information from reading.
- Build background knowledge.
- Build content knowledge.
- Anticipate content.
- Discover conventions of print and features of text structures.
- Learn models for the writer's craft.
- Increase word knowledge and language play.
- Develop and internalize self-questioning.
- Demonstrate effective use of reading strategies.
- Build world knowledge.
- Foster personal text connections.

Teachers working with students beyond the primary years also face the additional challenge of content area reading demands. Even if the initial reluctance is overcome by reading high-interest literature and nonfiction, teachers still grapple with the challenge of maintaining positive attitudes toward reading while teaching strategies for negotiating demanding texts that require sophisticated levels of thought and response. As I began to examine the approach of guided reading, it occurred to me that if I combined the voice support offered by shared reading and the cognitive questioning and modeling that accompanied guided reading, I could help students learn how to negotiate increasingly difficult and specialized texts. I now call this adapted approach shared strategic reading.

Adopting and Adapting the Approach
of Shared Reading

Recently, I worked with educators at a California inner-city school for students in grades 4–8. We quickly discovered that our questions with these students were the same as those that had plagued me in my own classroom. This time it didn't take me as long to start at the source: we went to the students and asked them what was getting in the way of reading for them. We asked twelve hundred students to tell us how we could best accomplish the dual goals of improved attitudes toward reading and increased ability to read. We also asked them to articulate for us the instructional practices they believe help them move toward improved attitudes and abilities in reading.

Not surprisingly, students cited many of the areas often highlighted in best practice research as roadblocks to reading: lack of interest, books too difficult or boring, not knowing how to read the text, too many big words, too much talking, and not enough reading. The largest number of comments on the student surveys came from students' opinions about teachers' choices for shared reading and the instruction that occurred connected to these choices. These young readers were adamant in their belief that choosing the right texts for shared reading is critical to positive attitudes toward reading. Many of them agreed that when the teacher stopped reading "good stuff," their interest in reading decreased, and when the teacher made them just read by themselves, it "was just too hard, so I stopped trying."

Once an interesting text is chosen, these students also had solid advice for us about the instruction related to shared reading. They didn't want the reading interrupted too much, but they did report enjoying and learning from instruction connected to read-alouds and shared reading in the following five categories: showing what good reading sounds like, learning new things together, getting ideas for books for independent reading, learning new words, and learning how to read hard texts (strategy demonstrations). The instructional implications for the advice these students offered are addressed in the chapters that follow. In this introductory chapter, I would like to focus on students' advice to us about the importance of beginning with the right book. I think we can all agree that if we have the right text as our foundation, many of the initial obstacles to reading are overcome. So, how do we get the text that is just right in meeting the interests and the needs of our students?

Choosing the Right Texts for Shared Reading

In Stephen King's *Hearts in Atlantis,* Bobby's reading mentor gives him some advice about how to choose books to read. "There are books full of great writing that don't have very good stories. Read sometimes for the story, Bobby. Don't be like the book-snobs who won't do that. Read sometimes for the words—the language. Don't be like the play-it-safers that won't do that. But when you find a book that has both a good story and good words, treasure that book" (25). I think this advice could serve us well as we think about text selection. We should choose some books because they have great stories and some because the language is incredible. Once we find books that fit our students, we should treasure those books and use them as anchors for making other choices.

With all of the possible choices that are available to us, how do we choose the right texts for the shared reading experiences we have with our students? And what about the texts we *have* to cover even when our students might consider them useless? Is shared reading still a viable approach under those conditions? Fountas and Pinnell, in *Guiding Readers and Writers Grades 3–6,* provide an excellent overview of multiple ways of knowing your students as readers so that appropriate texts can be chosen (224). Their survey questions help create a solid foundation for understanding students' reading interests. Summary highlights of their suggestions include the following:

- Examining independent reading choices
- Discovering patterns of personal connections (writing, home/community visits, parent conferences)
- Critical observations (what students talk about related to books and life)
- Content information (curriculum mandates, student inquiries, previous read-alouds)
- Student communication (questionnaires, interviews, conversations, class discussions, response journals, conferences)

Each one of these suggestions could provide hundreds of titles. We then have to look for patterns and advice so that we can choose the best books for our shared texts. To do that, I believe we have to look at our purposes for the shared reading: Are we choosing a text only for enjoyment or information, or do we want to use the text as a way of teaching concepts about reading? There are times when we wouldn't want to diminish the joy of a text with too much analysis and other times when an engaging text can also provide a vehicle for instruction.

Texts for Enjoyment and Information

In *Developing Life-Long Readers,* Margaret Mooney says the texts we share should have "charm, magic, impact and appeal" (4). The problem is that sometimes the texts that embody those characteristics for us are not the texts that will appeal to our students. Many of our students would find themselves in total agreement with the students in Mr. Fogelman's class in Gordon Korman's *No More Dead Dogs:*

> So when Mr. Fogelman had us write book reviews in eighth-grade English, I wasn't trying to be rude or disrespectful or even smart-alecky. I gave Fogelman what I give everybody—the truth, the whole truth, and nothing but the truth:
>
>> *Old Shep, My Pal* by Zack Paris is the most boring book I've read in my entire life. I did not have a favorite character. I hated everybody equally. The most interesting part came on the last page where it said "The End." This book couldn't be any lousier if it came with a letter bomb. I would not recommend it to my worst enemy.
>
> Mr. Fogelman scanned the few lines, and glared at me, face flaming in anger. "This isn't what I assigned!"
>
> I should say that I had nothing against Mr. Fogelman at that moment. He was okay—the kind of young teacher who tries to be "one of the guys," but everything he does only shows how out of it he is. I just wanted to set the record straight.
>
> "Yes it is," I told him. "The assignment sheet said to give our honest opinion, write what was our favorite part and character, and make a recommendation. It's all there."
>
> "*Old Shep, My Pal* is a timeless classic!" roared the teacher. "It won the Gunhold Award! It was my favorite book growing up. Everybody loves it." He turned to the rest of the class. "Right?"
>
> The reaction was a murmur of mixed reviews.
>
> "It was okay, I guess."
>
> "Not too bad."

"Why did it have to be so sad?"

"Exactly!" Fogelman pounced on the comment. "It was sad. What a heartbreaking surprise ending!"

"I wasn't surprised," I said. "I knew Old Shep was going to die before I started page one."

"Don't be ridiculous," the teacher snapped. "How?"

I shrugged. "Because the dog always dies. Go to the library and pick out a book with an award sticker and a dog on the cover. Trust me, that dog is going down."

"Not true!" stormed Mr. Fogelman.

"Well," I challenged, "what happened to Old Yeller?"

"Oh, all right," the teacher admitted. "So Old Yeller died."

"What about Sounder?" piped up Joey Quick.

"Don't forget *Where the Red Fern Grows,*" I put in. "The double whammy—two dogs die in that one."

"You've made your point," growled Mr. Fogelman. "And now I'm going to make mine. I expect a proper review. And you're going to give it to me—during detention!" (4–5)

Discovering those texts that are *not* "Old Shep" texts for our students is a constant quest for most teachers. I am never with a group of teachers that doesn't spend time trying to see who has read another book "just like *Holes* or *Freak the Mighty.*" When I'm with middle school teachers, we try to figure out which books would really interest students but not get us fired for reading them. With high school teachers, we often generate lists of books that meet the diverse reading and psychological needs their students have. I believe this is probably one of the most effective ways to choose books: talking with other teachers who teach students who are like those in your classes. It isn't that we just take someone else's reading list and use that in our own classrooms, but those conversations can help us look at the elements of a text that might ignite student interest in reading.

If you are doing multiple read-alouds in your classroom, keeping track of which ones students ask to read independently or ask you to read can give you feedback about the kind of books that could sustain their interest as shared reading texts. In Ann Bailey's eighth-grade class at Marshall Middle School in Long Beach, California, she highlights the books she has introduced during read-alouds by creating waiting lists for those who want to read one of the books. The lists themselves spark a great deal of interest in the books she has chosen, but they also give her an opportunity to examine patterns of student choices.

She photocopies the covers (see Figure 1.2) and puts each cover with a sign-up sheet for those in line to get the book. Often the list is so long and the com-

Figure 1.2

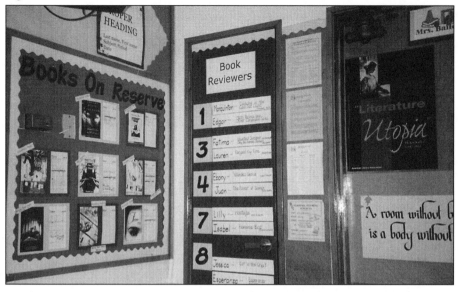

petition to get the book so fierce she is forced to buy multiple copies of the book. As students read the books, they sign up to be book reviewers so others can get their impressions of the books Ann has chosen. As Ann looks for a book that she can reasonably guarantee will be successful as a shared novel, she only has to find books like those that have been her bestsellers from the books on reserve.

In Jennifer Economos-Green's high school classroom in Baltimore, Maryland, she is able to discover the same patterns by examining the texts students are choosing for independent reading (see Figure 1.3). She can look at which genre students are reading by looking for patterns in the color of the Post-its, and she can look at individual titles represented. Both titles and genre help her make effective decisions about whole-class reading that would meet the interests of most of her students.

Critical Text Characteristics

I believe there are certain characteristics that help make rich shared reading experiences regardless of your instructional purposes. The first element that often secures the interest of students is a text that invites personal connections by students. Whether you are reading a text to experience the beauty of the language or for its content, readers are more likely to enjoy and learn from the experience if they can make personal connections. In Robertson Davies's book *A Voice from the Attic,* he tells us, "The best of novels are only scenarios, to be

Figure 1.3

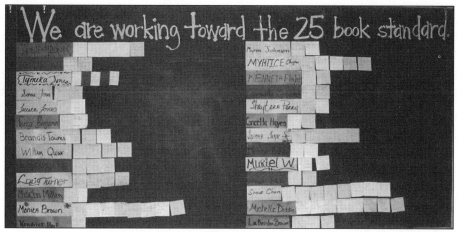

completed by the reader's own experience. They do not give us feeling: they draw out such feeling as we have" (13).

A text such as this one, from Sandra Cisneros's *The House on Mango Street,* offers all readers the opportunity to think about their names:

My Name

In English my name means hope. In Spanish it means too many letters. It means sadness, it means waiting. It is like the number nine. A muddy color. It is the Mexican records my father plays on Sunday mornings when he is shaving, songs like sobbing.

It was my great-grandmother's name and now it is mine. She was a horse woman too, born like me in the Chinese year of the horse—which is supposed to be bad luck if you're born female—but I think this is a Chinese lie because the Chinese, like the Mexicans, don't like their women strong.

My great-grandmother. I would've liked to have known her, a wild horse of a woman, so wild she wouldn't marry. Until my great-grandfather threw a sack over her head and carried her off. Just like that, as if she were a fancy chandelier. That's the way he did it.

And the story goes she never forgave him. She looked out the window her whole life, the way so many women sit their sadness on an elbow. I wonder if she made the best with what she got or was she sorry because she couldn't be all the things she wanted to be. Esperanza. I have inherited her name, but I don't want to inherit her place by the window.

At school they say my name funny as if the syllables were made out of tin and hurt the roof of your mouth. But in Spanish, my name is made out of a softer something, like silver, not quite as thick as sister's name—Magdalena—which is uglier than mine. Magdalena who at least can come home and become Nenny. But I am always Esperanza.

I would like to baptize myself under a new name, a name more like the real me, the one nobody sees. Esperanza as Lisandra or Maritza or Zeze the X. Yes. Something like Zeze the X will do. (10–11)

You might later reread this text in order to look at providing support for students writing memoirs. If you are introducing the literary organizer of genre, you could explore the elements of this piece of writing as if it were an exemplar of a "new" genre: the name piece. Students could reread the piece and discover that the elements of this genre might include a history of the name, personal connections, others sharing the name, family connections to the name, emotions or feelings about the name, and other names the narrator would choose. We could explore the beauty of language or the effectiveness of using sentence fragments as a tool for writing. I believe any or all of these instructional lessons would be enriched because the lesson has as its foundation a rich text that invites personal connections by the reader.

The second element that tends to make a strong shared text is one that creates an intense emotional experience for the reader. The emotion might range from intense humor to shared pain, confusion to satisfaction at questions answered. In Michael Dorris and Emilie Buchwald's edited collection *The Most Wonderful Books: Writers on the Pleasures of Reading*, Marion Dane Bauer synthesizes those experiences for a reader: "As a writer of stories, I am always reaching toward that moment when a reader will say, 'But I thought I was the only one who ever felt that, thought that, wanted that.' As a reader of stories, I search for that same experience, the moment when I will discover, yet again, the universal in the personal, the core of shared humanity beneath my isolation" (9).

I think Paul Jennings's short stories capture even the most reluctant of readers because of the intense range of emotion a reader experiences during the reading of one of his short stories. In "Licked," from *Covered with Nails and Other Stories to Shock Your Socks Off,* Jennings takes the reader on a wild ride of emotions that range from laughter to physical revulsion. It is indeed the stuff of reading memories.

Licked

Tomorrow when Dad calms down I'll own up. Tell him the truth. He might laugh. He might cry. He might strangle me. But I have to put him out of his misery.

I like my dad. He takes me fishing. He arm-wrestles me in front of the fire on cold nights. He plays Scrabble instead of watching the news. He tries practical jokes on me. And he keeps his promises. Always.

But he has two faults. Bad faults. One has to do with flies. He can't stand them. If there's a fly in the room he has to kill it. He won't use fly spray because of the ozone layer, so he chases them with a fly swatter. He races around the house swiping and swatting like a mad thing. He won't stop until the fly is flat. Squashed. Squished—sometimes still squirming on the end of the fly swatter.

He's a deadeye shot. He hardly ever misses. When his old fly swatter was almost worn out I bought him a nice new yellow one for his birthday. It wasn't yellow for long. It soon had bits of fly smeared all over it.

It's funny the different colors that squashed flies have inside them. Mostly it is black or brown. But often there are streaks of runny red stuff and sometimes bits of blue. The wings flash like diamonds if you hold them up to the light. But mostly the wings fall off unless they are stuck to the swatter with a bit of squashed innards.

2

Chasing flies is Dad's first fault. His second one is table manners. He is mad about manners.

And it is always my manners that are the matter.

"Andrew," he says, "don't put your elbows on the table."

"Don't talk with your mouth full."

"Don't lick your fingers."

"Don't dunk your cookie in the coffee."

This is the way he goes on every mealtime. He has a thing about flies and a thing about manners.

Anyway, to get back to the story. One day Dad is peeling the potatoes for dinner. I am looking for my fifty cents that rolled under the table about a week ago. Mum is cutting up the cabbage and talking to Dad. They do not know that I am there. It is a very important meal because Dad's boss, Mr. Spinks, is coming for dinner. Dad never stops going on about my manners when someone comes for dinner.

"You should stop picking on Andrew at dinnertime," says Mum.

"I don't," says Dad.

"Yes you do," says Mum. "It's always don't do this, don't do that. You'll give the boy a complex."

I have never heard of a complex before, but I guess that it is something awful like pimples.

"Tonight," says Mum, "I want you to go for the whole meal without telling Andrew off once."

"Easy," says Dad.

"Try hard," says Mum. "Promise me that you won't get cross with him."

Dad looks at her for a long time. "Okay," he says. "It's a deal. I won't say one thing about his manners. But you're not allowed to either. What's good for me is good for you."

"Shake," says Mum. They shake hands and laugh.

I find the fifty cents and sneak out. I take a walk down the street to spend it before dinner. Dad has promised not to tell me off at dinnertime. I think about how I can make him crack. It should be easy. I will slurp my soup. He hates that. He will tell me off. He might even yell. I just know that he can't go for the whole meal without losing it.

"This is going to be fun," I say to myself.

3

That night Mum sets the table with the new tablecloth. And the best knives and forks. And the plates that I am not allowed to touch. She puts out napkins in little rings. All of this means that it is an important meal. We don't usually use napkins.

Mr. Spinks comes in his best suit. He wears gold glasses, and he frowns a lot. I can tell that he doesn't like children. You can always tell when adults don't like kids. They smile at you with their lips but not with their eyes.

Anyway, we sit down to dinner. I put my secret weapon on the floor under the table. I'm sure that I can make Dad crack without using it. But it is there if all else fails.

The first course is soup and bread rolls. I make loud slurping noises with the soup. No one says anything about it. I make the slurping noises longer and louder. They go on and on and on. It sounds like someone has pulled the plug out of the bath. Dad clears his throat but doesn't say anything.

I try something different. I dip my bread in the soup and make it soggy. Then I hold it high above my head and drop it down into my mouth. I catch it with a loud slopping noise. I try again with an even bigger bit. This time I miss my mouth, and the bit of soupy bread hits me in the eye.

Nothing is said. Dad looks at me. Mum looks at me. Mr. Spinks tries not to look at me. They are talking about how Dad might get a promotion at work. They are pretending that I am not revolting.

The next course is chicken. Dad will crack over the chicken. He'll say something. He hates me picking up the bones.

The chicken is served. "I've got the chicken's bottom," I say in a loud voice.

Dad glares at me but he doesn't answer. I pick up the chicken and start stuffing it into my mouth with my fingers. I grab a roast potato and break it in half. I dip my fingers into the margarine and put some on the potato. It runs all over the place.

I have never seen anyone look as mad as the way Dad looks at me. He glares. He stares. He clears his throat. But still he doesn't crack. What a man. Nothing can make him break his promise.

I snap a chicken bone in half and suck out the middle. It is hollow and I can see right through it. I suck and slurp and swallow. Dad is going red in the face. Little veins are standing out on his nose. But still he does not crack.

The last course is baked apple and custard. I will get him with that. Mr. Spinks has stopped talking about Dad's promotion. He is discussing something about discipline. About setting limits. About insisting on standards. Something like that. I put the hollow bone into the custard and use it like a straw. I suck the custard up the hollow chicken bone.

Dad clears his throat. He is very red in the face. "Andrew," he says.

He is going to crack. I have won.

"Yes," I say through a mouth full of custard.

"Nothing," he mumbles.

Dad is terrific. He is under enormous pressure but still he keeps his cool. There is only one thing left to do. I take out my secret weapon.

4

I place the yellow fly swatter on the table next to my knife.

Everyone looks at it lying there on the white tablecloth. They stare and stare and stare. But nothing is said.

I pick up the fly swatter and start to lick it. I lick it like an ice cream cone. A bit of chewy brown goo comes off on my tongue. I swallow it quickly. Then I crunch a bit of crispy black stuff.

Mr. Spinks rushes out to the kitchen. I can hear him being sick in the kitchen sink.

Dad stands up. It is too much for him. He cracks. "Aaaaaagh," he screams. He charges at me with hands held out like claws.

I run for it. I run down to my room and lock the door. Dad yells and shouts. He kicks and screams. But I lie low.

Tomorrow, when he calms down, I'll own up. I'll tell him how I went down the street and bought a new fly swatter for fifty cents. I'll tell him about the currants and little bits of licorice that I smeared on the fly swatter.

I mean, I wouldn't really eat dead flies. Not unless it was for something important anyway. (1–6)

After reading this story, you might choose to focus on the reading strategy of predicting by revisiting the text to discover ways Jennings foreshadows the story's events. Students could look for clues that would have helped them predict and other clues that would have led them to reject an earlier prediction and create a new one. In writing workshop, this text could be revisited as a model of characterization. Students could analyze the story for techniques writers use to make their characters come alive for the reader. In either case, students have heard a great story that has provided emotional responses that make the story memorable. Those memorable qualities then provide a solid foundation for instruction.

Rich language that creates visual images is the third element that is characteristic of effective shared texts. Poetry often has language that evokes strong mental images, and the two poems that follow, "Summer Person" by Glenna Johnson Smith, and "Richard Cory" by Edwin Arlington Robinson, are no exception:

Summer Person
When Mrs. Ashley walks across a room
she leaves an almost-fragrance
so quickly blown away
it may be just a trick of memory,
a dream perfume.

    (White sheets blowing on a clothesline—
    the crumpled death of roses—)

Her tennis dress new-fallen on the bed
the saffron satin robe
shrugged off before her bath
hint the same bouquet.

The local high school girl,
lady's maid by summer,
breathes in the haunting message.
She longs to hold it
for a moment in her hands.

Eagerly and fearfully
while Mrs. Ashley's out to tea
the girl opens cut glass jars
to find the secret source.
But no bottle, tube or vial
contains the subtle essence.

The women of the village
smell of fried potatoes, onions,
Fels-Naptha soap and sometimes sweat
from scrubbing floors and making jam
in mid-July.
     (Cashmere Bouquet and Coty's Talc
     are saved for Saturday night.)

Perhaps only summer ladies
perspire sun and wind
and dying roses. (415–416)

Richard Cory
Whenever Richard Cory went down town,
We people on the pavement looked at him:
He was a gentleman from sole to crown,
Clean favored, and imperially slim.

And he was always quietly arrayed,
And he was always human when he talked;
But still he fluttered pulses when he said,
"Good morning," and he glittered when he walked.

And he was rich—yes, richer than a king—
And admirably schooled in every grace:
In fine, we thought that he was everything
To make us wish that we were in his place.

So on we worked, and waited for the light,
And went without the meat, and cursed the bread;
And Richard Cory, one calm summer night,
Went home and put a bullet in his head. (414)

In each of these poems, the richness of the language helps make the shared reading memorable. In "Summer Person," Smith evokes sensory images through the use of color, specific products, and memorable events. Robinson evokes strong images by describing Richard Cory as though we were seeing him through the eyes of the townspeople. These two poems have individual strengths, but when combined, they provide an excellent shared reading foundation for making text-to-text connections (see Harvey and Goudvis, *Strategies That Work*).

The two poems also offer readers the opportunity to make personal connections. The vivid images often help readers recall their own experiences with envying others and their possessions. An instructional strategy that supports readers' questioning their way through and between the two texts is taken from Aidan Chambers, *Tell Me: Children, Reading and Talk*. A complete application of this strategy is demonstrated in Allen's *Yellow Brick Roads* using two poems describing experiences of Japanese-Americans relocated to internment camps during World War II. Briefly, students generate three questions after the initial shared reading of the poems and exchange their questions with another student. They then use their six questions as a focus for discussion and out of that discussion create new questions to take to an expanded group or whole-class discussion. The richness of the questions is very dependent on students' having strong images of the characters, settings, and events because of the vivid language used.

Finally, a characteristic I believe should permeate most shared texts we use with children and adolescents is expanding the readers' worlds. In Margaret Meek's book *Learning to Read,* she reminds us that the texts we choose may stay with readers for the rest of their lives. Words, phrases, events, lines of poetry often find their way into our writing and speech decades after reading or hearing those words. "We gain more lives than one, more memories than we could ever have from what happened to us: in fact, a whole alternative existence, in our own culture or that of others. This is what the learner has to learn to do, and what we expect teachers to teach. Literacy has powerful consequences; not the least is that it changes one's view of oneself and the world" (21).

As we are choosing shared texts to read with our students, even for struggling readers, we can choose texts that challenge their thinking and enlarge their worlds. The approach of shared reading provides a great deal of decoding support, which allows the brain to do the cognitive work of reading a world larger than that we have experienced.

I was reminded of the truth of this Charles Schultz cartoon when one of the teachers in a San Diego genre studies class related her experience with students to me. When one teacher left and my friend was assigned to work with this

class, she gathered the materials available to study the genre of fairy tales because that was the next genre they were planning to explore. On her first day in the classroom, the students were adamant in their refusal to participate in reading fairy tales. My friend finally stopped and said, "Well, what do you want to read?" They responded by saying they wanted to read about the Holocaust because they had heard lots of people talking about it.

As teachers, we often fall prey to reading texts that are within the limited context of readers' previous experiences in order to ensure that the text is relevant for readers. In *"The Having of Wonderful Ideas" and Other Essays on Teaching and Learning,* Eleanor Duckworth reminds us that each reading should be accessible and interesting and that relevance can come out of that when readers make the text their own: "The material world is too diverse and too complex for a child to become familiar with all of it in the course of an elementary school career. The best one can do is to make such knowledge, such familiarity, seem interesting and accessible to the child. That is, one can familiarize children with a few phenomena in such a way as to catch their interest, to let them raise and answer their own questions, to let them realize that their ideas are significant—so that they have the interest, the ability, and the self-confidence to go on by themselves" (8).

World-expanding knowledge can happen each day in our classrooms within the context of shared reading. One of the most powerful picture books I've read in the last few years is John Marsden's *Prayer for the Twenty-First Century.* Two of the images and one line of the poem are shown in Figure 1.4. As you can imagine, the powerful images and the poem can't help but make each of us offer our own prayers and hopes for a safer, healthier world. A shared reading of this book helps adolescents see their roles in making our world a better place.

Following the events of September 11, students in Lee Ann Spillane's high school English class at University High School in Orlando, Florida, wrote and illustrated their own prayers for the world. Daryl's poem mirrored the thoughts of many as the student writers began to explore the notion that in a global society our personal prayers impact the lives of many:

A Prayer for the 21st Century
The world has changed,
Become deranged,
So I pray this prayer for me.

> To grant this plea,
> Of your sovereignty,
> I pray this prayer to Thee.

May rivers still flow,
And grasses still grow,
Please keep this planet free.

> Let justice be served,
> And criminals curbed,
> So peace is for all to see.

Let fear be vanquished,
And pain relinquished,
So the world is filled with glee.

> Let war be halted,
> And grace exalted,
> I pray this prayer for me.

In *On Learning to Read: The Child's Fascination with Meaning,* Bruno Bettelheim and Karen Zelan see the world-expanding feature of reading as being one of the most significant for developing readers who want to learn to read *and* those who will continue reading long after they leave school: "What is required for a child to be eager to learn to read is not knowledge about reading's practical usefulness, but a fervent belief that being able to read will open to him a world of wonderful experiences, permit him to shed his ignorance, understand the world, and become master of his fate" (49). Appendix F offers titles that help readers understand their world. If we choose diverse texts for shared reading that are just slightly out of a reader's range of experience, we can challenge students to learn something new each day. Each day's new learning creates a path that supports these students as they read independently both in terms of word and world knowledge.

Methods for creating effective instructional lessons and units using the approach of shared reading as a foundation make up the content of Chapters 2–7. Ways that we can assess the effectiveness of those approaches are described in Chapter 8.

This book begins and ends with the belief that shared reading provides an opportunity for students to experience texts that take them out of themselves and into a larger reading community—what Frank Smith describes as a literacy club. As students experience a diverse range of texts that invite personal con-

Figure 1.4

May we be outlived by our daughters,

nections, evoke emotional responses, employ rich language to create visual images, and expand their world knowledge, they begin to reap the rewards of a strong reading foundation. It is a time of being on the same page in order to support, nourish, and challenge us to discover the readers we can each become.

2

"Pleeeze, Just One More Chapter": Expanding Reading Fluency with Connected Shared Reading

[On interruptions to reading:] The spell will have been broken.

In fact the spell has already been broken. The panic itself is the

interruption. I have interrupted myself. Life is designed to

thwart ecstasy; whether we do it for ourselves or something

does it for us is a minor issue.

Lynne Sharon Schwartz, *Ruined by Reading*

One of the primary goals of shared reading or the shared book experience (SBE) is that readers leave reading with a sense of enjoyment or satisfaction. Connected shared reading is often enjoyable and satisfying for students because it is a relatively uninterrupted reading of a substantial portion of text. If the whole class is sharing a novel, the teacher might choose to read fifteen to twenty pages during one class period. If a short story, informational text, or poem, the entire text is read and perhaps reread in that same amount of class time. Students follow along with individual copies of the text or by using an enlarged version of it on an overhead transparency, chart, or monitor. In these cases, the teacher often chooses a text that meets the needs of an entire class.

The level of student engagement is equally good when book choices are made by individuals or small groups. In Figure 2.1, a student at Gompers

Figure 2.1

Secondary School in San Diego is enjoying the benefits of assisted reading during independent reading time with the help of audiotapes and accompanying books.

A similar form of reading assistance is extended when students participate in shared reading through partner, or paired, reading (see Figure 2.2). These students at Los Nietos Middle School in Whittier, California, demonstrate the high level of engagement that occurs when students choose to share a text in paired reading. Readers value the independence of choosing their own books and reading partners while still benefiting from the support of another reader's voice. Even the most struggling readers can participate in this valuable approach by reading books with an appropriate level of support. Books such as those listed in Appendix G are high interest and offer multiple reading supports.

Regardless of whether the shared reading is teacher-initiated or part of independent, assisted reading, there is little in it of what Richard Allington calls "bothering kids." In fact, unless readers get lost in the text—either because they lose track of where they are or because they are so confused it has interrupted their reading—the teacher does an uninterrupted shared reading. Teachers may

Figure 2.2

choose to anticipate the shared reading with word study, some form of prereading experience such as anticipation guides (Readence, Bean, and Baldwin) or K-W-L (Ogle), or by reading a short related text. They will probably also follow the shared reading with discussion, analysis, and synthesis, and connect the reading to writing. But during the course of the shared reading, the teacher is not interrupting the flow of the text. Strategic shared reading (see Chapter 3) is based on interrupting text in order to get an "interacting voice" (Tovani) as part of a reader's thinking through reading. Connected shared reading is based on students' experiencing a portion of text in large enough chunks to be able to examine the text as a whole.

An example of a typical connected shared reading of a complete short story is described here. The lesson might begin by anticipating some of the content through word study. Using a Words in Context form, we can explore and build on students' background knowledge of the word *miser* (see Figure 2.3).* In this case, the teacher has offered as an example, "In the portion of *A Christmas Carol* that we just read, Scrooge's employees think he is a miser. What does he

---

*The graphic organizers, or forms, shown in the figures are provided in Appendix I as blanks for reproduction.

Figure 2.3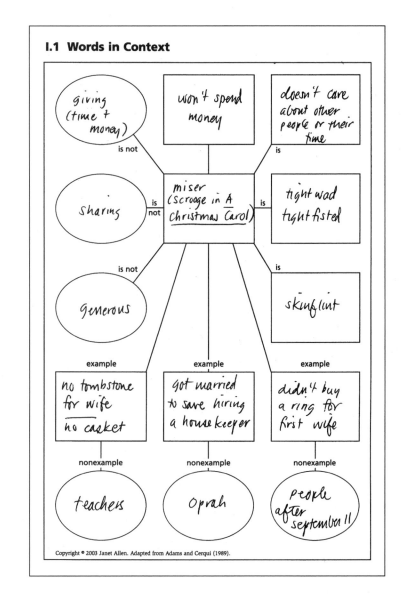

do or not do that make them think that?" Students generated his being mean, not caring about people's time, and not spending money as part of a possible description of a miser. The teacher then says that the group will read a story about a miser and then come back to the word study. The story is from Judith Gorog's collection of short stories *When Nobody's Home: Fifteen Baby-sitting Tales of Terror:*

Poppy

On Friday, Poppy was done with school forever. On Monday morning pretty darned early, Poppy's mother handed Poppy the want ads and pushed her out the door, saying, "Find a school or find a job. Today."

That's how Poppy came to be the baby-sitter for the Banner children, all four of them. Their mama, Mrs. Banner, had up and died, leaving Mr. Banner with the four little ones, ages two, three, four, and five. Poppy thought that of all the possible jobs she might have to get, baby-sitting certainly would be the easiest. For sure, she could do the job sitting down. After all, the Banners, tightfisted as old Mr. Banner was, did have a large television set.

And that's the way it was. Poppy got the job. Mr. Banner went out the front door. Poppy turned on the television set and sat herself down to watch. The four Banner children, who had grown pretty wild during their mother's illness, continued as they had been doing.

That whole first day, and the second, and the third, Poppy took her eyes off the television screen only when she made herself something to eat. Because there was not a single clean knife in the kitchen, Poppy used a spoon to scoop peanut butter out of the jar onto a piece of bread. Because there was not a single clean mug or glass, Poppy drank from her hands, which she cupped under the kitchen faucet, noticing as she did so that the kitchen sink, like all the others in the house, smelled of urine.

Stepping carefully around the lumps of food, worms of toothpaste, remains of dirty diapers, and unidentifiable splotches on the kitchen floor, Poppy wiped her wet hands on the legs of her jeans. She wished Mr. Banner would buy some soda for her to drink, but of course he wouldn't. Mr. Banner was known to be pretty tightfisted.

And that is how Mr. Banner came to court Poppy. When he got home at night, he could see that Poppy had done nothing all day but sit. Mr. Banner wanted Poppy to cook and clean, to wash and iron, but he knew Poppy wouldn't so long as she was paid only to baby-sit. Mr. Banner could not bear to part with enough money to pay someone to do all the work that needed to be done in that house. As it was, it pained Mr. Banner terribly to pay Poppy, or anyone else, to baby-sit.

Poppy was young. Mr. Banner was sure he could train her to be a good wife. As a good wife, Poppy would work for free.

After Poppy had been baby-sitting for a few days, Mr. Banner set out to charm Poppy just as he had charmed the young girl who had become Mrs. Banner all those years ago.

And, as long as it did not cost any money, Mr. Banner could be very charming. Mr. Banner praised Poppy until she blushed. Mr. Banner said that Poppy deserved a wedding ring of gold, a gold ring heavy with diamonds, so heavy it would take both her hands to lift the hand that wore it. His smile was bright when he said it, his eyes full of the sadness of love. Poppy laughed, sighed to picture herself so laden with diamonds that she could not raise a hand to work.

Mr. Banner knew exactly the look of the ring he was describing. It was the ring Mrs. Banner had worn, still wore. It was the ring Mrs. Banner was given by her grandmother when she married Mr. Banner, who had with immense charm convinced the family that he was good, noble in fact, but too poor in worldly goods to provide a ring for his bride.

Poor Mrs. Banner suffered for years in her marriage to the tightwad who so charmed his baby-sitter. Oh yes. Mrs. Banner had been worn to death by the sleazy skinflint who described her wedding ring to a breathless Poppy.

And that ring? It could be found easily enough, in a grave, on the third finger of the left hand of the Mrs. Banner who lay wrapped in her shroud. With her last breath she had clasped her hands, and had not opened them when Mr. Banner tried to get the ring from her finger. After that moment, it had been impossible for him to take the ring. There were people who could see, and others who knew that Mrs. Banner insisted she be buried with the ring. After all, it was her very own. For Mr. Banner at the time, it had been only a small problem. After all, he knew where to find the ring when the time came to take it.

Now. Now was the time. First, Mr. Banner charmed Poppy into accepting his offer of marriage. After that it was an easy matter to convince her that only that particular ring of gold, heavy with diamonds, would do as a wedding ring for Poppy. Together they would fetch the ring. Poppy agreed.

Together they drove out of town, up the hill to the old cemetery. Together they carried their shovels along the path, around one tombstone after another, to the place where Mrs. Banner lay, no tombstone above her head. Together they dug away at the soil above the body. Six feet down, they touched the body; no coffin for Mrs. Banner. Together they brushed away at the dirt, unwrapped the shroud.

Mrs. Banner lay, hands clasped, the gold of the ring glowing softly even there deep in the ground. The diamonds sparkled, even there deep in the ground.

Together Poppy and Mr. Banner tried, tried with all the force they could muster, to pry open those fingers, to slip the ring over the knuckle of that dead hand.

29

The hands held fast. The ring remained on that finger. Together they sweated in the chill night air, gritting their teeth, pulling at those fingers with all their might. At last Mr. Banner let go of the hand, reached into his pocket for a knife.

"No," said Poppy. "That won't do. Use the edge of the shovel."

Together, they used the shovel to chop the finger from the hand. At last, the ring was free.

Breathless, Poppy slipped it onto her finger. How beautiful it was. Even down there, deep in the earth, crouched over that corpse, you could see how spectacular a ring it was.

"Lovely, isn't it?" asked the first Mrs. Banner, as she reached up to clasp both of them, together, to her breast.

They struggled, oh how Mr. Banner and Poppy struggled, but the first Mrs. Banner was stronger than both of them.

They sobbed. They pleaded. Poppy pulled at the ring, trying to wrench it from her finger. She tried to give it back, but the ring did not budge. Mrs. Banner held them fast. The earth fell in upon them, as she dragged them down, down, down, together, with her forever. (26–31)

Adolescent readers love this story and are quick to make judgments about errors that Mr. Banner and Poppy made. As a way to weave the word study into the context of the story, the Words in Context form can be revisited. Students go back to reread sections of "Poppy" to find other words Gorog uses as synonyms for *miser: tightwad, tightfisted, skinflint.* They then find examples of *miserly* activity on the part of Mr. Banner: no tombstone, got married rather than hire a housecleaner, didn't buy his wife a ring, and didn't get her a casket when she died. As a class, students generate characteristics of someone who is the opposite of a *miser:* giving, spends time or money, sharing, generous. This leads to their finding nonexamples of miserly activity in our society by talking about people or events that indicate someone is generous and giving. In this class, students decide that teachers are not misers because they spend money and time on students; Oprah isn't a miser because of the money she donates; and people who gave time and money to help victims and their families after September 11 are not misers. The word study used to anticipate content also helps focus and extend the discussion after the reading.

The postreading discussion leads naturally to discovering ways to analyze characters. At this point, readers are familiar with the text and can work as partners or small groups to reread portions of the text to discover Mr. Banner and Poppy's characteristics and infer traits they believe Mrs. Banner possessed. In order to maintain focus during this activity, students use a Character Chart (I.2, Appendix I) to record their thinking and discussion. When students then return to a whole-class modeling and discussion of how to write a character analysis, they have had three "readings" of the same text, gathered information about the characters, been part of a collaborative discussion, and highlighted dialogue that indicates something of the characters' personalities. The writing lesson becomes richer for the word study and character analysis lessons, and those lessons can occur pre- and postreading so as not to interrupt the flow of the text.

Students thrive on the kind of support offered by connected shared reading. Many struggling readers have not had the experience of reading an entire text or book. In classes where they are given a certain amount of time to finish an assignment, such students seldom manage to get to the end of the reading. But in a lesson like the one just described, students had the experience of reading an entire text and an opportunity to reread portions of it for word study, discussion, and writing. Through developing familiarity with the text, each rereading becomes easier and leaves more cognitive energy for the related aspects of analyzing, synthesizing, and extending knowledge. In a middle school, students were asked about what makes them want to read and what they believe is helping them become better readers. They highlighted shared reading as the instructional approach they enjoyed the most *and* found the most helpful:

> The thing I notice now is that I feel confident. Before I didn't like to read. I always used to say that reading was boring. In shared reading I hear the teacher say the words for me and I think hearing her pronounce them is making me a better reader. It seems like every single book gives me new words I haven't read before. It's the first time I knew what good reading was supposed to sound like. When I'm reading now I think differently.

These words capture the important aspects of students' taking part in shared reading each day: enjoyment, language acquisition, gaining confidence, and thinking about reading in new ways.

We surveyed over twelve hundred students in this school and found over a thousand students who reported that the large volume of connected shared reading they were doing was helping them become better readers. They commented on the new words they were learning because they could "see and hear the words at the same time." These students were reaping the benefits of volume of reading. In *What Really Matters for Struggling Readers,* Allington states, "What all these studies have consistently shown, regardless of how volume of reading was measured, was that there exists a potent relationship between volume of reading and reading achievement" (33).

Allington goes on to suggest that ninety minutes of reading a day should be a minimum goal based on the data provided by the studies. The ninety minutes might be met and exceeded if language arts teachers read with students for twenty to thirty minutes a day, students participated in a schoolwide independent reading program for thirty minutes a day, and each content area teacher made it a priority to read to and with students every day (see Chapter 5). As students become more competent and engaged readers, they will exceed this amount of time because they will begin to read outside school hours. Hearing many voices reading fluently on many occasions from many different texts gives students experience of "what good reading sounds like."

Modeling Reading Fluency

In a graduate course in Marion County, Florida, one of the teachers shared a student's beliefs about good reading. She had been working with this middle school student for several months and was impressed with the incredible progress he had made as a reader. One day, she was partner-reading with this student. When it was his turn to read, he read in a very halting, word-for-word manner. She stopped him and asked him to listen to the way she read and then gave him another opportunity to read. He still read in the same manner, so she repeated her modeling of fluent reading. Finally, in exasperation, she asked, "Why are you reading like that? Listen to the way I'm reading." She once again started reading in her best fluent voice, and the boy exclaimed, "Oh, I get it. You want me to read like a girl!"

Many middle and high school students have lacked the time, opportunity, resources, and supportive environment to clock the kind of reading mileage that makes a difference in one's ability to read. Providing students with a wide range of high-interest books and audiobooks so that they can read along with books that are interesting and challenging provides the kind of supportive reading opportunity many students have missed at an early age. If students had access to such materials during all advisory periods, in-school suspensions, independent reading, and extended-day programs, they would probably read about forty books a year. With that kind of increased background knowledge about the way words work and how they sound, most students would improve significantly in attitudes toward and aptitude for reading.

For our students to have the best shared reading experience possible, we have to make sure we have practiced reading the chosen text. In *Bad,* Jean Ferris's novel of a young girl remanded to a girls' rehabilitation center, Dallas is shocked when a voice comes over the loudspeaker after lights out:

> The lights in the room dimmed and some music came over the intercom. It was classical, I knew that much, but I didn't know what kind. It was nice.

Then a voice began to read, a grandmotherly sort of voice, warm and quiet. The words of the story were both formal and intimate, and the rhythm of them was lulling. I couldn't remember anybody reading me a bedtime story before. (43–44)

Over time, the nightly read-alouds in the rehabilitation center change Dallas as a person and as a reader, and that is the impact we hope for with our students. While we certainly don't want our voices to lull readers to sleep, we do want the experience to be memorable because it contains the excitement, emotion, and rhythm of the language we are bringing to life. In *I Know Why the Caged Bird Sings*, Maya Angelou says, "Words mean more than what is set down on paper. It takes the human voice to infuse them with the shades of deeper meaning" (82). It is this model of reading that our struggling readers need to create and solidify their own fluent reading voices.

To model effective reading for our students, we have to be familiar enough with the text to change the pace of reading, use a range of voices for multiple characters, and provide enough inflection to keep the interest of readers. Our reading speed has to be fast enough to maintain interest yet slow enough for readers to track the words. Reading aloud with these parameters requires practice. Each shared reading will add another level to your ability to bring the text to life for students who need to hear a fluent reader.

As reading fluency is modeled during reading and rereading of texts, students are developing as fluent readers. Fortunately, reading fluency has a positive impact on comprehension, so many students seem to improve in several areas simultaneously once they develop the expertise and habits of fluent reading. As one of my students told me, "I like to hear you read every day because you are my competition. I try and read along with you in my head to see if I'm getting better each day." Part of that challenge is overcome when we are able to enter shared reading with confidence because we have chosen a text that is meaningful and memorable and also has substance that can extend to other literacy lessons.

Shared Reading: Foundations for "Beating the Odds"

In her research study *Beating the Odds: Teaching Middle and High School Students to Read and Write Well*, Judith Langer highlights six features of effective instruction that increase students' achievement in literacy (45). These six instructional methods came out of a study designed to discover the common elements of curriculum and instruction in schools where students scored higher in English and literacy than in other schools with similar populations of students. Researchers discovered the following six patterns:

- Tests deconstructed to inform curriculum and instruction
- Connections made across content and structure
- Strategies for thinking and doing emphasized
- Skills and knowledge taught in multiple types of lessons
- Classrooms organized to foster collaboration and shared cognition
- Generative learning encouraged

Each of these features of instruction was examined individually, but the study determined that it was their integration that effected the most significant improvement. Shared reading can provide a solid foundation for the individual elements as well as the integration of these elements within the context of longer texts and units of study.

Guiding Readers Through Texts

If we are reading shorter texts such as poetry, short fiction, essay, or informational texts, our natural inclination is to read through the text in its entirety before looking at deeper levels of the text. However, when we move to novels, we often feel compelled to stop and explain language or events for which our students might lack background knowledge or understanding. In an attempt to move my own practice away from interrupting texts during shared reading, I began creating guides for myself that would highlight the text's teachable moments, word study opportunities, and writing or research extensions (see Figure 2.4 and Appendix J). In this way, I could look at the number of pages I wanted to read with students on a given day and the range of options those pages represented for using the text to examine author's purpose, language, style, and related information. Rather than interrupt the text during the reading, I could read through the section knowing I could use the guide to take us back to areas of the chapter where we could reread in order to make some new discoveries about the reading.

In my initial read through the book, I took notes about words from the text that could become part of our daily word study, writing we could do to anticipate content and extend reading, literary devices readers could examine, and areas of interest students might want to research. I then organized my notes into guides

Figure 2.4

1.3 Guiding Readers Through the Text

Title: *Freak the Mighty*

Page Nos.	Possibilities to Explore	Additional Ideas
1–20	(1) I never had a brain until Freak came along and let me borrow his for a while, and that's the truth . . ." (discuss self-image) (1) Begin Methods of Communication graphic as a way of discussion how we let people know what we're feeling and thinking. (2) Discuss memories: "remembering is a great invention of the mind" (2) Names we give ourselves: "I'm Robot Man" (3) Names "Mad Max they were calling me, or Max Factor . . ." (4) Read 1st paragraph for writing: Places we find to get comfort/hide. (5) Stop and discuss how Max sees himself and what he's used to. Make those opinions. (15) use "sobriquet" and "demeanor" to discuss context as word attack. (16) Revisit context with "quest." Use Making Connections graphic. (17) Revisit context with "robotics" (18) Opiate (19) OH: "I also read tons of books so I can figure out what's true and what's fake, which isn't always easy. Books are like truth serum—if you don't read, you can't figure out what's real." Do a class chart: "Books are like . . ." (20) Use "Jumping to Conclusions" as a way to pull together understanding of the characters.	
21–40	(21) Writing: Description of place to hide/escape/feel comfortable. (27) Crying because of happiness (something new for Max) (31) Language play: "Close encounters of the turd kind" (39) Discuss Max's fears at this point.	

so that the page numbers and information were readily accessible to me each day during our shared reading time. These are not study guides for students; rather, they are teaching guides for us as we support students in enjoying texts and deepening their understanding of the structures and events from the text.

Lee Ann Spillane's teaches ninth-grade English at University High School in Orlando, Florida. In the pages that follow, she has documented her teaching and reflection as she uses Reading–Thinking–Responding, one of the guides I created as a support for her teaching of Jan Cheripko's *Imitate the Tiger* (see Figures 2.6–2.9, 2.11–2.12, 2.14–2.16). Throughout her teaching of this text, we can see evidence of Langer's six features of instruction. On some days the pages I indicated on the guide as possible novel breaks are just right, and on other days Lee Ann divided the reading into more manageable chunks. (Each figure represents approximately one class period.) Lee Ann didn't use all of the teaching suggestions connected to the reading; they were there as possibilities for her teaching. In some cases her students had already discovered the strategies and information there, and in other cases they may not have been ready for that instruction yet. The center column in the guide lists another shared text that Lee Ann could use as a way to anticipate some aspect of the content of each day's reading or as a prompt for small-group collaboration to extend the reading. The third column is Lee Ann's place for making notes—a rich source of information about her teaching moves. We are able to see her thinking about the teaching and learning occurring in this classroom as she adapted her plans based on the kind of support students needed.

Several abbreviations are used in the Reading–Thinking–Responding guide:

H&N	Here and now
WS	Word study
WC	Writer's craft
GO	Graphic organizer
PR	Personal response question
CN	Connection response question
ST	Surface feature question
CR	Critical response question
MC	Metacognitive question

Each day's reading has an H&N, here and now (Kirby, Liner, and Vinz) used to jot down a central point of the shared reading anticipated for that day. For example, the H&N for the first day is from an inspirational poster with a quote by Kurt Vonnegut: "We are what we pretend to be, so we must be careful what we pretend to be." The here and now one of her students wrote combines his feelings about pretending with a prediction for the novel:

I think pretending is the number one way to get into big trouble. I believe that the truth will catch up to you sooner or later and when it does, the more you pretended, the worse it will be. Pretending is the same as lying unless it is used for entertainment. Prediction: In *Imitate the Tiger* I think the person in the picture pretends to be something he either is not or does not like and it affects him drastically.

Another abbreviation, WS, indicates a word study directly related, specifically or conceptually, to the text read that day. WC, writer's craft, is noted when the text offers an opportunity to explore the author's craft of writing. For example, page seven of *Imitate the Tiger* could be the basis for a writing craft lesson to help readers establish ways to develop setting in their writing.

GO indicates that a graphic organizer is available to support the teaching of a concept or as a help for students during small-group collaboration. The abbreviations PR, CN, ST, CR, and MC represent types of questioning that Lee Ann could model as she collaborated with students through a discussion of the text (Allen, *Yellow Brick Roads,* 93–94). *Personal response* questions ask readers to put themselves in the context of the story; *connection response* questions ask readers to do the cognitive work of seeing the events or characters and imagining someone else's response; and *surface text* questions ask readers to examine an author's purpose for using features such as bold, italics, white space, illustrations. *Critical response* questions challenge readers to read with a critical eye for effective or ineffective uses of language and technique, and *metacognitive* questions ask readers to examine their thinking as they read so that they can become adept at noticing their own confusions and what they need to do to sort through the text.

Lee Ann used the connected shared reading approach for all or part of the pages listed at the top of the guide's reading section for each day. On some days she read eight to ten pages and had students continue to read independently, either in school or at home. I have included here the beginning of *Imitate the Tiger* in order to give you a context as you examine Lee Ann's teaching in relation to the text and the features of effective instruction:

They're asking me to remember. They're asking me to write down everything I can remember that led up to this. To this school. Sitting here all alone in a rehab for drunks and druggies that they call a school. Some school! First thing they do is go through all my luggage—pants, socks, even my underwear—just to make sure I don't have any booze or drugs. They tell me I can't make any phone calls. Then they hand me a stack of paper that has all these rules on it. And I got to remember them all. First one I see says I've got to get up at six in the morning. Six in the morning!

Now some short, skinny lady is looking over my shoulder, telling me I'm supposed to write down what I remember. I'm supposed to tell my story.

Okay. I'll tell you my story. I'll tell you all of it. You want to know what I remember? Here's what I remember. I remember a football game. That's right, a football game.

It already seems like a long time ago. But I will never forget that game, what he said, and how it hurt.

"YOU'RE CHICKEN!"

John Papano, my football coach. He yells across the field at me. He stands on the sideline, surrounded by his army of assistants, and yells at no one but me. His voice rips through my head like a rifle shot. It tears through my heart and stomach and settles there.

"Chicken!" he yells again, just in case I didn't hear him the first time.

But I heard him just fine. He didn't need to say it again. He didn't need to yell at all. He didn't need to embarrass me in front of all those people. I would do anything for him. He didn't have to yell at me.

I know I blew it. But now everybody knows that I, Christopher Serbo, outside linebacker for the Valley View Dragons, had let that touchdown score. I stand alone in the end zone, staring at the ground.

For days, weeks, and months I've played that scene over and over again in my mind.

We're ahead of the High Falls Raiders, 14–7, but High Falls has the ball on our two-yard line. It's fourth down and two to go for a touchdown.

High Falls splits their wide receiver and flanker to my right. Since I'm the linebacker on the opposite side, I move to the inside of Neil Lounsbury, the defensive end. My teammates shift to their right to counter the High Falls overload. It looks like the play is supposed to go away from me, where High Falls has its strength. I hope that it will, but I know it won't. I know instinctively that their big fullback, Billy Dunmore, is coming right at me.

I watch their quarterback fake to the halfback running to my right. Neil shoots wide into the backfield. Then I see the quarterback give the ball to that fullback, Dunmore. Damn, he is big!

They figure that we'll go with the fake to the halfback, leaving Dunmore a huge hole to run through for the touchdown.

I am well coached. I know what's going to happen. I see it all in slow motion. High Falls's guards and tackles blocking down the line away from me, the halfback shooting to his left. Dunmore starting left, then coming back toward me. The handoff. Dunmore coming right at me. It's all just like I've seen High Falls do so many times in game films. Just like we've practiced so many times in scrimmages. High Falls is running their fullback counter, and I am right where I am supposed to be.

But instead of stepping into the hole, instead of hitting Dunmore hard and stopping him before he gets too much momentum, I wait. I have no idea why I wait. Well, yes, maybe I do. I remember thinking how big he is and how painful it's going to be to hit him. I remember being afraid. Yeah, I admit it, I am afraid to hit Billy Dunmore.

It can't be more than a split second that I wait. But like I said, it's all in slow motion. And then it is Dunmore who hits me.

God, does he hit me! His two big thighs smack into my right shoulder and face mask. I drop to my knees and claw at him. I'm like a drowning man grabbing for a piece of shipwrecked boat. I scratch and tear at any piece of Dunmore I can get, hoping to hold on until my teammates can rescue me. But they do not come. I am left alone, and Dunmore runs through me in seconds.

Touchdown.

I just lie on the ground—alone. Humiliated. Nobody helps me up. For a second I hope my shoulder is broken so I can hide my shame in an honorable excuse. But it isn't. So I lie there staring up into the clouds, watching the High Falls players dance around my head.

There's no avoiding it. I have to stand up sometime. When I do, all I hear is, "You're chicken!"

It doesn't matter that on the next play I stop the two-point conversion by racing across the field and hauling down the quarterback from behind. Pappy doesn't pat me on the back and say, "Great job!" Nobody does.

It doesn't matter that we win the game 14–13. It doesn't matter that I am not the only one who plays lousy. Even the stars, Bobby Kidrow, Timmy Van Vleet, and Tommy Zodac, stink. All that matters to me, all that I remember clearly, is that coach John Papano calls me chicken. That's what I remember. (7–10)

Now that you have a context for the novel, let's look at the way Lee Ann used shared reading as the foundation for each of the six features highlighted in the Langer study. For each feature, a figure shows a page from the *Imitate the Tiger* guide with Lee Ann's teaching notes.

Tests Deconstructed to Inform Curriculum and Instruction

In the higher-performing schools in the study, teachers understood the demands of mandated tests and therefore integrated the test-taking skills and strategies into the teaching and learning that was a part of the work they did together on a daily basis. Since students took part in reading the shared text, Lee Ann was able to assess and evaluate student learning using the common text as a springboard. At Lee Ann's school, they use mandated vocabulary books. She did other word studies with her students as well, but she was also required to do lessons from the programmed vocabulary book and to test students on those words. In order to accommodate her school directives as well as her individual teaching goals, Lee Ann created her own tests (see Figure 2.5) where students applied their knowledge of the vocabulary words to the context of *Imitate the Tiger*. In this way, they demonstrated both their understanding of the words and their knowledge of the shared text.

Figure 2.5

English I

Directions: Answer each of the following questions as completely as possible and in complete sentences. Be sure that your answer demonstrates your knowledge of the vocabulary word's meaning and usage and that it answers the question posed. 4 points each. Be sure to use the word and a one word or phrase definition in your answer

Example: How might a person revile someone?
An immature student may revile someone by calling them bad names or attacking them with words; when you "talk trash" you are reviling a person.

Honors students answer all questions (60 points). Regular students, choose five of the short essay questions (40 points).

1. Describe something that is arduous for you to do? Give two specific details in your description. *Something that is arduous or hard to do, is remembering to clean my room and teach myself hard math.*

2. Is Chris Serbo intrepid when he plays football? Why or why not? Give two examples from the book. *Chris Serbo is intrepid or brave when he plays football because he knows when he gets hit it will hurt but he never back down.*

3. Is Mrs. Whittaker biased against football players? Why or why not? *I think Mrs. Whittaker is biased or prejudiced against football players because she always tries to get them in trouble.*

4. How does football act as a reprieve for Chris Serbo? What is it a relief from? Be specific. *I think football is a reprieve or a relief from something to Chris. I think its a relief from all his problems.*

5. Chris Serbo reviles who in the novel? Why? Is the attack justified? *Chris reviles or calls bad names to a few people. When he is drunk he mostly reviles Marrisa.*

6. What daunts you? Why?

7. How does Chris Serbo hoodwink his Aunt and steal alcohol from her house? *Chris hoodwinks or decieves his aunt and steals alcohol from her house by waiting until she isn't looking and puts it in a shampoo bottle.*

In Figure 2.6 we see that use of the Reading–Thinking–Responding guide constitutes another type of test prep. Lee Ann modeled inferring, connecting, and literary devices such as flashback, and she provided students with an opportunity to make text-to-text (Keene and Zimmerman) connections by asking them to discuss and write about the connections they saw between *Imitate the Tiger* and Sara Holbrook's poem "Bang, I Gotcha." Thus, for the students in these classes, the kinds of question they would encounter on a state-mandated test would be familiar to them, both in terms of content and of understanding the task of test taking.

Teachers Make Connections Across Instruction, Curriculum, and Life

This feature of effective instruction is predicated on a teacher's willingness to establish opportunities for students to see their reading as part of a larger goal: understanding themselves and their world in new ways. Teachers attempt to show students how they can apply and transfer the strategies they are learning to other texts and life: "They point out these connections so that students can

Figure 2.6

I.4 Reading . . . Thinking . . . Responding . . .

Title *Imitate the Tiger* by Jan Cheripko		
Reading	Thinking	Responding
pages 7–27 H & N: "We are what we pretend to be, so we must be careful what we pretend to be." Kurt Vonnegut. How can pretending get us into trouble? (21) WS: "I know I've overstepped my boundaries." (7) ST Why might the author start the book with italics? (7) ST Cheripko uses flashback on this first page. Does this hint at the structure? (7) WC What techniques does the author use to help us "see" the setting? *flashback, description* (8-10) TW Use the scene from Mighty Ducks video where the coach yells at his players. Compare Chris' feelings to the player's in the video. What would make a coach act this way? Impact on players? (8-10) PR How would I be feeling at this point? Would there be long-term effects of feeling this way? (26-27) CN Where does Chris' anger come from?	Bang, I Gotcha "I never needed you anyway, so there!" I shoot from the hip . . . "I don't even care what you have to say," Words shot intended to rip a bulls-eye wound near your nowhere heart. "I'm better off on my own, apart." I candle puff my smoking gun, holster my hurt. Turn, and run. by Sara Holbrook from *Walking on the Boundaries of Change*	

see how the skills and knowledge they are gaining can be used productively in a range of situations" (Langer, 8).

As Figures 2.7 and 2.8 show, Lee Ann created opportunities for students to connect their developing understandings of guilt, regret, and choices to the text of their lives. She asked students to look at the main character's life and his choices in order to examine how our choices affect everyone in our lives. The thinking, writing, and connecting these students did in the course of their response to the shared text took them into their own lives, Greek tragedies ("fatal flaw," "hubris"), memories of effective teachers, and the responsibility students have for their own learning.

Students Learn Strategies for Thinking and Doing

In classrooms where this feature is thriving, students learn to think about the work they are asked to do and develop procedural strategies for doing that work. Because strategies are "how-to" lessons, students are then able to transfer and apply that shared learning to other contexts. "They guide students through the process and overtly teach the steps necessary to do well" (Langer, 10).

Figure 2.7

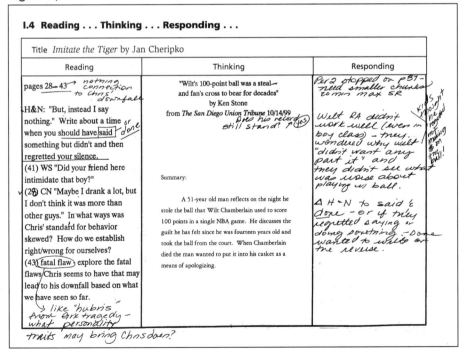

Figure 2.8

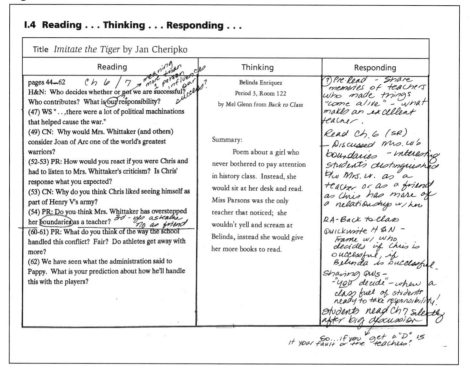

Figure 2.9 shows that Lee Ann elicited multiple text connections with the Bible and Chris Crutcher's *Ironman*. She began the process here of asking students to collect data about the main character, Chris Serbo, from the text and by comparison to other characters with similar traits. In this way, she modeled for students how they could begin to find concrete traits to help them write a character analysis.

As a way to document their discoveries, students used the graphic organizer Fleshing Out a Character (see Figure 2.10). They then worked collaboratively to analyze their thinking and try out their ideas on members of their learning groups. This organizer provided students with a beginning focus for analyzing character development: actions, words, emotions, thoughts and feelings, and motivations as well as strengths and weaknesses. Students could return to their notes from this discussion on another day as they moved toward a more formal written analysis. In this way, Lee Ann scaffolded the steps toward a finished product by showing them multiple ways of doing the work.

Figure 2.9

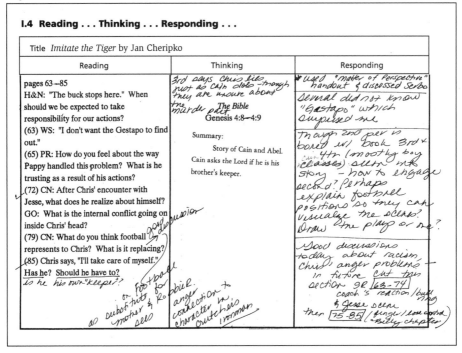

I.4 Reading . . . Thinking . . . Responding . . .

Title *Imitate the Tiger* by Jan Cheripko

Reading	Thinking	Responding

pages 63–85

H&N: "The buck stops here." When should we be expected to take responsibility for our actions?

(63) WS: "I don't want the Gestapo to find out."

(65) PR: How do you feel about the way Pappy handled this problem? What is he trusting as a result of his actions?

(72) CN: After Chris' encounter with Jesse, what does he realize about himself?

GO: What is the internal conflict going on inside Chris' head?

(79) CN: What do you think football represents to Chris? What is it replacing?

(85) Chris says, "I'll take care of myself." Has he? Should he have to?

Skills and Knowledge Taught in Multiple Types of Lessons

When effective teachers determine students' literacy needs, they look at ways to teach to those needs by isolating the area needing support and giving students the opportunity to do activities that apply what they have learned and then to integrate that learning back into the class text. One of the advantages of a common shared reading text is that all the students have the text and so teaching points can be pulled out, isolated, talked about, applied, and then reconnected to the text. Another significant aspect of this approach is that students are always able to try out their ideas on others who have read the same text.

As Figures 2.11 and 2.12 show, Lee Ann helped students isolate the skill of writing a character analysis. She used a variety of ways of getting students to think through who the person is from evidence they gathered and inferences they made based on that evidence. The Fleshing Out a Character form gave students a beginning, and that information then was applied at the inferential level by using the graphic organizer It's a Matter of Perspective (see Figure 2.13).

As students continued to examine Chris's character, they did so by getting inside the main character's thinking and the thinking of those around him.

44

Figure 2.10

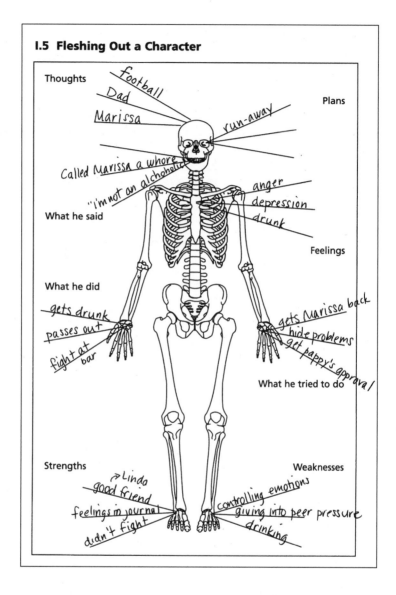

1.5 Fleshing Out a Character

Thoughts
football
Dad
Marissa

run-away

Plans

Called Marissa a whore
"i'm not an alchoholic

anger
depression
drunk

What he said

Feelings

What he did
gets drunk
passes out
fight at bar

gets Marissa back
hide problems
get pappy's approval

What he tried to do

Strengths
Linda
good friend
feelings in journal
didn't fight

controlling emotions
giving into peer pressure
drinking

Weaknesses

These discussions and focused analysis and writing moved students toward a synthesis of their thinking. Students synthesized their thinking in an "I Am" poem for Chris:

> I am scared and alone.
> I wonder why my life is going in
>   the wrong direction?
>   I hear people dying and can't get them out of my head.

Figure 2.11

I.4 Reading . . . Thinking . . . Responding . . . *afraid to face "right" problems - use wrong ones to hide what we really need to fix*		
Title *Imitate the Tiger* by Jan Cheripko		
Reading	**Thinking**	**Responding**
pages 86–109 *define right & wrong problem w/ Chris Serbo — example* H&N: In the book *Winnie-the-Pooh* on *Problem Solving*, Pooh says: "I think," said Pooh, "that if you don't pick the right problem, it's the wrong problem which means that you still have to solve the right problem after you've solved the wrong problem, if you do. Right?" Why do you think we have so much trouble finding the right problems to solve in our lives? *father figure* WS: vindication (86) CN: Chris plans not to tell his adviser anything, but quickly spills his guts. What role do you think Chris sees for Mr. Lake in his life? (96) CN: Why do you think this victory means so much to the team? To Chris? What does it represent? *?* (97) WC: Look for ways Cheripko consistently uses his response journal to lead us back to the action of the story. (109) What is your prediction for what is ahead for Chris?	"Everything I Need," by K. Moore & C. Streetman , sung by Keb' Mo' on *slow down* Summary: Singer laments having nothing to hold onto in life, and no one who cares. But he realizes he has his heart and soul and that's all he needs. *reminds you of Serbo* *what does this ending suggest?*	Set up quickwrite by discussing right/wrong problems in relation to Serbo RT WR drinking football loss of mother ex-girlfriend father gone Do fleshing out character handout Aing- using specific details from fleshing out for a Ft on Serbo's character Check mastery of Ft studies Describe football scene- - define safety blitz - ask student to demonstrate?

I see myself as a coward and chicken.
I want to forget about the accident and fight.
I am scared and alone.
I pretend that I am perfect in every way.
I believe I am in trouble and need someone to talk to.
I touch alcohol every day.

I feel alone and worried.
I worry that I am not going to survive.
I cry because nobody likes me.
I am scared and alone.
I finally understand that I need help.

Lee Ann established multiple opportunities for students to organize their thinking about Chris's character, choices and motivation, and hopes for a better life. By the time students were asked to write a formal character analysis, they had had several lessons to organize their thinking and collaborate with others working on the same task.

Figure 2.12

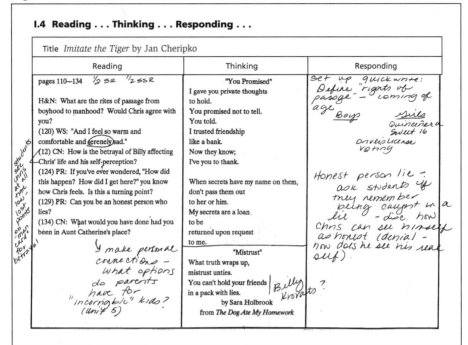

Classrooms Organized to Foster Collaboration and Shared Cognition

We have all experienced the "best of times and the worst of times" with respect to collaboration in our classrooms. And we have learned from those experiences that all collaborative talk is not worthwhile talk. In effective classrooms, the kind of talk we try to model, and the kind we hope our students will engage in, is what Lauren Resnik describes as accountable talk: "Accountable talk seriously responds to and further develops what others in the group have said. It puts forth and demands knowledge that is accurate and relevant to the issue under discussion. Teachers can intentionally create the norms and skills of accountable talk in their classrooms" (4).

While accountable talk should be the norm for any classroom talk, I find the best place to foster accountable talk is in conjunction with shared reading. When students have been part of a shared book experience, they have access to the text, so as they put forth their opinions, respond and question the opinions of others, and use knowledge to increase knowledge, they have access to a common text to support their thinking and talk.

Figure 2.13

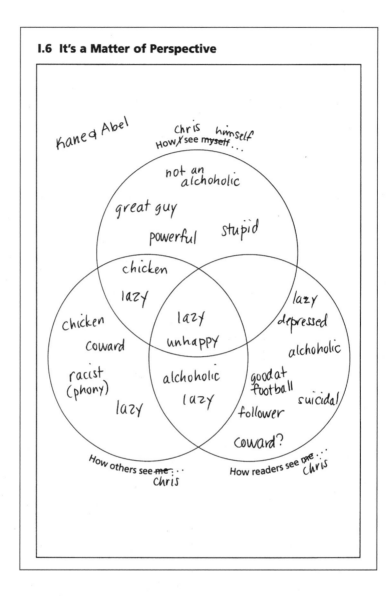

1.6 It's a Matter of Perspective

How do we get students to the point where their accountable talk will promote cognitive collaboration and active learning? I believe there are three kinds of influence by the teacher that will promote or diminish accountable talk: making an environment safe for accountable talk; providing texts students find worthy of talk; and modeling accountable talk with think-alouds.

For students to begin the process of engaging in talk that is academically and personally challenging, the environment has to be safe enough for that to occur. Teachers can do several things to promote this kind of environment:

- Build classroom community, not just at the beginning of the year but at frequent intervals.
- Create rules for disagreeing in agreeable ways.
- Invite comments from all students.
- Allow time for everyone to think before sharing.
- Use small-group structures (think-pair-share, literature circles, inquiry groups) so students have the opportunity to try out ideas and accountable talk with less risk than in whole-group discussions.
- Teach students how to support comments and assertions.
- Give value to talk by saving highlights (class scribes, charting, synthesis, or exit slips).

Regardless of the environment, students will engage in talk that is academically productive only if they find common texts worthy of talk. We can create a foundation for that talk by choosing texts for shared reading with some parameters in mind:

- Use a variety of text types (narrative, essay, poetry, information, visual, musical) so all students find a genre that is accessible and engaging.
- Use multiple text sources for major concepts or themes.
- Use texts that offer a point of entry because of personal connections or background knowledge.
- Offer students texts that provide divergent or unique points of view.
- Provide texts that are accessible in terms of language and context.

In an age when students hear a great deal of talk that is not accountable, we have to model talk that is accountable. This is talk that comes from forming our own opinions and supporting those opinions with evidence, actively listening to the opinions of others, extending others' thinking by challenging their rationales, and developing ways to disagree without being disagreeable. We can model that talk in honest ways as part of the cognitive collaboration that occurs after a connected shared reading:

- One thing I noticed that intrigued me . . .
- I was surprised to hear you say . . . What made you make that connection?
- When you point out . . . it reminds me of . . .
- Although I agree with you, I couldn't help but notice . . .
- I see a connection between what _____ and _____ said, which makes me wonder if that was part of the author's intention.
- My thoughts are similar to _____'s, but I also noted . . .

- Although _____ already mentioned something similar, I think my ideas take this in another direction.
- One thing I disagree with in what you said was _____ because of these words (or this statement) . . .

This was actually one of the most difficult aspects of collaborative discussions in my classroom. Many of us came into the profession at a time when right answers were valued. We wanted students to get the answer quickly, and if they didn't, we didn't spend much time giving them support to think their way through to an answer that could be justified by the text. A few students always dominated those discussions, and I tended to be the center of all the talk. Collaborative cognition demands that students try out their thinking on others and that we do everything we can to bring all thinking into the center. Figure 2.14 shows that Lee Ann and her students found support for their text discussions by connecting the shared novel to the "thinking" text offered each day.

Figure 2.14

I.4 Reading . . . Thinking . . . Responding . . .

Title *Imitate the Tiger* by Jan Cheripko

Reading	Thinking	Responding
pages 135—156 H&N: Some people say, "I know what I see," and others say, "I see what I know." How does what we expect to see in others influence what we see? (152) WS: ". . . this is what I love. To see all of the intricate parts of the offense start to move." (135) CN: Why do you think Chris is feeling such a connection to Jackie? (141) CN: "Something has got to change." Do you think Chris sees himself changing or in need of change? (142) CN: GO—It's a Matter of Perspective. Use the GO to discuss how Chris sees his relationship with Pappy; how Pappy sees his relationship to Chris; and how we (as readers) see their relationship: Does tension arise from these perspectives? (149) PR: "You really are a coward, you know that?" Does Chris exhibit characteristics of cowardice? (156) PR: Do you think football makes Chris' life feel in or out of control? *Do : I am poem for Chris using the "Matter of Perspective go completed earlier*	"Fear" by Shel Silverstein from *A Light in the Attic* Summary: Poem about Barnabus Browning who had a fear of drowning, so he would never go near water. Instead he locked himself in his room and drowned from his tears. *read last*	*2nd - did not understand "expectation" + how they influence perceptions - explain in terms of Serb - how does Mrs W expect him to be? explain in terms of 1/2 bull, 1/2 empty glass* *"He is a coward." discussion went well - Chris doesn't do anything to overcome his fears or problems so he's like Barnabus Browning says one student*

Generative Learning Encouraged

Langer's research pointed to the importance of students' moving beyond the acquisition of discrete skills: "All of the teachers in the higher-performing schools take a generative approach to student learning. They go beyond students' acquisition of skills or knowledge to engage students in creative and critical uses of their knowledge and skills" (12). When we teach in ways that encourage creative and critical thinking, we have an opportunity to see students at their best. I believe there are times when we underestimate students' abilities to think critically about a text and respond in ways that affect our thinking.

Figures 2.15 and 2.16 show that Lee Ann's students moved to that critical stage. They examined the text from the perspective of both reader and writer. In those dual roles, they began to make demands of the text that might not have occurred to them just weeks before. With each shared text that is read, students layer a new level of understanding and expectation on the author's work. As my students became more literate, I was always shocked to see the demands they placed on texts in terms of coherence and consistency. They began to see other options the author could (or should) have taken, and it seemed as though I

Figure 2.15

I.4 Reading . . . Thinking . . . Responding . . .		

Title *Imitate the Tiger* by Jan Cheripko		
Reading	Thinking	Responding
pages 157–195 *157-177 / 178-195* *"Think of yourself first & everything else will fall into place"* *(Point)* H&N: Some people think we should think of ourselves first in case no one else does. Do you agree? *(I just red yes)* (183) WS: "I know in my heart that this is the reckoning about my getting drunk." (157) PR: Chris says, "Suffering in silence is what being a man is all about." Is this right? (178) CN: If we could get inside Chris' head at the moment, what would we see there? Are his perceptions of others' feelings and actions changing as he goes downhill? *unrealistic* (195) CN: After the intervention, how do you think Chris is feeling? Are there feelings he isn't admitting to here? Do you think he feels any relief? *some day yes* *students stumped on this or one wall but relief*	The Beatles *Sgt. Pepper's Lonely Hearts Club Band* "With a Little Help From My Friends " Summary: Song about friendship and loneliness and how we all help each other through the difficult times. *www.beatlesfan.de/walhfmf.htm*	*H&N discussion good – is it being selfish to think of yourself?* *(162)* *⑧ Do you know "friends" like Chris & Polly? Is Chris really Polly's friend?* *good discussion about Chris' friends help him with homework, support etc* *(157) most groaned at this line & said No admitting problem & asking for help is what being a man is* *Have students read on-line & connect to novel in R/response*

Figure 2.16

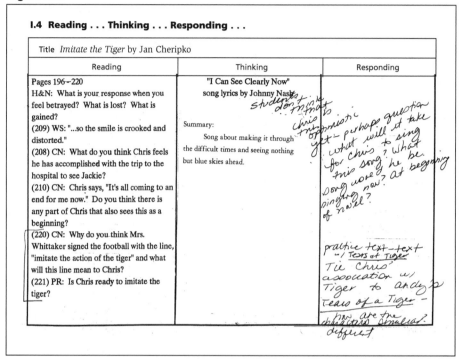

often had to remind them that each of us gets to tell a story in our own way. Lee Ann's students were no exception.

Their reader response journals indicate the diversity of opinions about the quality of the shared text. If we look at three different responses, we can see the range of expectations students began to articulate:

> I thought the book was very slow at the beginning. It was all about football. Then in the middle of the book, it started getting better. I was right. It's like *Tears of a Tiger*. The main character is depressed and gets into arguments. So basically it was bad at first but then it got you.
> —Jon

> To tell you the truth, I really didn't care much for this book. I thought it was basically boring and pointless. I don't know much about football, so some of the book was confusing and hard to understand. I did like the way that you presented the book to us and made connections to our life. In that aspect it made me understand how Chris was feeling and

how I would feel if put in the position of having no friends and no one to turn to. Overall, I would not read the book again.
—Amanda

I truly enjoyed *Imitate the Tiger* for many reasons. First, the story could have easily been nonfiction since it describes what happens all the time all around the U.S. Second, it was thoroughly and smoothly written to give that "hook" to catch the reader. Third, it's easy to relate to many of the characters. Finally, it was just a good book, end of story.
—Daryl

We may not agree with students' opinions, and we may not even like those opinions at times, but we can appreciate the way these readers have begun to extend their thinking to the role of text critic. As I read through the students' responses, I chose ones that represented the range of thinking and response, and I found it interesting that most students appreciated learning something new or making connections between and among texts and their lives even if they didn't enjoy the book. For me, these are clear indications that students have moved to a more demanding level of reading.

Another indicator of generative thinking was that students acted on the challenge to determine whether Johnny Nash's song lyrics, "I Can See Clearly Now," would represent Chris at the end of this book, or whether he would have a song that better represents who and where he is at this point. Many students believed "I Can See Clearly Now" would be appropriate but offered other suggestions:

I picked the song "I Will Survive" because I think while Chris is in this school he will learn to find his spirit even though he didn't want to change. I think Chris finally realized he was in the ditch.

Other songs I believe he could identify with are "Break Stuff" when he breaks the window on the door; "We Are the Champions" when he wins the championship; "Chop Suey" because he pretends to be something; and "Survivor" because he survives through a lot of things.

Perhaps the ultimate evidence of generative thinking is when readers can take the evidence from one text and apply the thinking represented there to other texts. These responses demonstrated the careful and respectful way these readers treated Chris Serbo. They didn't always like him, but they did try to help him find his way.

Through an analysis of Lee Ann's study of a common shared novel, we can conclude that even though there were students who didn't like the main character and those who didn't enjoy the writing, they all learned from the teaching and learning opportunities that this shared reading offered. By anticipating reading with word study and writing; synthesizing reading with strategy lessons; and facilitating collaborative discussions and writing after reading, Lee Ann was able to have an uninterrupted time of shared reading with her students every day.

Guthrie, Alao, and Rinehart cite characteristics of engaged readers as being committed to the subject matter, wanting to learn the content, believing in one's own ability, and wanting to share understandings from learning (439). Connected shared reading provides a solid foundation to support student engagement. The shared reading approach gives all readers access to texts they might not otherwise choose or be able to read. Each shared reading provides a foundation not only for the next whole-class text but for students' independent choices for reading.

Will students become so addicted to shared reading that they never want to read on their own? I doubt it. As we sit in workshops or seminars, most of us still enjoy a great read-aloud or shared reading. We enjoy it knowing that it will never replace our choosing our own books for our own purposes and listening to the fluent reader voice we have created for ourselves. In *The Book of Learning and Forgetting,* Frank Smith reminds us that as student readers find their way, we become less critical to their development as readers because the authors of the books they read will then teach them how to read: "There's a simple yet powerful reason why children will never become dependent upon other people to do anything they think they can do for themselves—they don't have the patience" (26). Readers' independence is a reflection of the success of shared reading—a time when they are given enough support so they can eventually find their own ways.

3

Learning to Read and Reading to Learn: Understanding Strategic Shared Reading

Successful comprehension depends in part on readers' ability to allocate their limited attention efficiently and effectively to the most relevant pieces of information within the text and within their memory.

Paul van den Broek and Kathleen Kremer, "The Mind in Action"

While connected shared reading provides a powerful model of how texts come together in order to entertain, inform, motivate, or persuade us, many readers need more assistance before they can independently read a variety of texts that may be more complex in terms of structure and language. Like Peppermint Pattie in the Peanuts cartoon, many of our students read without paying attention.

So, how can we get students to "pay attention" inside their heads without losing the joy of reading we have instilled with connected shared reading? We know there are many sound academic reasons for students' needing strategic reading, but we also know we have lost ground if students do not want to read on the other side of our instruction. I believe we can accomplish both goals if we help students understand that our instructional purposes are different when we move from connected shared reading to strategic shared reading. While both connected and strategic reading can be done with a shared reading approach (eyes past print with a fluent reader's voice support), I believe each has unique instructional purposes:

Connected Reading	*Strategic Reading*
Relatively uninterrupted reading	Reading interrupted to demonstrate strategies in action
Purposefully allows students to experience the whole before examining the parts	Strategically examines the way thoughtful readers experience texts
Goal is to give students the opportunity to experience the global aspects of text: story grammar, characterization, cause and effect, character motivations, etc.	Goal is to give students the opportunity to use strategies to make sense of text: inferring, questioning, visualizing, etc.
Clocks reading mileage	Develops strategy-conscious readers
Texts chosen to offer readers experience with a diverse range of texts and authors	Texts chosen to support needs-based strategy focus

With these purposes in mind, I would use strategic reading when I could tell my students were struggling with the structure of the text or understanding the text purpose or language; missing supports of text or genre; or not using strategies that would help them gain meaning from the text. In each of these cases, I would want students to understand why we were examining the strategy, how and when they might use this strategy to help them gain more proficiency as readers, and how to transfer experience with this strategy to other texts and contexts.

In schools where there is a heavy emphasis on strategic reading, it has been interesting to talk with some of the students who are recipients of strategic reading instruction. I often ask them why they are learning the strategy and how it will help them as readers, and they tell me they are learning this because that's what good readers do. They point to a list of strategies displayed on the bulletin board. On further questioning, I find their purpose is circular: I'm learning to predict because good readers predict so that's why I'm learning it. If students do not understand the purpose and transfer pieces of a strategy lesson, perhaps little has been gained toward their independence as readers. In the *Handbook of Reading Research,* Paris, Wasik, and Turner cite research in support of students' understanding why they are learning strategies: "Understanding *why* the strategy was important helped children to identify main ideas and made them feel capable of completing the task" (613).

Students' understandings' of when and how to apply the strategy is perhaps the most important aspect of strategy instruction. In *I Read It, but I Don't Get It,* Cris Tovani reminds readers of the critical role of purpose in strategy instruction: "A reader's purpose affects everything about reading. It determines what's important in the text, what is remembered, and what comprehension strategy a reader uses to enhance meaning" (24). For many students, both purpose setting and transfer have been overlooked as part of the modeled instruction and guided practice that are critical to strategic reading.

The actual teaching of the strategy usually does not take much time. Most readers learn a strategy fairly quickly and can demonstrate they know the strategy through guided practice or with assessment tools. However, knowing the strategy and actually using the strategy are two different problems. Paris, Wasik, and Turner cite Raphael and McKinney's 1983 research in which they reported that "eighth graders were unmotivated to use the strategy over the ten weeks of instruction and appeared to need only a ten-minute orientation in order to understand the strategy" (613). Their lack of strategy use did not result from lack of understanding but from lack of motivation. If students have no desire to read, the strategy won't be employed anyway because the strategy has no purpose for them.

Strategy vs. Skill

There are many definitions for what a strategy is. The practice that emerges from those definitions can lead to effective support for readers and writers or to more stumbling blocks for those students. I like the definition Cris Tovani uses with her students: "A strategy is an intentional plan that readers use to help themselves make sense of their reading. Strategies are flexible and can be adapted to meet the demands of the reading task. Good readers use lots of strategies to help themselves make sense of text" (5). I like this definition because it incorporates several important characteristics of a strategy: flexibility, intentionality, and multiple uses.

As I work with teachers and students, I find students involved in all kinds of activities that teachers have labeled strategy lessons: workbook pages where readers are underlining main ideas, graphic organizers where students are filling in cells, Post-it notes for each paragraph or page of a text, or student think-alouds after each paragraph they read. Any or all of these might have something to do with a strategy, but that is not always the case. In observing these classes, I like to tell teachers and students the mark of a strategy lesson for me is evidence of a "how-to" lesson. As part of both the modeled lesson and the guided practice, I would expect instruction in how to employ a tactic or strategy in order to reach a larger goal. Therefore, as teachers list their instructional purposes for the day, I look for a commitment to teaching a strategy as one way to get to a larger goal. For example, we might look at learning the strategy of inferring as a way to look beneath the literal level to the subtleties of the text, such as authors' intentions or characters' motivations.

I define a skill as something one obtains after the strategy has become automatic. When a strategy is at the conscious level, we are able to observe how and under what conditions the strategy is being used. The real value becomes apparent, and ironically less able to be seen as a discrete strategy, when a reader is using the strategy to meet the ultimate goal of making sense of text. Paris, Wasik, and Turner discuss a skill as a strategy gone "underground" (Vygotsky). In their view, "Strategies are more efficient and developmentally advanced when they become generated and applied automatically as skills" (611). (For the contrast between strategy and skill, see Figure 3.2.) If the ultimate goal of strategy instruction is movement toward this automaticity, then our purposeful teaching has to include changing our levels of support as students become more sophisticated in their strategy use and integration.

Planning for Strategy Instruction

When I think of planning for a strategy lesson, I'm always reminded of the beautiful model Elizabeth Berg paints for us in her novel *Durable Goods*. In this book, a young girl is lonely after the death of her mother and often gravitates to a neighbor's house so she can be with the maid who works there.

> "You can help me bake," she says. "I've got to make a cake today . . ."
> "I might mess up," I warned her, the shame already curled low in the bottom of my belly.
> "Try it," she said. Her voice was as comfortable as a quilt. I held my breath, cracked the shell against the side of the bowl. The yolk

smashed; pieces of shell fell into the bowl with it. I was so sorry, and feeling scared to look up, and all she did was give me a clean bowl and another egg. "Try again," she said, and walked away. She started humming. Country western was what she really liked.

"But I messed up," I said.

She stopped singing, came to stand by me. "Do you like scrambled eggs?"

"Yes, ma'am."

"Well, you didn't hardly mess up, then."

I had to keep my smile tight, so much was in me. And that wasn't all. Next she said, "You know if you didn't like scrambled eggs, you still wouldn't have messed up. You're just learning, Katie. That's all. You go ahead and mess up all you want. Hell, I got a million eggs. They're on sale over to Piggly Wiggly."

I didn't do anything else wrong. I figured I might not. I'd been taught tenderly, and that's how a lesson stays. (96–97)

Katie was able to learn a strategy for cooking because her teacher knew that a strategy lesson has several important aspects: it is a model that clearly defines the task and its purpose; offers an opportunity to practice; provides time and support for learning from mistakes and tools for trying again; and discovers a way to make the learning memorable. As teachers, we can take that model into our classrooms as we design strategic reading lessons.

In *Mega Memory*, Kevin Trudeau examines four steps for charting progress toward learning: unconscious incompetence, conscious incompetence, conscious competence, and unconscious competence. While these terms can seem to be complicated ways of obscuring the obvious, I have found the concepts embedded in them helpful for looking at how we support learners at each of these stages. If we look at these stages as a progression toward automaticity, we can examine each stage for learner characteristics and then determine how we could best support learners with strategic shared reading in order to help them move toward and into the next stage. In order to look at the stages logically, I discuss the interconnected strategies of questioning, predicting, and inferring at each of the stages.

Unconscious Incompetence

At the unconscious incompetence stage, readers are unaware of the wide range of strategies fluent readers use (unconscious), and therefore they are unable to read some texts (incompetence) beyond basic decoding. This stage is characterized by students' saying, "Why do we have to do this anyway? Who cares about

Achieving Automaticity

this stuff? I'll never use this—why am I wasting my time?" Does this sound familiar? If so, your role at this stage is one of awareness. Students will need to see and hear ways that questioning, predicting, and inferring can help readers gain meaning from a text.

Introducing the strategies of questioning and predicting through a shared reading of Jack Gantos's *Joey Pigza Loses Control* helps students understand both the importance of questioning and how too many questions can lead us away from a text or task:

We were on our way to Dad's house and Mom was driving with both hands clamped tightly around the wheel as if she had me by the neck. I had been snapping my seat belt on and off and driving her nuts by asking a hundred *what if's* about Dad. She's been hearing them for two weeks already and wasn't answering. But that didn't stop me. What if he's not nice? What if he hates me? What if he's as crazy as you always said he was? What if he drinks and gets nasty? What if I don't like him?

What if Grandma tries to put me in the refrigerator again? What if they make Pablo sleep outside? What if they don't eat pizza? What if I want to come home quick, can I hire a helicopter? (3)

After our reading of this delightful book, we could look at the kinds of questions Joey asks and decide whether the questions move him toward his goal or serve to overwhelm him. We can then compare what happens when our questions have a specific focus that leads us to our goals by doing a lateral thinking puzzle together. Paul Sloane's book *Test Your Lateral Thinking IQ* is an excellent resource for helping students learn how to ask focused questions. Each lateral thinking puzzle can be done as a shared reading. Students are then given the opportunity to ask questions that would help them solve the puzzle, but you can respond to the questions only with yes or no. One of the puzzles, "The Cabin" (29) is given here:

In the mountains there is a cabin. Inside, three people lie dead. The cabin is locked from the inside and there is no sign of a struggle or of any weapons. What happened?

If students' questions lag, you can give them additional clues:

1. All three died at the same time. Their deaths were violent but accidental.
2. They knew they were going to die immediately before they died. They died because they were in the cabin. If they had gotten out of the cabin three hours earlier they would have lived. If they could have gotten out three minutes earlier they would still have died. (32)

As students generate lots of questions and narrow their focus to the questions that seem to be leading them toward a solution, their ability to ask effective questions increases. By the way, the answer to the puzzle involves seeing multiple meanings for *cabin*. In this case, it is an airplane cabin after a plane crash that has killed both pilots and the passenger.

After these two readings, we can list the kinds of questions that help us maintain focus and gain deeper understanding of a text (e.g., "I wonder what I already know about . . .") and the kinds of questions that would get in the way of understanding (e.g., "Why do we have to read such stupid stuff?"). As students reach higher levels of competence, we could move to more challenging texts, but at this stage we want to make sure that the texts we choose are interesting enough for readers so they will want to ask questions. Engagement at this awareness stage helps us move readers into the next stage (conscious incompetence), where they begin to benefit from our modeling of ways fluent readers use thinking strategies. At this stage, readers would not be adept at using these strategies on their own (incompetence) but they are aware (conscious) that the use of these strategies will make a difference in the reading of a text.

Conscious Incompetence

In order to demonstrate strategic reading where questioning and predicting lead to inferring, I would use a Paul Jennings short story, "Ex Poser," as my text. This story is interesting enough so that readers will want to get to the end even with the interruptions. They may even ask you to return to the story for a connected shared reading so that they can get the entire story again. Here, I separate the story as if I were using one portion of it at a time on overhead transparencies so all students could see the text while we read it together. I include my thinking aloud with predicting and questioning as italicized text following each "transparency." The first transparency has only the story and book titles and the author's name. An uninterrupted copy of the text is provided in Appendix H.

> **Overhead 1:** "Ex Poser" by Paul Jennings
> From *Unmentionable!*, pp. 85–88
>
> *(I'm wondering what a poser is. I know what a model does when he/she is posing, but I'm not sure this is related to that kind of posing. I do know that the other stories I've read by Paul Jennings usually use the title as some kind of twist for the story. I'm thinking the same will happen here.)*

> **Overhead 2:** There are two rich kids in our class. Sandra Morris and Ben Fox. They are both snobs. They think they are too good for the rest of us. Their parents have big cars and big houses. Both of them are quiet. They keep to themselves. I guess they don't want to mix with the ruffians like me.
>
> Ben Fox always wears expensive gym shoes and the latest fashions. He thinks he is good-looking with his blue eyes and blond hair. He is a real poser.
>
> *(I think "poser" is being used like "posing for a modeling job." I think the narrator of the story sees being good-looking as a negative thing but I'm not sure why. I wonder if I'm going to find that the narrator resents Ben's good looks because the narrator feels like he doesn't look good. In any case, that makes me wonder why Ben would want to be an exposer.)*

Overhead 3: Sandra Morris is the same. And she knows it. Blue eyes and blond hair too. Skin like silk. Why do some kids get the best of everything?

Me, I landed pimples. I've used everything I can on them. But still they bud and grow and burst. Just when you don't want them to. It's not fair.

(*I think my prediction was pretty close. Seems like he resents Ben and Sandra's looks. I'm wondering if he's going to do something to try and take them down a notch.*)

Overhead 4: Anyway, today I have the chance to even things up. Boffin is bringing along his latest invention—a lie detector. Sandra Morris is the victim. She agreed to try it out because everyone knows that she would never tell a lie. What she doesn't know is that Boffin and I are going to ask her some very embarrassing questions.

Boffin is a brain. His inventions always work. He is smarter than the teachers. Everyone knows that. And now he has brought along his latest effort. A lie detector.

(*I'm wondering what he could possibly ask Sandra with this lie detector that would "even things up." He says he's going to ask embarrassing questions and my guess is that he won't be gentle.*)

Overhead 5: He tapes two wires to Sandra's arm. "It doesn't hurt," he says. "But it is deadly accurate." He switches on the machine, and a little needle swings into the middle of the dial. "Here's a trial question," he says. "Are you a girl?"

Sandra nods.

"You have to say yes or no," he says.

"Yes," replies Sandra. The needle swings over to TRUTH. Maybe this thing really works. Boffin gives a big grin.

"This time tell a lie," says Boffin. "Are you a girl?" he asks again.

Sandra smiles with that lovely smile of hers. "No," she says. A little laugh goes up, but then all the kids in the room gasp. The needle points to LIE. This lie detector is a terrific invention.

"Okay," says Boffin. "You only have seven questions, David. The batteries will go flat after another seven questions." He sits down behind his machine and twiddles the knobs.

This is going to be fun. I am going to find out a little bit about Sandra Morris and Ben Fox. It's going to be very interesting. Very interesting indeed.

(If I stop here for a second, I can't help but think of some of the questions I'm guessing he will ask her. It almost seems like he has some secret information about her. Because I've read other Jennings stories like "A Mouthful" and "Licked" I can't help but think the joke is going to turn on him.)

Overhead 6: I ask my first question. "Have you ever kissed Ben Fox?"

Sandra goes red. Ben Fox goes red. I have got them this time. I am sure they have something going between them. I will expose them.

"No," says Sandra. Everyone cranes his neck to see what the lie detector says. The needle points to TRUTH.

This is not what I expected. And I only have six questions left. I can't let her off the hook. I am going to expose them both.

"Have you ever held his hand?"

Again she says, "No." And the needle says TRUTH. I am starting to feel guilty. Why am I doing this?

(Well, it seems like the narrator is at least feeling guilty. I'm wondering if those were the most embarrassing questions or if there are some that are going to be worse. I wonder if she will do something to turn the tables or whether he will cause his own downfall.)

Overhead 7: I try another tack. "Are you in love?" I ask.

A red flush starts to crawl up her neck. I am feeling really mean now. Fox is blushing like a sunset.

"Yes," she says. The needle points to TRUTH.

"Does he have blue eyes?" I ask.

"No," she says.

"Brown?" I say.

"No," she says again.

I don't know what to say next. I look at each kid in the class very carefully. Ben Fox has blue eyes. I was sure that she loved him.

(I'm thinking he has worked himself into a corner here but I can't figure out what is going on. In fact, I don't think he wants to embarrass her as much as he did when he started. How many questions does he have left?—I've lost track.)

Overhead 8: "This thing doesn't work," I say to Boffin. "I can't see one kid who doesn't have either blue eyes or brown eyes."

"We can," says Boffin. They are all looking at me.

I can feel *my* face turning red now. I wish I could sink through the floor, but I get on with my last question. "Is he an idiot?" I ask.

(*Oh, no. I think my prediction about the story turning on him is happening. Even he sees that it is happening. I'm wondering if he will be a good sport about this. I'm also wondering how the other kids will react.*)

Overhead 9: Sandra is very embarrassed. "Yes," she says in a voice that is softer than a whisper. "And he has green eyes."

This modeling of questioning and predicting our way through the text allows emerging strategic readers to see inside our heads. At this stage of awareness, we are trying to get them to understand the active nature of reading. Typically, after several shared strategic readings of diverse texts, the reader is aware of the kinds of interacting voices fluent readers have going on inside their heads while they read, but they have not developed their own internal reader voices. In fact, one of my students told me that when she tried to read, she heard my voice in her head reading to her. I told her that she could use my voice only until she found her own. After our modeling of a strategy, we have to give our readers a chance to transfer these reader actions to another text. In this way they can begin to use these strategies while they still have the support of shared reading. At this transfer stage, they are moving into conscious competence.

Conscious Competence

Conscious competence occurs when the reader has internalized the strategies of a good reader and is able to use those strategies because he is following the actual "how to" that was demonstrated in the model lesson. The following text sample demonstrates eighth-grade, student-generated questioning throughout a shared text. I broke the text for overhead transparencies in places I thought would give students a good opportunity to practice strategic questioning. Students' questions are italicized. An uninterrupted copy of the text is provided in Appendix H.

Overhead 1: "Reptiles and Children Don't Mix"
by Susan Okie
From *The Washington Post,* November 16, 1999, p. Z12
(*What kind of reptiles? How old are the children? Who ever thought they would mix anyway? Who gets hurt—the kids or the reptiles? I wonder if this is a lateral thinking puzzle kind of thing with the word "mix"? If it says "new study," I wonder if there was an old study? Who pays for this stuff anyway?*)

Overhead 2: Got a baby or a toddler in the house? Get rid of that iguana.

(Well, we know that it is at least an iguana. I'll bet there are other reptiles though. We know how old the kids are now. I'm still looking for answers to my other questions.)

Overhead 3: Pet reptiles—including all types of lizards, snakes and turtles—can be a source of life-threatening infections and do not belong in households that have children younger than 5, according to a recommendation issued last week by the federal Centers for Disease Control and Prevention.

Reptiles also shouldn't be handled by small children or by anyone whose immune system doesn't work well, the agency cautioned. In addition, the animals should not be kept as pets in preschools and day-care centers.

With the growing popularity of snakes and lizards as pets, health officials are concerned about a recent increase in reptile-related salmonella infections. Although most cases of salmonella are caused by food contamination, reptiles account for about 93,000 cases of such illness each year, or about 7 percent of the total.

(Well, now we know that it isn't just iguanas—it's lizards, snakes, and turtles. We now know why they did the study—salmonella—but I'm still wondering how somebody catches it. We also know who did the study— Centers for Disease Control and Prevention. I wonder if everybody knows this stuff. I think lots of day care centers have turtles and fish and stuff. I'm wondering what I would do if my kid had a pet and I read this article. I wonder what the symptoms are.)

Overhead 4: Many people are aware turtles can carry salmonella bacteria—in fact, the sale of small turtles as pets was banned for that reason in 1975—but most consumers and even many pet-store owners apparently don't know that lizards and snakes can be carriers, too.

Salmonella infections can cause fever, vomiting, bloody diarrhea and sometimes blood poisoning, meningitis or death.

(Hey, there are the symptoms. I still don't know how you catch it. I guess lots of people don't know this because it says that even pet store owners don't all know.)

Overhead 5: People can become infected by handling the animal or objects contaminated with the reptile's feces. Touching the reptile isn't necessary. According to the CDC, some cases of reptile-associated illness have occurred in infants who never even touch the scaly family pet, presumably resulting from having been held by people whose hands were contaminated.

Reptiles carry salmonella in their digestive tracts and shed the bacteria in their feces. The microbes don't make them sick. There is no reliable test or treatment to ensure a pet reptile won't carry the bacteria. "You can test it one week and it will be negative, two weeks later and it will be positive," said Stephanie Wong, a veterinarian with the CDC's food-borne and diarrheal-diseases branch. "We feel there is no way to say that a reptile is salmonella-free."

(That is gross! I guess that would answer the question about what a parent would do. The CDC would say that you should get rid of the pet. I wonder if there was a test. Shouldn't the article end here—that sounds like an end. What else could they say about this?)

Overhead 6: Wong said CDC officials are so concerned about the risk to young children they decided last week to strengthen one of the new guidelines after it had been printed in the agency's weekly bulletin. Originally, the recommendation had said reptiles should not be kept in households with children less than 1 year old; this was revised to include households with children younger than 5.

About 3 percent of U.S. households have reptiles, according to a CDC estimate based in part on an industry survey. "They're becoming more common household pets," Wong said.

The symptoms of salmonella infection—typically abdominal cramps, diarrhea, fever and sometimes vomiting or headaches—begin 24 to 72 hours after exposure. Severe cases are treated with antibiotics. Drugs usually aren't necessary in mild cases of illness, Wong said, and their use is discouraged because they may promote the emergence of resistant strains. *(Nothing new here but I wonder why they didn't put a phone number to call for information. They should've put the symptoms back with the other symptoms. I wonder why they talked about it twice? I kind of felt like this was a game, so I didn't stop reading. If I were a mother, I'd just want all the important stuff in a box or something so I'd know exactly what to do. I don't care about all that mess about the CDC, whatever.)*

Overhead 7: **Play It Safe**
To help prevent the transmission of salmonella from reptiles to humans, the CDC recommends:

- Pet stores, veterinarians and pediatricians inform owners and potential owners of reptiles about the risk of salmonella infection.

- People always wash their hands thoroughly with soap and water after handling reptiles or reptile cages.
- Children, people with compromised immune systems and others at increased risk for infection or serious complications of a salmonella infection should avoid contact with reptiles.
- Pet reptiles be kept out of households with children younger than 5 and with anyone with a compromised immune system. Families expecting a new child should remove the pet reptile before the infant arrives.
- Pet reptiles not be kept in child-care centers.
- Pet reptiles not be allowed to roam freely throughout a home.
- Pet reptiles be kept out of kitchens and other food-preparation areas. Kitchen sinks should not be used to bathe reptiles or to wash their dishes, cages or aquariums. If bathtubs are used, they should be cleaned thoroughly and disinfected with bleach.

Students were relieved to see that the important stuff was "in a box somewhere" by the time they reached the end of the article. This also provides an excellent opportunity for students to reread after the initial reading and questioning in order to create bulleted items that they think should go in the information insert at the end. This gives students the opportunity to summarize important details, analyze ways those details could be communicated, and synthesize that information into a concise format.

In *What Really Matters for Struggling Readers,* Richard Allington points to the significance of this kind of strategic teaching: "Because of the increase in the unfettered flow of information, American schools need to enhance the ability of children to search and sort through information, to synthesize and analyze information, and to summarize and evaluate the information they encounter" (7). In this process, students move to another level of questioning that leads to a critical analysis of the article:

- Why did the author write the article?
- What are readers supposed to learn from reading the article?
- How is this like anything else I've ever read?
- How could this have been written so it would have been easier to read?
- What is missing from the text in terms of information or interest?
- How could I rewrite or represent this text so that it would be understandable for others?

When students reach this level of questioning competence, they are moving into the final stage of learning: unconscious competence.

Unconscious Competence

At this stage, a reader has internalized the repertoire of strategies that knowledgeable readers use to make sense of diverse challenges of text. The reader is able to move between and among these strategies depending on the challenges of the text and her purposes for reading. She is able to do this without knowledgeable others prompting or giving concrete patterns of action. At this stage, a reader has internalized what Cris Tovani calls an "interacting voice."

As I worked with Jennifer in my ninth-grade classroom, I started to suspect that she had internalized the reading strategies that were the focus of our reading lessons to the point that the strategies had become skills for her. These strategies had become so automatic for her that I felt my teaching was getting in the way of her reading. As a way to test my assumptions, I asked Jennifer to do a think-aloud for me as she read a portion of the novel she was reading independently. Our discussion of that reading follows:

Janet: OK, Jennifer, if you could just read the way you would read normally, but this time I'd like you to stop each time you realize you are thinking about your reading and tell me what you're thinking.

Jennifer: You want me to tell you what I'm thinking—you mean after I think it?

Janet: Well, as soon as you're aware you are thinking.

Jennifer: Well, if I'm aware of it, then maybe I'm not really concentrating on my reading.

Janet: Maybe this is the way you do concentrate on your reading.

Jennifer: I don't think so, but I'll try.

[*Jennifer read three paragraphs from her novel and then stopped.*]

Jennifer: I'm not thinking anything. Well, I am thinking about how beautiful this island might be, but I didn't know I was thinking about it. Now that I've stopped, I realize I was thinking about it or maybe I'm only thinking about it now. I don't know. Is this what you want?

Janet: I'm not sure. I'm just trying to figure out what is going on inside your head while you're reading. I don't really know how to figure that out. I know that you've been doing such a great job with your reading and you're making all kinds of connections, and I wanted to see if I could figure out what was happening with you so I could help some other kids who are still struggling.

Jennifer: I can tell you for sure that this isn't going to help you—it's too confusing. I don't really know what I'm thinking until after I read. If I stop and think about what I read, I just kind of have a sense of the book—I don't know how to explain it to you.

Janet: Any idea how I could figure that out?

Jennifer: Hey, isn't that what you get paid the big bucks for? Only kidding—why would you want to figure it out?

Janet: I want to see if there is something else I should be doing so other kids could make the same progress you made.

Jennifer: Make them read more. I started reading with the tapes you made me, and then I read on the bus. Then I started reading at night. I don't know if I should tell you this part.

Janet: Just say it—it will be okay.

Jennifer: Well, I started stealing the books you read to us during shared reading. Well, not really stealing—I brought them back—well, most of the time.

Janet: Stealing the books?

Jennifer: Yeah. At first I wanted to reread what you read that day in case I missed something. Then I started reading ahead to see if it would sound like it did when you read the next day. Then I thought it would be fun to see if I could figure out what you would try to teach us. I don't know—it sounds kind of stupid now that I've told you.

Janet: Not stupid—smart. You were thinking like a reader.

Jennifer: Well, now I'm reading like a reader, so don't get in my way with this stuff.

This is the kind of interacting voice we would wish for all our readers. A voice that is so adept and flexible it supports readers in discovering their options, challenges them to be active and not passive, and helps them solve their own literate challenges. Jennifer has even created a voice that overcomes distractions such as the ones I was putting in her way. At this stage of strategic reading development, teachers have two critical roles: getting out of the way as students find their way through texts that are at their independent reading levels, and providing increasingly diverse and challenging texts at students' instructional levels so readers are challenged to make use of strategies in order to make sense of text.

When Lee Ann Spillane wanted to see if her students were able to transfer the strategic reading she had been doing with them to an independent reading of a more complex text, she was able to determine that she needed to spend more instructional time on helping students transfer strategies. She gave students a copy of Maurice Ogden's poem "The Hangman" and asked them to read the poem independently and mark the text for places where they had to use reading strategies to make sense of the text (see Appendix H for complete poem). She left wide margins so students could make notations about the thinking they were doing in the process of making meaning from the reading. Students were asked to note where they questioned a word but read on, visualized, questioned, made a text connection, predicted, inferred, or stopped reading because they were confused. In Figure 3.1 we can see the complex web of thinking that accompanies even the initial reading of a challenging text.

After students did an independent reading of the poem, Lee Ann read the poem aloud to them, asking that they follow along and note anything new during a shared rereading of the poem. In this way, she provided students with an opportunity to collaborate, discuss strategies that worked for them, and note challenges they still weren't able to overcome. She was also able to assess what the group and individual challenges were for this reading, which gave her the opportunity to plan her next strategy lessons for the entire class or with small

Figure 3.1

The Hangman

By Maurice Ogden

Into our town the Hangman came
Smelling of gold and blood and flame
And he paced our bricks with a diffident air
And he built his frame on the courthouse square.

How can you smell of gold?

The scaffold stood by the courthouse side,
Only as wide as the door was wide,
A frame as tall, or little more,
Than the capping sill of the courthouse door.

And we wondered, whenever we had the time,
Who the criminal, what the crime,
The Hangman judged with the yellow twist
Of knotted hemp in his busy fist.

This reminds me of a saying: "don't worry what people think of you, because you don't know what their doing behind the doors."

And innocent though we were, with dread
We passed those eyes of buckshot lead;
Till one cried. "Hangman, who is he
For whom you raised the gallows-tree?"

what is buckshot lead?

And a twinkle grew in the buckshot eye,
And he gave us a riddle instead of reply:
"He who serves me best," said he,
"Shall earn the rope of the gallows-tree."

reminds me of what my father tells me. "You have to earn my trust, impress me."

And he stepped down. and laid his hand
On a man who came from another land
And we breathed again, for another's grief,
At the Hangman's hand was our relief.

And the gallows frame on the courthouse lawn
By tomorrow's sun would be struck and gone.
So we gave him way, and no one spoke,
Out of respect for his hangman's cloak

what is a cloak?

The next day's sun looked down
On the roof and street in our quiet town
And. stark and black in the morning air,
The gallows-tree on the courthouse square.

"every day is a new day. The world won't end."

And the Hangman stood at his usual stand
With the yellow hemp in his busy hand;
With his buckshot eye and his jaw like a pike
And his air so knowing and businesslike.

reminds me of a judge or lawyer.

71

Figure 3.1 *(continued)*

reminds me when some one is caught guilty because they have someting to hide or to save themselves.

And we cried: "Hangman, have you not done,
Yesterday with the alien one?"
(Then we fell silent, and stood amazed;
"Oh, not for him was the gallows raised..."

reminds me of someone being accused of an affair.

He laughed as he looked at us;
"...Did you think I'd gone to all this fuss
To hang one man? That's a thing I do
To stretch the rope when the rope is new."

reminds me of an olden day punishment. more in a western movie.

Then one cried "Murderer!" One cried, "Shame!"
And into our midst the Hangman came
To that man's place. "Do you hold," said he,
"With him that was meat for the gallows tree?"

This reminds me of the book, Witch of Black bird Pond when everyone screams, Witch!

And he laid hid hand on that one's arm,
And we shrank back in quick alarm,
And we gave him way, and no one spoke,
Out of fear of his hangman's cloak.

That night we saw with dread surprise
The Hangman's scaffold had grown in size.
Fed by the blood beneath the chute?
The gallows-tree had taken root.

what is this?

Now as wide or a little more,
Than the steps that led to the courthouse door,
As tall as the writing, or nearly as tall,
Halfway up the courthouse wall.

Reminds me of a long walk to your punishment after an act or crime (Bryron's ride to Grandma sords)

The third he took - - we had all heard tell - -
Was a usurer and infidel.
And: "What," said the Hangman, "have you to do
With the gallows-bound, and he a Jew?"

Reminds me of the Hollocaust.

And we cried out: "Is this the one he
Who has served you well and faithfully?"
The Hangman smiled: "It's a clever scheme
To try the strength of the gallows-beam."

The fourth man's dark, accusing song
Had scratched our comfort hard and long;
And: "What concern", he gave us back,

....

groups who experienced common challenges while reading the text. The difficulty often comes when we are left wondering whether students actually have moved to a level of independence where they are using the strategies to help them understand their reading.

Assessing Strategic Reading

In order to determine whether individual students have internalized thinking strategies to the point where they can use them successfully when reading independently, teachers have to develop ways to carefully assess readers' progress with familiar texts and scaffold support for transfer of those strategies to unfamiliar texts. At Wilson Middle School in San Diego, where I spend many of my days, teachers were so involved in the instructional practice of teaching strategies that they kept offering lessons on how to use a strategy long after many students seemed to have internalized the strategy. When we talked with some of the teachers on that faculty, some said they were uncertain about when to stop teaching a strategy because they weren't sure what to look for as evidence that students truly understood how and when to use it.

I pointed out that in many cases we could be reasonably sure students were using strategies in helpful ways because they were able to sustain reading engagement for significant periods of time. In addition, teachers were conferring with students about the use of strategies during their independent reading, and students could articulate times and places where they had used the strategies as part of their independent reading. However, there were still some teachers who remained uncertain about the evidence they should see if students really knew how to employ a specific strategy.

In an attempt to support careful assessment by the teachers, the principal Mary Louise Martin, the staff developers Bernie Nguyen and Kathy Burns, and I developed a strategic reading checklist. In the course of teaching these strategies, you might find other characteristics of each strategy, but this offered the teachers at Wilson a place to start in order to look systematically at the kinds of behaviors teachers could expect from strategic readers. They are offered here as our thinking-in-progress about strategic teaching and learning. A copy of the complete assessment tool, Critical Indicators for Developmental Reading Process, is included as form I.29 in Appendix I.

Strategic readers develop ability to . . .

B1. Visualize
_____ 1.1 identify language in a text that would help create images in the mind
_____ 1.2 use descriptive language to describe connections to the text
_____ 1.3 use sensory language (five senses) in a text to create images
_____ 1.4 describe oneself as if in the context of the text
_____ 1.5 use mental images to infer, make connections, and predict

B2. Question
_____ 2.1 create questions prompted by the text (title, cover, pictures, events, author)
_____ 2.2 create literal questions to help with recall, sequencing, and summarizing

_____ 2.3 create complex inferential questions that lead to deeper understanding of the text

B3. Infer

_____ 3.1 identify text clues (words, illustrations, title, cover, pictures, etc.) that help reader infer

_____ 3.2 identify background knowledge that helps reader infer

_____ 3.3 articulate how reader combines text clues and background knowledge to infer

_____ 3.4 use inferences to make predictions

_____ 3.5 modify inference as new text clues are presented

_____ 3.6 use inferences to draw conclusions or make a judgment

B4. Analyze/Synthesize

_____ 4.1 differentiate between essential ideas and nonessential ideas based on a specific purpose

_____ 4.2 combine related ideas to formulate an original idea, a new line of thinking, or a new creation

_____ 4.3 recognize the relationship between the author's intention and the author's words

_____ 4.4 determine the author's purpose

_____ 4.5 understand that each "part" of the text works together to create the total effect of the author's intentions

_____ 4.6 use the text to support reader response to the text

This careful assessment gives teachers the opportunity to form needs-based guided reading groups. As increasing numbers of students demonstrate proficiency in using strategic processes, the necessity of whole-group instruction for these strategies diminishes. Our goal for these readers is expressed by Alexander and Jetton: "Skilled readers, like skilled cooks or skilled accountants, have honed essential domain procedures to a level of automaticity" (295). When that occurs, our role with these students moves toward giving them more challenging and diverse texts so that their repertoire of strategies remains flexible and transferable as they take new reading risks.

Planning for Shared Strategic Reading

As we plan instruction using the shared strategic reading approach, it is important to keep in mind the distinctions between a strategy and a skill (see Figure

3.2). If one is providing a strategy lesson for learners, that lesson should be a "how-to" lesson that brings the strategy to a conscious level. For example, we might construct strategy lessons for our students on how to predict, how to question, how to write persuasively, or how to read boring texts. These lessons would include guided support for helping students discover the purpose of the strategy (e.g., "We question in order to gain a deeper understanding of the text

Figure 3.2

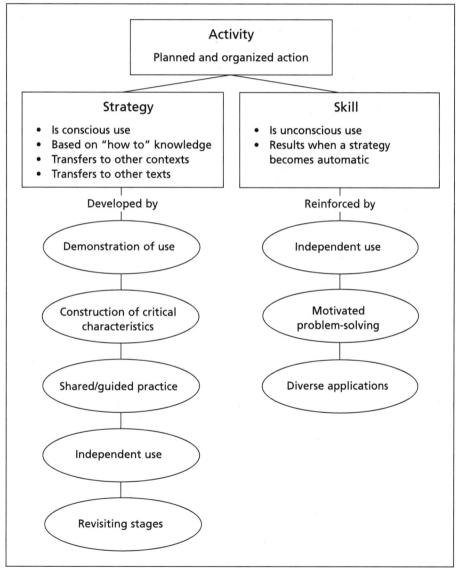

or help ourselves maintain reading focus"). The lessons would give students the opportunity to discover the benefits or outcomes of the strategy and the steps or stages to be taken in order to use the strategy effectively. As part of the instruction, students should also examine ways to transfer the strategy to other texts and other contexts.

A strategy becomes a skill when learners no longer need our support in reminding them to use incremental steps of the strategy. At the skill level, the strategy is used unconsciously and automatically when a task requires the use of strategy for comprehension.

As we plan instruction, we create activities that help develop a strategy through introduction, demonstration, and construction of critical indications for each strategy. These can be charted so that students can use them for reference while they are involved in guided practice and independent use of the strategy. On subsequent days, the strategy can be revisited in order to support the transfer to other tasks. If the strategy is reinforced through diverse applications, and students are motivated to use the strategy, it will become a skill.

The need to change our levels of support as students' expertise increases is grounded in Vygotsky's stages of the zone of proximal development. The zone of proximal development is characterized by four levels of support:

- Performance is assisted by more capable others.
- Performance is assisted by the learner.
- Performance is developed, automatized, and fossilized.
- The first three stages are repeated because of new levels of difficulty or regression from lack of use.

These stages are the basis for the incremental introduction, modeling, guided practice, and independent use stages detailed in this chapter. As Lee Ann found out from her students during their reading of "The Hangman," when they encountered new levels of challenge in terms of reading, she had to go back to some beginning stages of assistance in order to help support the transfer.

In Seligman's research on "learned helplessness," he notes that if a learner does not believe he is capable of taking action that will foster independent success, academic progress will be halted: "They had learned that nothing they did mattered—and they therefore expected that no actions of theirs would matter in the future. Once they formed this expectation, they would no longer engage in action" (25). Strategic reading is meant to build students' levels of confidence in the belief that what they do does matter so that they will begin to make conscious moves that will support them in reading independence.

4

"When Do I Teach Vocabulary?" Shared Reading and Word Study

Words are all we have.

Samuel Beckett

Shared reading is the ideal time for word study because it provides a rich context for enjoying new words, discovering word meanings, connecting new words to familiar reading, and creating word banks for those words connected by concept or association. While all readers benefit from the combined richness of shared reading and word study, poor readers derive extra support. In *Three Arguments Against Whole Language and Why They Are Wrong*, Krashen discusses the importance of rich context for these readers: "Poor readers appeared to be influenced more by the overall context. In addition, poorer readers appeared to profit more from helpful context" (22).

As students encounter a wide variety of words during these shared reading experiences, they are also more likely to take language risks in their speech and writing. We have all been amused by students' humorous experiments with language, such as the incident where a student in Alaska was role-playing a historical figure and claimed to be "Erik Thorgood, king of the Orgies" or when an English teacher in Ohio learned that Aphrodite was a "skank ho'." While these students missed the mark just slightly, the good news is they saw the ultimate goal of learning words as the ability to use language.

Baker, Simmons, and Kameenui remind us that "an individual does not need to know all definitions of a word and all its contextual meanings to use a word successfully. What is important is that instruction parallels the expectation of word usage" (5). These researchers describe three critical instructional roles for the teacher in leading students to increased word knowledge and

77

usage: incidental, mediated, and explicit instruction. I believe shared reading can support word learning at each of these levels.

Incidental Word Study

Incidental word study is characterized by the reading of a variety of texts that include repeated general knowledge and high-frequency words as well as content-specific, specialized vocabulary. These texts are read aloud in shared reading so that students have the opportunity to see and hear words at the same time. These repeated exposures, when combined with rich, interesting texts, add significantly to the word knowledge base for readers. According to Nagy, "It should be stressed that repetition is necessary and worthwhile, at least for some words. According to available research, many encounters with a new word are necessary if vocabulary instruction is to have a measurable effect on reading comprehension" (23).

To demonstrate this principle of incidental word study, I'd like to look at a selection from Daniel Butler and Alan Ray's *The World's Dumbest Criminals*:

That's a Spiceeeeeey "Meatball"!

A group of American college students on an archeological summer study program in Italy were having the time of their lives. During the day they dug and sifted through the fine Tuscan soil, uncovering Roman relics; at night they collapsed exhausted under the stars. Some evenings though, they visited a restaurant in a nearby village to enjoy sumptuous seven-course dinners of pasta, fish, chicken, beef, and, of course, wine.

On one such evening, while the college kids were safely settled at Mama Dominici's restaurant, a drifter wandered into their dig. He helped himself to food, CD players, radios, and clothes, packed everything into a stolen backpack, and made off into the night. Actually, he stumbled into the night, falling several times in the moonless evening before giving up and deciding to wait for daylight.

The college kids returned to their camp too tired and tipsy to notice that they had been robbed; they all just crawled into their sleeping bags and started snoring. But the next morning one of the boys went for his toothbrush and realized his whole backpack was missing. He woke up his friends, and they were making an inventory of missing items when they heard a series of blood-curdling screams from nearby in the woods. They seemed to be coming from an animal in pain, and they would not stop.

The howling came closer and closer. Then they saw him. The drifter was stumbling into trees and bushes, clutching his throat, and screaming while flames shot out of his mouth! Yep, his mouth was on fire. He ran blindly into camp, collapsed to his knees, and plunged his whole head into the water bucket. His screams gurgled to a stop. Then he jerked his head up, gasped for air, and spat before plunging his head back under.

While some of the students attended to the fire-breathing drifter, two of the boys retraced his steps. Within moments they found the stolen backpack with the missing items. Lying together on the ground were a toothbrush, a pack of cigarettes, a toothpaste-like tube, and a lighter. When one boy picked up the tube, he solved the mystery.

Back in camp, they told the others what they assumed had happened. The drifter had awakened and rummaged through the backpack to find a toothbrush and what he thought was toothpaste. The tube actually contained Liquid Fire, a flammable paste used to start campfires. After giving his teeth a good brushing with it, the drifter had then decided to have his first smoke of the day—with dramatic and incendiary results. (79–82)

Students will encounter many previously unknown words within the context of this story. Words such as *sumptuous, incendiary, rummaged, flammable, relics, tipsy,* and *inventory* might not have been a part of their speaking or written vocabulary, but with discussion readers will connect those words to this interesting text and the humorous outcome. Additionally, some of these words have what is described as rich local context—context that by definition, example, or illustration offers enough support for readers to make a fairly accurate definition. For example, *sumptuous* is followed by an example of a sumptuous meal: "seven-course dinners of pasta, fish, chicken, beef, and, of course, wine." The details of the example would help most readers posit a definition that would be fairly accurate.

Incidental word learning occurs as we offer students opportunities to discover some words based on the surrounding language and illustrations. Those connections, when repeated with subsequent encounters with the words or repeated readings of the words in the same context, lead to the addition of these words to readers' individual word banks. The teacher's role for language acquisition at this level is twofold: choosing texts that contain interesting, intriguing, and usable language, and demonstrating for students how they can use context to assist in learning new words.

While context is seldom a reliable word-learning strategy when used in isolation, it does have benefit when used as part of a repertoire of word-learning strategies. Nagy writes, "One motivation for having students try to figure out word meanings from context is to help them develop word-learning strategies to use on their own" (8). Making a habit of following occasional shared readings with an opportunity for students to discuss possible contextual clues helps them understand how to approach difficult or unfamiliar words and has significant benefits for moving students toward independence.

For example, after reading the first few chapters of Louis Sachar's *Holes,* the teacher might take students back to the description of the setting for Camp Green Lake:

> The land was *barren* and *desolate.* He could see a few rundown buildings and some tents. Farther away there was a cabin beneath two tall trees. Those two trees were the only plant life he could see. There weren't even weeds. (11)

As students work together to look for other words or mental images that would help them offer broad definitions for the italicized words in this excerpt, they might point to words like *only* in relation to plant life or to "rundown buildings" or "weren't even weeds" as indicators of the absence of life. At the incidental word level, readers are often left with a sense of the word rather than a clearly articulated definition. That sense of the word is added to a reader's schema for the word or concept and then refined during subsequent encounters with the word.

Since at this level word learning is heavily dependent on context, I find it important to help my students understand that context is more than just the other words in the targeted sentence. Context could include readers' experiences and background knowledge as well as any of the following text supports:

- Surrounding text
- Knowledge of language
- Sound-spelling correspondence
- Pictures and illustrations
- Charts and graphs
- Voice and tone
- Text structure
- Glossary
- Surface features of the text (bold, italics)
- Footnotes
- Parentheticals

This knowledge requires teachers to ask several questions when choosing a passage for an example to introduce or reinforce using multiple sources of context for word meaning. We have to question whether there is sufficient context for the target word and whether that context has supporting graphics, examples, or other supports that would help students determine a broad definition. Finally, we have to ask whether readers have limited or extensive background knowledge for the word and its context. I believe the following example from Paul Many's *These Are the Rules* demonstrates a case where the context is rich in terms of concrete examples but some readers would still not understand that context because they lack the background knowledge for the event that is occurring:

> Then I got in, but hit the rear barrel . . . And I tried it again, this time coming in too shallow. "Again." You could see his ears going way red now.
>   It was like the car and barrels were those little magnetic dogs. First the barrels pulled me in and I couldn't get far enough away, and then I couldn't get close enough. None of this was helped, of course, by having to be all the while furiously pushing down pedals and shifting and turning the wheel and looking over my shoulder. (81–82).

For those of us who spent hours learning to parallel-park, this description has details that critically define that process. But for readers who have missed that delightful learning experience, this passage would be difficult to understand.

With repeated partner and whole-class study of context, students begin to see the many ways they are combining their world knowledge and their knowledge of reading to make sense of unknown words in a text. They participate in the behaviors of mature readers by determining if they need to know the word in order to comprehend the text. If the reader determines the word is necessary, she chooses from a repertoire of word-learning strategies: using resources such as the dictionary or another reader; determining meaning from looking at known parts of the word such as prefixes or root words (structural analysis); or combining text clues (context) with background knowledge. These strategies can be demonstrated and reinforced with shared reading of a text such as Adam Rapp's novel *The Buffalo Tree*.

Before the shared reading of the text, students are asked to work in groups to determine possible meanings for the following words or phrases:

Bust those naps
Crib
Patch mate
Juvy pound
Carped
Clip
Hash house honeys

A group of high school students responded with the following possible definitions for these words:

Bust those naps: comb your hair, wake up, hit someone in the head
Crib: house, bed, home, neighborhood
Patch mate: cell mate, friend, homeboy
Juvy pound: juvenile detention, school, jail for kids
Carped: complain, steal, bust on, nagged
Clip: part of a gun, hit, hit someone in the head
Hash house honeys: waitress, cook in the school cafeteria

After a class list of definitions is created, students are asked to read the text and to refine the definitions by using local context (the words directly connected to the unknown word or phrase) and global context (the larger sense of the story that comes with reading extended passages of text, such as dialect, setting, character motivations). As you read this passage, you might think about the strategies you use to determine meaning for these words.

Coly Jo plays floor hockey in his jeans 'cause that's all he's got. His unbreakable comb keeps falling out of his pocket and he keeps picking it up. He's always trying to bust those naps with that comb. Sometimes he'll just stick it in his afro and walk around.

Coly Jo is my patch mate. When someone throws me into the wall Coly Jo goes after him and gets that juvy with his stick.

Coly Jo and I have been here six weeks and after blackout we take turns sleeping cause Hodge or Boo Boxfoot will creep into your room and crib shit. Hodge and Boo are on their third clip. A clip is like a year but it ain't the same. Mostly juvy homes don't give clips. They let you go when you make reform. But Hamstock is different. It's like Hamstock wants to keep you.

Boo and Hodge know the halls and the shadows and the tricks in the showers. I've seen how Hodge sweet-talks those old hash house Honeys into extra slices of pie. I've seen the Mop man slip a fifth of Old Crow into Boo's laundry bundle.

They cribbed most of Coly Jo's shit his first two days. I heard them in our room after blackout, creeping like some cats. Boo sports Coly Jo's Barnum Fletcher squirrel-skin cap around Spalding like it's something his mom sent him. He's sporting it right now and the tail keeps flipping up.

Boo's got a harelip and he makes me rent a bedside table for six tenths a week. That's half your juvy pound. And you get that only if you don't get carped. They'll carp you with the quickness for walking into Spalding with your shoes on and cut away two tenths. And you'll be in line for your weekly juvy pound and they'll just take out their little notebook and cross off some digits and hand you four or six tenths instead of that full bone-and-twenty. And they don't even look at you either; they just shove that change at you like it's some medicine you got to take. (8–9)

Incidental word learning occurs every time we share texts with students as long as readers understand the strength of context in the word-learning experience. For some students, it is that first sight recognition of a word they knew only as part of their listening vocabularies, such as *rendezvous* or *hors d'oeuvres.* For others, it is a reinforcement of frequently used sight words that need to be automatic during the reading experience. At times, it is the introduction of a word these students would otherwise not encounter. Each word learned at this level builds a foundation for new words that are connected by concept, topic, root word, or background and that might be studied in more depth at the mediated or explicit level.

Mediated Instruction

Mediated instruction differs from incidental word study in the extent to which teachers use this time to help students develop effective strategies for learning and remembering new words. This can be supported in a variety of ways as teachers demonstrate for learners how to anticipate or use words to develop and cement background knowledge, or model interactive reading as a way of predicting words that logically fit context and topic. Shared reading is the ideal place for such demonstrations because students and teachers have a common text for reading and rereading.

Language Collection

Showing students how they can connect words by concept, topic, or function aids them in developing independent strategies for learning and remembering new words. Graphic organizers can provide excellent support for such language collection because they offer students a concrete model for the abstract process of expanding individual word banks. A poem by Christopher Morley, the first of "Nursery Rhymes for the Tender-Hearted," lets us look at how this might work:

Nursery Rhymes for the Tender-Hearted
(dedicated to don marquis)
Scuttle, scuttle, little roach—
How you run when I approach:
Up above the pantry shelf.
Hastening to secrete yourself.

Most adventurous of vermin,
How I wish I could determine
How you spend your hours of ease,
Perhaps reclining on the cheese.

Cook has gone, and all is dark—
Then the kitchen is your park:
In the garbage heap that she leaves
Do you browse among the tea leaves?

How delightful to suspect
All the places you have trekked:
Does your long antenna whisk its
Gentle tip across the biscuits?

Do you linger, little soul,
Drowsing in our sugar bowl?
Or, abandonment most utter,
Shake a shimmy on the butter?

Do you chant your simple tunes
Swimming in the baby's prunes?
Then, when dawn comes, do you slink
Homeward to the kitchen sink?

Timid roach, why be so shy?
We are brothers, thou and I.
In the midnight, like yourself,
I explore the pantry shelf!

Our first reading of this poem would be for the sheer joy of the language and rhythm it contains. After talking about and making connections to the poem, we could revisit it for the specific purpose of gleaning words. I might use this poem if I noted that my students were using weak verbs in their writing.

Over several days of shared reading, I would read a variety of texts that offer examples of robust action words. We would use the Language Collection form (I.7, Appendix I) as a way of collecting words for future writing or word study. Words collected from this poem as interesting action words might include *scuttle, approach, secrete, determine, recline, browse, trek, whisk, linger, slink,* and *explore.* Shared reading provides the opportunity for us to do repeated readings of the poem as we collect words and connect them to the actions of a roach—certainly a memorable context!

On other days this experience can be repeated by returning to texts that have been used for other purposes. For example, we had read a news article, "New Study Says Reptiles, Children Don't Mix," as a way of reinforcing the role of questioning during strategic reading of informational text. We could now revisit it as a way of collecting words that experts use to inform, to persuade, or to support their premises. From that article, we can gather expert language as follows: *recommendation, issued, cause, necessary, according to, resulting from, reliable, guidelines, estimate,* and *prevent.* Those words can be collected on the Language Collection II form (I.8, Appendix I) and used as a word study basic in a craft lesson on persuasive writing. In this case, students had the opportunity to collect words around a single concept, and we modeled for them the value of returning to familiar texts for models of language usage and writer's craft.

Collected words can be kept in students' academic journals or in writing/language folders. They can also be gathered on charts, bulletin boards, or word walls for whole-class use. Figure 4.1 shows effective and "wimpy" descriptive words collected by Jennifer Economos-Green's high school students in Baltimore, Maryland, from their reading and writing. As new texts are read and descriptive language is encountered, this collection will expand.

Anticipating Content

Anticipating words based on titles, content, illustrations, graphs, charts, and text type supports the critical role of word connections and offers students a strategy for activating background knowledge prior to reading. I have found this especially effective before reading expository texts. As a way to demonstrate this strategy, I have chosen an informational text, "Kids drink too much juice, doctors say" (see Figure 4.2). Before reading the article with students, I would give each group a copy of the form Words We Can Read, A–Z (I.9, Appendix I). I would write the article's title and subtitle on the board, chart, or overhead. After reading these titles to the students, I would say I had found several really important words in this article that related to the title and subtitle, and that began with the letters C, N, O, R, S, or W. They would then have several min-

Figure 4.1

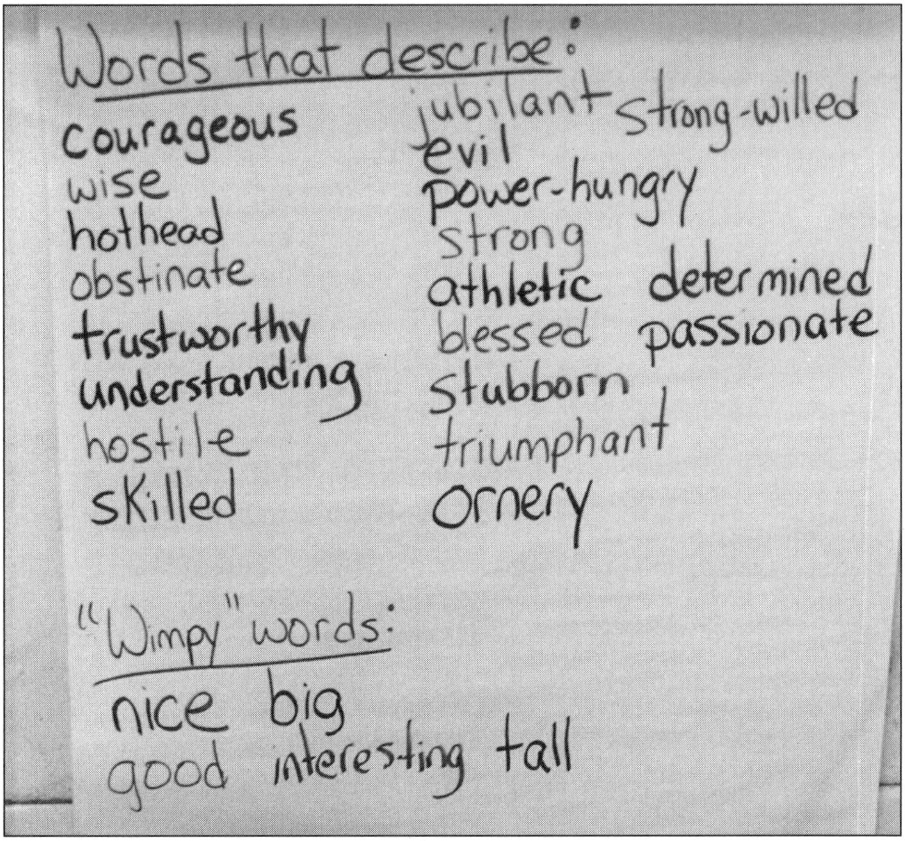

Words that describe:

courageous   jubilant strong-willed
wise   evil
hothead   power-hungry
obstinate   strong
trustworthy   athletic determined
understanding   blessed passionate
hostile   stubborn
skilled   triumphant
                    ornery

"Wimpy" words:

nice big
good interesting tall

utes to brainstorm words beginning with those letters that they think they will encounter in reading this article. As students report the anticipated words for the group A–Z chart, we talk about why they chose those words and how they think the words are connected to the title or subtitle. Typical predictions from students would include *caffeine, consume, vitamin C, calories, can't, concern, no, not, nutrition, nutritious, negative, obese, obesity, overweight, open, orange (juice), reduce, restrict, rapid, resist, sweet, sugar, snacks, water, well,* and *weight.*

These words can be revisited after a shared reading of the article to talk about ways in which their predicted words matched those found in the text. Students can list words that surprised them or ones they wouldn't have expected, and talk about why those words didn't occur to them. Again, we find that this kind of mediated word study provides a strong basis for using words to anticipate content and reinforces strategic prereading as well.

Figure 4.2

Kids drink too much juice, doctors say

Parents urged to limit intake to aid health

By Marilyn Elias
USA TODAY

U.S. pediatricians have a new message for parents: Hold the juice.

For the first time, parents are being advised to give no fruit juice to infants younger than 6 months and to restrict juice for all children and adolescents. Concern over kids' rising consumption of high-calorie juice and sugar-laden "juice drinks" prompted the policy,

which was issued Monday, says Susan Baker of the American Academy of Pediatrics.

Fruit juice is healthy in moderation, "but some children are drinking too much of it, and it's replacing other nutritious drinks," Baker says. "We know it's given often to babies. ... There's no earthly reason to give babies juice."

An 8-ounce glass of juice averages 120 calories, "and lots of kids I see are just drinking so many calories, they're getting overweight from it," says the new policy's senior author, William Cochran of the Geisinger Clinic in Danville, Pa.

"Juice snack habits might be contributing to the recent upswing in childhood obesity and obesity-related diabetes, he says. About 13% of children 6 to 11 and 14% of those 12 to 19 were overweight in 1999, ac-

Doctors' guidelines

► No juice before 6 months.
► 4 to 6 ounces of juice a day for children ages 1 to 6.
► 8 to 12 ounces of juice a day for children ages 7 to 18.
► Encourage children to eat whole fruit. It has beneficial fiber that is missing in most juices.

Source: American Academy of Pediatrics

Q&A ■ 8D

cording to the Centers for Disease Control and Prevention.

Not all agree that juice is a factor. Sue Taylor of the Processed Apples Institute says new research finds no link between consuming 100% fruit juice and obesity.

The American Academy of Pediatrics also cautions that excess fruit juice can lead to malnutrition, dental cavities, abdominal pain and diarrhea.

The academy recommends breast milk the first year of a child's life. Formula can be used for babies who aren't nursing. Older children ought to drink milk as the preferred staple beverage, the group says. Kids also should be encouraged to drink water when thirsty.

"Many parents don't distinguish between juice and water," says William Dietz, director of the division of nutrition and physical activity at CDC.

"If a child's thirsty, they think juice is better than soda because at least it has vitamin C. But when kids are thirsty, what they need is water, not water with added calories."

The new policy "is just common sense," says Brian Taber, public relations director at Northland Cranberries, manufacturer of Northland, TreeSweet and Seneca brand juices.

"We know our juice is a healthy product. But it's like any other food — overindulgence is not good for you," Taber says.

Interactive Word Study

Creating opportunities for learners to use words in an interactive study as a way to anticipate content and look at the connections between and among words gives support to students as they learn how language can be used in predictable ways. Baker, Simmons, and Kameenui write, "The research support is clear that to incorporate new words into their receptive or expressive lexicons, students need multiple exposures to words and multiple opportunities to practice using words" (13). A useful strategy in applying this research is one described by McGinley and Denner as "story impressions."

McGinley and Denner cite the use of story impressions for a variety of purposes: note taking, summarizing, memory retrieval, generating and answering questions, and sequencing. Additionally, I have found success in adapting the activity as an interactive word study method before beginning a novel for shared reading. The following story impressions chart is for Bel Mooney's historical novel *The Voices of Silence*:

Romania	she's	lucky	she
1989	for	dress	save
It's	granted	eat	his
unthinkable	parents	well	
for	best	everyone	
criticize	daily	poor	
leader	altered	Flora's	
Thirteen	frightening	crumbles	
Flora	changes	she	

can't	connected	closer
revolution	Daniel	truth
like	new	father
Suddenly	Why	danger

Students work in groups from the chart to create logical sentences that would contain these words. They are instructed that the words have been taken from the book jacket and should be used in the order they appear, reading each column from top to bottom and then going back to the top of the next column. Words have been left out that the teacher believes the students could anticipate with the support of their peers. After groups have had the opportunity to create story impressions for *The Voices of Silence,* the teacher brings them back together to create a class story impression. A typical class story impression would read as follows, with student-inserted words in italics:

The story takes place in Romania in 1989. It's unthinkable for *anyone to* criticize *the* leader. Thirteen-*year-old* Flora can't *understand* a revolution like *this.* Suddenly she's not *taking* for granted *her* parents and her best *friends. Her* daily *life is* altered *by* frightening changes connected *to* Daniel, *her* new *friend.* Why *is she* lucky *enough to* dress *and* eat well *when* everyone *else is* poor? Flora's *life* crumbles *as* she *gets closer to the* truth. *Her* father *is in* danger *and* she *must* save his *life.*

As you can see, students are inserting words that would typically be part of their usage vocabulary. This interactive strategy supports students at the mediated level by helping them make conscious language connections and anticipate content via the words (students now can anticipate the setting, characters, conflict, and exciting elements), and by providing models for students as they write advertisements for their choices of independent reading texts.

Another interactive word study strategy I have used successfully during shared reading is asking students to take part in creating a poem based on the kinds of words we choose to fit the pattern of the poem. One of my favorites is Douglas Florian's "Mr. Backward" from his collection *Bing, Bang, Boing.*

Mr. Backward
Mr. Backward lives in town.
He never wakes up, he always wakes <u>down</u>.

He eats dessert before his meal.
His plastic plants and flowers are <u>real</u>.

He takes a bath inside his sink
And cleans his clothes with purple <u>ink</u>.

He wears his earmuffs on his nose
And a woolen scarf around his <u>toes</u>.

He loves his gloves worn inside out.
He combs his hair with <u>sauerkraut</u>.

His black dog, Spot, is colored green.
His grandmamma is <u>seventeen</u>.

He rakes the leaves still on the trees
And bakes a cake with <u>antifreeze</u>.

He goes to sleep beneath his bed
While wearing slippers on his <u>head</u>. (71)

Our first reading of the text is a shared choral reading with the underlined words omitted. In the first couplet, readers discover a pattern of a single word that (1) rhymes with the last word of the previous line, and (2) creates an "opposite" or unexpected image. The next three couplets reinforce that pattern with very predictable words. But in the couplets that follow, students stumble in their reading because no one word *automatically* comes to mind that meets both of the pattern criteria—more than one word could be chosen. After our initial interactive reading of the poem, we choose words that meet only one critical criterion of the pattern (rhyme) and create a new poem. We can change words often, but we end by doing another shared choral reading of the original "Mr. Backward" poem with Douglas Florian's words intact. This kind of interactive shared reading helps students see that language has patterns and that those patterns can support their independence in reading.

Explicit Word Study

Explicit word study is a way of teaching words or concepts critical to a successful experience with a text. This would typically include a structure or system for helping students understand the word in the context in which they will encounter it. In addition, this method might also help them understand that the word has multiple meanings and word parts. The explicit word study lesson would typically end with students' creating examples of the word in use, making personal or literature connections to the word, or illustrating the word as a way of remembering the word and its meaning. This final stage of the lesson provides students with a concrete model for transferring the word or concept to future encounters in different contexts or with related words.

Explicit word study can be used judiciously prior to the reading experience for the big-idea words that are critical to understanding a text but that probably could not be learned through context or structural analysis (word parts). Explicit study could also be done during or after text reading when readers have a more complete understanding of the text as a whole.

Using an article from *USA Today* as an example, we can identify places where we could do explicit word study as a support for readers:

Beaten unconsciously: Violent images may alter kids' brain activity, spark hostility

Media violence may trigger aggression in kids by stimulating brain regions involved in fighting for survival and storing readily recalled traumatic memories, a scientist will report Friday.

Functional magnetic resonance imaging (MRI) scans show that violent film clips activate children's brains in a distinctive, potentially violence-promoting pattern, says Kansas State University psychologist John Murray. He will speak at the Society for Research in Child Development meetings in Minneapolis.

The brain scans were done on eight youngsters, ages 8 to 13, as they watched TV for 18 minutes, six minutes each of boxing sequences from *Rocky IV,* nonviolent PBS clips and just a blank screen marked with an "X."

Compared with MRIs done before the study, and scans taken during nonviolent scenes, the boxing images evoked much greater activation of three brain regions:

* The amygdala, which registers emotional arousal and detects threats to survival.
* The premotor cortex, an area believed to rev up when a person thinks about responding to a threat.
* The posterior cingulate, reserved for storing long-term memory of important, often troubling events. For instance, this area activates when Vietnam combat veterans and rape victims recall their trauma.

Although children may consciously know violence on the screen isn't real, "their brains are treating it as real, the gospel truth," Murray says. There's no proof this brain activation will spur aggression, "but it does give us great reason for concern."

Flashbacks readily occur after post-traumatic stress; images of on-screen aggression also may recur and influence kids, he says.

One Yale University study showed a delayed effect a few days after youngsters watched aggressive TV spots: When prompted with cues similar to those in the TV scene, they, too, behaved aggressively.

But Murray's study "is way too small to make a case" for the brain-aggression link, says Yale psychologist Dorothy Singer, an expert on how TV affects children. "It's very important stuff, but we need larger numbers."

And kids' TV viewing habits don't promote belligerent behavior nearly as much as exposure to real violence and parents' failure to monitor their youngsters' activities, a recent study of 2,245 students showed.

Still, "if your child is watching lots of TV, then you have reason to be concerned, " says Mark Singer of Case Western Reserve University in Cleveland. "Many, many studies show it isn't healthy."

Since the word *aggression/aggressive* is used six times in this short article, that word is worthy of explicit study prior to reading the article. If there are students in the class who don't have any understanding of this word, they would have great difficulty comprehending the article. In this case, we also use the pre-reading word study as a way for students to activate personal background knowledge for a relatively difficult reading. Lynnette Elliott, an eighth-grade teacher at Odyssey Middle School in Orlando, Florida, chose to use the graphic organizer Word in My Context (see Figure 4.3) to support those connections and provide opportunity for whole-class predictions of content based on the background knowledge students bring. For this graphic, students looked at dictionary definitions of the word and connected those definitions to feelings that could be associated with the word from the point of view of an aggressor or a victim of aggressive behavior. After a class discussion of aggression, students wrote about their experiences with aggression. Following Lynnette's reading of the article, students revisited the graphic organizer to illustrate the main point of the article by visualizing the reporter's opinion of the relation between viewing violence and responding to it.

It could be argued that terms such as *amygdala, premotor cortex,* and *posterior cingulate* are complex words and therefore should be the focus of prereading word study. But specialized vocabulary like this is often taught more effectively within the context of the reading or through comparison/contrast or charting after the reading. The words taught explicitly before reading should be words or concepts central to understanding the text in its entirety. Since this was a shared reading, Lynnette read through the text once to bring out the main idea and then revisited it with students to look at subtleties of the specialized vocabulary. In this way she offered explicit support to help students discover

Figure 4.3

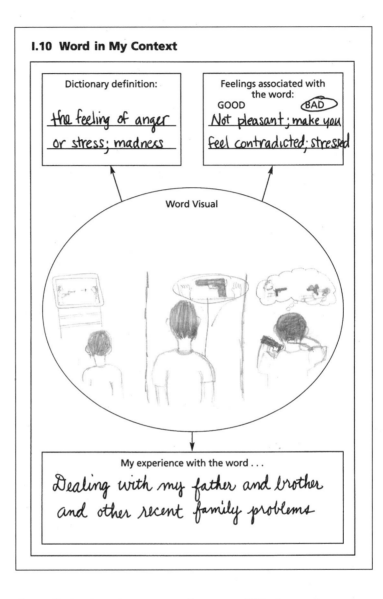

I.10 Word in My Context

Dictionary definition:

the feeling of anger or stress; madness

Feelings associated with the word:
GOOD   BAD

Not pleasant; make you feel contradicted; stressed

Word Visual

My experience with the word . . .

Dealing with my father and brother and other recent family problems

strategies for making distinctions between and among difficult words or concepts and for remembering those distinctions. This is often one of the most challenging aspects of word study in science: several words are connected because they are related, so students remember that they are related but not what makes them different from each other.

Using the Alike but Different graphic organizers (see Figure 4.4), students were asked to look at what these words or concepts had in common. In this case, they discovered that these terms are tied together because they all refer to

Figure 4.4

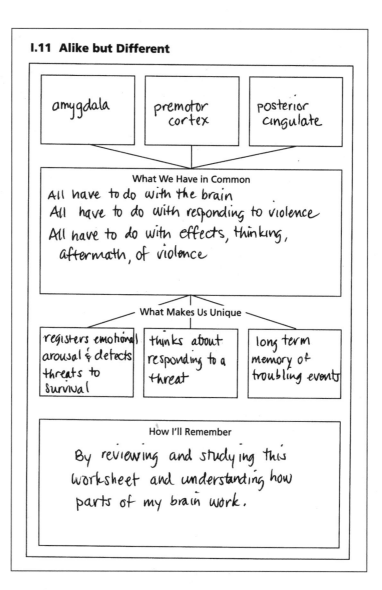

I.11 Alike but Different

| amygdala | premotor cortex | posterior cingulate |

What We Have in Common
All have to do with the brain
All have to do with responding to violence
All have to do with effects, thinking, aftermath, of violence

What Makes Us Unique

| registers emotional arousal & detects threats to survival | thinks about responding to a threat | long term memory of troubling events |

How I'll Remember

By reviewing and studying this worksheet and understanding how parts of my brain work.

regions of the brain that trigger behavioral responses. They made distinctions among the terms by noting how each region is responsible for causing a different kind of behavioral response.

In this way graphic organizers helped learners break down information they would have overlooked because it seemed too abstract or difficult. Graphic organizers are readily available in professional books and teacher resource books, and are easily created using software programs. However, it is important to modify published organizers to fit the purposes of your word study.

It is easy to get so involved in using graphic organizers and varying the types of reading texts that we could miss the real value of shared reading and word study—words encountered in the context of interesting texts are memorable. In a chapter entitled "How Teachers Make Children Hate Reading," John Holt describes an argument he had with his sister when she criticized her child's teacher for making students look up and analyze every difficult word in Cooper's *The Deerslayer*. Holt lost the argument when his sister reminded him of how he had actually learned most of the words he knew:

> My sister answered that until this year her boy had always loved reading, and had read a lot on his own; now he had stopped. (He was not really to start again for many years.)
>
> Still I persisted. If children didn't look up the words they didn't know, how would they ever learn them? My sister said, "Don't be silly! When you were little you had a huge vocabulary, and were always reading very grown-up books. When did you ever look up a word in a dictionary?"
>
> She had me. I don't know that we had a dictionary at home; if we did, I didn't use it. I don't use one today. In my life I doubt that I have looked up as many as fifty words, perhaps not even half that.
>
> Since then I have talked about this with a number of teachers. More than once I have said, "According to tests, educated and literate people like you have a vocabulary of about twenty-five thousand words. How many of these did you learn by looking them up in a dictionary?" They usually are startled. Few claim to have looked up even as many as a thousand. How did they learn the rest?
>
> They learned them just as they learned to talk—by meeting words over and over again, in different contexts, until they saw how they fitted. (455–456)

One of our tasks in terms of word learning is making sure we aren't killing the experience of shared reading for the sole purpose of studying words. Books such as Debra Frasier's *Miss Alaineus: A Vocabulary Disaster* or Mary Amato's *The Word Eater* make great shared reading experiences *and* they explicitly encourage the wide and wild use of language. Our daily teaching should be filled with readings that are so interesting they mesmerize students with the sheer beauty of the ways words are used. Appendix A provides titles for reading that supports words study, but rich language is everywhere. A shared reading of a poem like the Kormans' "Vocabulary" from *The D- Poems of Jeremy Bloom* illustrates this. The poem reminds us all that words are not only "all we have" but, sometimes, all we need.

Vocabulary

I think that today I'll invent a new word.
An adjective. See how you like it. It's *glurd*.

When something is *glurd*, it's especially nice,
Like chocolate, and hockey, Nintendo, and *flice*.

Of course I mean red *flice*, 'cause *flice* that are green
Are not *glurd* at all; they're depressingly *sveen*.

With *glurd flice*, not *sveen flice*, a guy's in great shape.
He can *wazzle*, *perfuffle*, *kazyme*, and *terflape*.

You wonder why I use new words like *kazyme*?
It's so I can get these dumb poems to rhyme. (61)

5

Building on Common Ground:
Shared Paths to Content Literacy

David Hawkins has said of curriculum development, "You
don't want to cover a subject; you want to uncover it." That, it
seems to me, is what schools should be about. They can help to
uncover parts of the world that children would not otherwise
know how to tackle.

Eleanor Duckworth, *"The Having of Wonderful Ideas" and*
Other Essays on Teaching and Learning

A few weeks ago I was visiting a school and observing classes, so I stopped to visit a social studies class. In the half hour I was there, I noted the teacher repeating isolated facts (in response to students' questions related to a worksheet they were completing); students discussing an upcoming school dance; students drawing on the brown-paper covers of textbooks (none actually opened while I was there); and four students sleeping. Now, I will admit that there have been days in my classroom when you could have noted the same behaviors, but it still saddened me to witness the behaviors on this day. The most distressing aspect was that the content to be covered that day could and should have been very interesting because it was related to the internment camps for Japanese-Americans during World War II. Students were filling in blanks with numbers—dates, the number of the executive order remanding citizens to the camp, the number of Japanese-Americans who fought for the United States, and the number of the amendment in the Constitution that was violated. Students were filling in the blanks as though this event had happened only on the pages of a textbook rather than to real people who had homes and families, jobs and professions, all of which were lost on a single day. These students were covering, instead of uncovering, the curriculum.

Our goals for content literacy do not change because of our use of the shared reading approach. In fact, these goals should be easier to reach because students are more engaged, can see our modeling of independent learning strategies, develop knowledge of text structures and supports, and begin to understand the role of an active learner. In the *Handbook of Reading Research Volume III,* Thomas Bean states, "The degree to which adolescents are motivated to engage in learning science, mathematics, history, and other content is heavily influenced by the nature of the material they encounter and opportunities for discussion" (637). Using literature as shared texts in content classes supports growth in both literacy and content knowledge. Literature can supplement textbook instruction by giving readers opportunities to explore events more extensively than textbook coverage allows.

In addition, some students can learn from a narrative format when they might have difficulty with expository texts. If a concept is introduced to those readers with a story, they are then able to take the character or story line into their expository reading to make the content information seem more real. In *Student-Centered Language Arts, K–12,* Moffett and Wagner support the use of multiple texts as a way of helping students develop as independent learners: "Students learning to operate their language must learn to send and receive any sort of message, regardless of abstraction level or mode of discourse (such as fictional or factual). Furthermore, comparing one level or mode with another brings out the uniqueness of each. It is with subjects as with students: differences teach" (38).

The shared reading approach in content classes can make content reading accessible; the materials chosen for shared reading can make the study engaging. I believe that shared reading can support and extend content learning in several areas: building background knowledge for content inquiry, making content connections, understanding content textbook structures, internalizing and applying content vocabulary, and extending and synthesizing content knowledge.

Building Background Knowledge
for Content Inquiry

When I first read Michael Harper's poem "American History," I thought it would make a great opening for a social studies teacher at the beginning of a school year. Wouldn't it be interesting to explore with students the very events and ideas that some might hope we "can't see"? We are fortunate to have writers who offer us texts that build background knowledge in interesting ways and also challenge our thinking.

> ### American History
> Those four black girls blown up
> in that Alabama church
> remind me of five hundred
> middle passage blacks,
> in a net, under water
> in Charleston harbor
> so *redcoats* wouldn't find them.
> Can't find what you can't see
> can you? (19)

After reading Harper's poem, who among us would not be anxious to read historical texts that give some answers to the many questions we would have about the Sunday school bombing in Birmingham or the five hundred blacks in Charleston harbor? When the texts we share with students precipitate content questions, our teaching role changes from someone who transmits information to one who facilitates questioning, critical thinking, and research. When our shared texts offer enough background information to leave students wanting to know more, we will have overcome one of the major impediments to content literacy—lack of motivation or interest. Our goal is that students would echo the sentiments of the main character in Kathryn Lasky's novel *Memoirs of a Bookbat:* "I prefer books that answer no questions but raise millions; that do not simplify the laws of nature but deepen the mystery of the universe" (189).

For students who have had a passive role in making connections and developing questions that would lead them to deeper understanding of texts, it is often important to support these learners through modeling and helping them get their own thoughts on paper. Using the Information Quest form (I.12, Appendix I) during the shared reading of several texts can give students a way to record information, connections, comparisons and questions for discussion, writing, and further research. Harper's poem led students to list as fact that four girls were blown up in a church in Alabama. Students had many questions, including who was responsible, reasons for the explosion, what happened, was anyone caught, and why those little girls were the target.

The information quest can then be continued with a different shared text. In *Classroom Instruction That Works,* Marzano, Pickering, and Pollock note that identifying similarities and differences and summarizing/note taking had the highest rank ordering in terms of instructional power. Moving from a poem to an informational article offers readers the chance to compare text structures and information. This article is from Bullard's *Free at Last: A History of the Civil Rights Movement and Those Who Died in the Struggle:*

Schoolgirls Killed in Bombing of 16th Street Baptist Church, Birmingham, Alabama

It was Youth Sunday at Sixteenth Street Baptist Church in Birmingham, Alabama. The preacher had prepared a sermon especially for the children. The youth choir would lead the congregation in music, and children would serve as ushers.

For the youngsters, many of whom had marched proudly with Dr. Martin Luther King, Jr., it was another in a series of momentous events that year. That spring, their own church had been the center of a campaign against segregation. The long struggle was won mainly because children were brave enough to march into the overpowering water hoses and vicious dogs of Police Commissioner Bull Connor. After television news cameras revealed the brutal force unleashed on the children, city officials were forced to reform their harsh segregation laws.

Now lunch counters were no longer closed to blacks, and a federal court had just ordered white schools in the city to admit black children. The whole world had watched in awe as the children in Birmingham made history. Before this day was over, the whole world would mourn.

The Sacrifice of Children

In the basement ladies' lounge of Sixteenth Street Baptist Church, four girls were chatting nervously and straightening their fancy white dresses. In a few minutes the worship service would begin. Addie Mae Collins, 14, and Denise McNair, 11, were in the choir. Carole Robertson and Cynthia Wesley, both 14, had been chosen to serve as ushers.

Only a few feet away, beneath a stone staircase along the outside wall of the church, a dynamite bomb had been planted eight hours earlier. At 10:22 it exploded. The whole church shook. Plaster and debris fell around the people in Sunday School upstairs. The four girls in the ladies' lounge were killed instantly.

For a few minutes, there was only screaming and chaos. Then people began to search through the rubble for victims. In the end, more than 20 people were hospitalized with injuries. One of them was Addie Mae Collins' sister Sarah, who was blinded in one eye.

There had been many bombings in Birmingham designed to stop the black struggle for equality. Ministers' homes, a black-owned hotel, and other churches had been wrecked. But there had been nothing so evil as the dynamiting of children during Sunday School. The news spread quickly, and it sickened people of all races and all political allegiances throughout the world.

"We All Did It"

The FBI immediately investigated the bombing, and discovered it was planned by Klansmen in response to the new school desegregation order. An eyewitness saw four white men plant the bomb. Unexplainably, no one was charged with the crime.

Then 14 years later, Alabama Attorney General William Baxley reopened the case. A 73-year-old Klansman named Robert Chambliss was charged with first-degree murder, and the jury found him guilty. Chambliss was sent to prison, where he died. No one else has ever been tried for the Sixteenth Street bombing.

September 15, 1963, was remembered as a day of victory for the Klan. Shortly after the church bombing, white supremacist leader Connie Lynch told a group of Klansmen that those responsible for the bombing deserved "medals." Lynch said the four young girls who died there "weren't children. Children are little people, little human beings, and that means white people . . . They're just niggers . . . and if there's four less niggers tonight, then I say, 'Good for whoever planted the bomb!'"

The Sixteenth Street bombing, perhaps more than any other event of the period, brought national attention to the evil of racism. The tragedy sparked a surge of support for federal civil rights legislation, and it led to an intensive voting rights campaign in Selma, Alabama.

But more importantly, it made the pain of racism felt among whites who would never experience it themselves. The day after the bombing, a white lawyer named Charles Morgan gave a speech in Birmingham. He asked his audience: "Who did it?" and gave his own anguished answer: "We all did it . . . every person in this community who has in any way contributed . . . to the popularity of hatred is at least as guilty . . . as the demented fool who threw that bomb." (58–59)

As students participate in the shared reading of this text, they discover answers to many of their questions. In the second column of the Information Quest form, they connect this new information to what they already know about this event. The patterns they discover in the reading are patterns of hatred and forgiveness.

The third column of the form provides an opportunity for students to work with partners or small groups reading one other text related to the same event. Students might watch a video such as Spike Lee's *Four Little Girls,* read portions of Curtis's *The Watsons Go to Birmingham—1963,* or read other newspaper articles, such as Farley's "The Ghosts of Alabama," describing the indictments of two men thirty-seven years after the bombing. With the partner or small-group, students can read, compare and contrast new information to the previous knowledge base, and develop questions for whole-class research.

When the acquisition of background knowledge is supported through multiple texts, shared reading, and conspicuous note taking that includes questions, connections, and comparisons, the background knowledge is memorable. Students come to "know" the individuals who were part of these historical events as real people and not just as objects connected to dates and time lines. The content knowledge gained gives readers confidence in their abilities to learn and makes them more motivated to continue learning. The strategic processes they learned for recording information, conducting comparisons, making connections, and asking questions create a foundation for ongoing text connections.

Making Content Connections

In order for readers to make connections between their existing background knowledge and new learning, the text building the bridge for that learning has to be meaningful and memorable. Eleanor Duckworth says, "Tools cannot help developing once children have something real to think about; and if they don't have anything real to think about, they won't be applying tools anyway. There really is no such thing as a contentless intellectual tool" (13).

One of the ways we can make those connections is by trying to imagine what an event or situation might have been like for someone who experienced it. We can look at a single event from several perspectives by sharing texts that offer diverse insights. In this case, the reader's work becomes one of gathering clues from the text that would help visualize the event, inferring what that must have been like, and asking questions that would help lead to a deeper understanding.

Using the graphic organizer Multiple Sources, Multiple Perspectives (I.13, Appendix I), students were given the opportunity to look at relocation camps during World War II from the perspective of a child experiencing the confusion of the event. Unlike the students described at the beginning of the chapter, these students were allowed to make critical, cognitive, *and* affective connections before examining the information from a textbook. As each of the following poems by Marnie Mueller was shared, students were given the opportunity to discover factual information, infer motivation and emotions, and ask questions they hoped would be answered:

Santa Anita Racetrack Assembly Center—March 1942
They put us in horse stalls.
They crowded us in,
sometimes three people
where one horse had lived.
Good enough for Japs
I guess they believed.
We found bits of manure
with straw stuck in.
Eeeouw, it was disgusting
and my mama-san cried.
She cried all day long
and couldn't be stopped
until my papa-san went out
and said he wouldn't come back.
After that she banged her head
against the side of our stall,
like a horse that's gone mad,
I heard some people say.
Like a horse gone mad,
my mama-san did,
in front of all those strangers
we were living with. (39–40)

Train Ride to Tule Lake Internment Camp—May 1942
We were riding all night on the train,
all night on the train,
all night, with the shades pulled down,
and the lights turned out.

I lean against mommy,
I lean my head in her lap,
I lean against mommy all through the night.
The only lights are two little red ones
in the front and the back of the car.

When I open my eyes in the middle of the night
I can see heads shaking,
bobbing, swaying,
I can see heads
of our neighbors in the dim red light.
I have my coat on, it's cold in the train,
my blue Easter coat, my new-bought one.

They called us dirty Japs
and mommy didn't dare
let us go to church
on White River Street.

So my coat is brand-new on the train,
on the train to I don't know where. (40–41)

First Week at Tule Lake
Papa won't talk
not one single word
no matter what mama says.
"Papa-san, you stop that,"
she says. "You be a man.
Your children cry.
Your children ashamed."
But papa only sits by the window
and stares out.
He doesn't move the whole day.

We bring him food
from the mess hall—
American food
like in my school back home,
not so bad, I think.

He turns and looks
when I give it to him.
For a minute it seems like
he's going to smile—
his mouth goes up that way.
Instead he spits
fat and disgusting
right in the middle of the tin plate. (41–42)

Teenage Boy at Tule Lake
Mama measured me
today, I grew one more inch.
Papa grew smaller. (42)

Issei Bachelor at Tule Lake
It good to be bachelor here,
no children
to see your shame. (42)

Understanding Content Textbook Structures

Many of our content classes are still heavily dependent on textbooks, but many students remain unwilling or unable to break the code of textbook reading. Common barriers to learning from textbooks include lack of background knowledge for the content, lack of vocabulary, failure to use relevant background knowledge or interference from inaccurate background knowledge, unfamiliarity with common textbook structures and supports, and lack of strategies for comprehending challenging textbooks.

Added to these challenges, we know that many students believe it is the teacher's job to explain the textbook to them. They take on a passive role, waiting for the content to come to them with little evidence of cognitive work on their part. In *Reading for Meaning,* van den Broek and Kremer contrast that attitude with that of students who successfully negotiate their textbooks: "Less skilled readers set lower standards for comprehension, such as by relaxing or even totally abandoning their need for these kinds of coherence. The standards that readers adopt also differ by such factors as their metacognitive skills, motivation, reading goals, and pragmatic concerns" (7).

In order to move students from passive to active engagement (as opposed to active refusal to learn), I recommend that teachers begin each content lesson with shared reading as a foundation. We know from Richard Allington's research and our own experience that if students get frustrated early in the process of learning content, they won't learn the content and they may also cause disruptions and management problems: "Students given tasks where success was low were far more likely to cease work on the task and engage in nonacademic behaviors than were students working at high success rates. Thus, many classroom management difficulties were linked to the relative difficulty of school work students were given" (45). I've outlined here a lesson plan that uses shared reading in different ways so that students will have multiple ways to access the content information and to apply what they are learning both about reading and about content.

Each of the five stages of this literacy-based content lesson has a distinct purpose and builds on process and content established in the previous stage. For each stage I detail the purpose in terms of content knowledge and reading process. The content purpose is helping students understand the body's nervous system, and the strategic literacy purpose is helping students develop independence as readers by teaching them how to use text supports to comprehend their textbooks.

Shared Reading

Beginning a lesson with the teacher reading aloud using a shared reading approach while students follow along with individual copies of the text or with enlarged text on an overhead allows readers to begin to build content knowledge in a risk-free way. They can connect with a character's dilemma as the shared text offers real-world applications and connections to the content. Other texts might offer the opportunity to share information from content experts or provide students with a content challenge from their reading.

In "Night of the Pomegranate," a short story by Tim Wynne-Jones, Harriet has waited until the last minute to create her science project. When she arrives at school with her project, she discovers that other kids have created masterful projects (some she suspects have had parental help). As it gets closer to the time when she will present her project, she becomes extremely nervous and just a bit sick to her stomach.

> She was using the tape on Ms. Krensky's desk when Clayton Beemer arrived with his dad. His solar system came from the hobby store. The planets were Styrofoam balls, all different sizes and painted the right colors. Saturn's rings were clear plastic painted over as delicately as insect wings.
>
> Harriet looked at her own Saturn. Her rings were drooping despite all the tape. They looked like a limp skirt on a . . . on a ball of scrunched-up newspaper.
>
> Harriet sighed. The wires that supported Clayton's planets in their black box were almost invisible. The planets seemed to float.
>
> "What d'ya think?" Clayton asked. He beamed. Mr. Beemer beamed. Harriet guessed that *he* had made the black box with its glittery smears of stars.
>
> She had rolled up her own project protectively when Clayton entered the classroom. Suddenly one of the planets came unstuck and fell on the floor. Clayton and Mr. Beemer looked at it.
>
> "What's that?" asked Clayton.
>
> "Pluto, I think," said Harriet, picking it up. She popped it in her mouth. It tasted of grape gum. "Yes, Pluto," she said. Clayton and Mr. Beemer walked away to find the best place to show off their project.

Dargit arrived next. "Hi, Harriet," she said. The project under her arm had the planets' names done in bold gold lettering. Harriet's heart sank. Pluto tasted stale and cold.

At this stage students begin to connect with the range of emotions Harriet is experiencing. Most of them can sympathize with her because of their own experiences with procrastination and feeling "less than" other students. They have now made a personal connection to Harriet's nervousness, which leads us to the next stage of the lesson.

Thinking/Learning/Problem-Solving Group Challenge

Following the shared text with an opportunity for students to use the text in some kind of creative problem-solving activity gives students the opportunity to think critically and creatively about the content they are going to study. They can both anticipate the content of the lesson and continue to build background knowledge for that content. At this point, I would ask students which emotion is most obvious for Harriet. Students always mention that Harriet is obviously nervous. Students are then given the graphic organizer Cause and Effect in Science (I.14, Appendix I) and asked to examine the details for external indicators of Harriet's nervousness. Then they are asked to collaborate with their group members to make a hypothesis of the biological triggers that would have caused these external indicators. When they read their textbook, they can revisit their hypothesis for confirmation or rejection after they have investigated the biological triggers.

Modeled Lesson: Direct Instruction

The purpose of the modeled lesson is to demonstrate for students a process for thinking through a concept we want to introduce. During this time, we can model strategic paths to content literacy, connections between and among previously taught concepts, and transferring of new information to personal understandings and other contexts. I see the modeled lesson as a time to teach content for transfer rather than content for the sake of content.

An important aspect of this lesson that could be taught through direct instruction and modeling is helping students figure out what the text supports in their textbooks are for. Students can use their textbooks in a type of scavenger hunt facilitated by the teacher as they determine the purpose of the text supports there. Using the Text to Text form (I.15, Appendix I), the teacher could think aloud to model for students how text supports help determine meaning. In this case, the form could help us focus on the following text supports: titles, subtitles, photographs, boldfaced words, italics, first paragraph and last paragraph, diagrams, focus questions, and glossary/key words.

Using a previously read chapter of the textbook, we could revisit it and think how each support could help us read the textbook independently. We are still using the shared reading approach as we reread the chapter in order to discover the supports and the purposes of those supports. Students can use the Text to Text organizer to record the text supports we find and how those supports would help them comprehend the text. The modeled lesson is then followed by guided learning so that students can apply what they have just learned and the teacher can see if students have understood the instruction.

Guided Learning

Guided learning is an important stage in this lesson. During guided learning, students are given an opportunity for shared construction of meaning around the modeled lesson. Our role at this stage is to provide a task that would let students apply the information to a new text or in a new context. We can also use this time to assess students' understanding of the process or of strategies they have been taught. We often don't know what we don't know until we get to the point of trying to apply or use information.

In this guided learning, we are attempting to give students an opportunity to extend the modeled lesson about using supports to comprehend textbooks by applying those supports to a chapter about the nervous system. Students now take their image of nervous Harriet from "Night of the Pomegranate" and their knowledge of how to read a textbook into shared reading of the chapter with a partner. The teacher continues to scaffold that transfer by providing a textbook activity guide for the chapter that will focus students on those supports as a way to gain knowledge.

The textbook activity guide (TAG) was created by Davey as a way to help students organize their thinking while reading through texts. I have used a TAG often in order to help students make a conscious transfer of whatever was taught in the modeled lesson. A TAG has the following directions for students: P = discuss with partner; WR = write a written response; Skim = read quickly for a stated purpose and discuss with partner; Map = complete a semantic or visual map to represent information; and PP = predict with your partner. Each time students are given a direction in the TAG, they are also provided with the page numbers for applying that direction.

To help students gain content knowledge about the nervous system by comprehending a textbook chapter, the following guide leads them to use supports taught in the modeled lesson. These TAG prompts are specific to this topic ("The Nervous System") and connected to a middle school textbook (*Silver Burdett Science*, 1985), but they can be easily adapted for other textbooks and chapters. As a way to offer several prompt models, I have included eleven prompts for this guide. This would actually be a larger number than we might need for five pages of the text because the TAG is dependent on choosing the most crucial pages of the text for students to read.

TAG: "The Nervous System," pp. 316–320

1. PP—Look at the pictures on pages 317–319, and list two things you and your partner predict you might learn in this selection.
2. Skim—List the boldfaced words on pages 316–320.
3. P—Discuss with your partner some possible ways these words might be connected.
4. MAP—Illustrate the ideas you and your partner discovered for connections in (3) above by drawing a map that connects at least three of the key words (316–320).
5. P, WR—Read, discuss, and write or draw your conclusions about how the central nervous system is related to the peripheral nervous system (316–320).
6. WR—What is the purpose of the nervous system? (318)
7. MAP—Draw a map that illustrates what nerve cells look like (318).
8. P, WR—Discuss the jobs that each type of nerve cell performs. Write a job description for each one (319).
9. P, WR—Read this page with your partner. Discuss the relation between reflex and reaction time. Work with your partner to write your summary of this connection. Include at least one example of reaction time in your summary (320).
10. MAP, WR (Activity)—Do the meterstick experiment on page 321 with three or four people. Draw a graph to show the results of your experiment.
11. WR—Write a conclusion statement from your experiment that would complete this sentence: Based on our research, we think we see the following patterns:

_____.

As students read passages to each other, they are using the approach of strategic shared reading for comprehending content from their textbooks. This leads to the final stage of the lesson: connecting the new to the known so that students have a way to keep track of both the strategic processes and the content they are learning.

Connecting the New to the Known

In *Starting from Scratch: One Classroom Builds Its Own Curriculum*, Steven Levy says that a measure of true understanding is the ability to apply a principle to a different context: "When students learn by discovery, they are much more likely to understand, remember, and apply their knowledge to other situations. The challenge is always to give them a chance to discover it themselves" (78). In the course of demonstrating these understandings, we take the opportunity for more shared reading. The purpose of this stage is helping students demonstrate they have acquired new learning by recording that learning so that they can apply the processes in their independent reading for this and other classes.

The following example of writing is connected to the short story we used initially and to a TAG for the solar system, but I think it is a wonderful example of students' demonstrating their content knowledge in creative ways. The writer combined Harriet's love of the solar system from "Night of the Pomegranate" and the writer's textbook knowledge of the solar system to take an imaginary journey through the solar system with her hero:

> If I would have to travel with a hero, I would pick Dad. We would pack all sorts of clothes, 5 jackets for Pluto, and underwear for Mercury. My dad is a musician and on our trip we would sing happily. We would fly by Saturn and see its pretty rings. We would go to Mars and look at aliens. I would catch one, or take a picture of one so when I get home everyone would believe me. I would pass by earth and see its beautiful colors (which are mostly green, blue, and white). Also I would go to Jupiter. I believe I would see a couple of rings. I would count how many moons it has. I would do the same for Neptune, but would wear three jackets. I would go to each planet in order, which are Mercury, Venus, Earth and Mars.

At this stage, it is also important for students to assess their use of strategies as a way to provide feedback for us to determine the next modeled lesson we might need to offer. The Student Self-Assessment of Strategic Reading form (I.16, Appendix I) serves as a checklist for students in their continued use of text supports and effective reading strategies. As students assess and report areas where they continue to struggle, the content for the next literacy-based lesson emerges.

Internalizing and Applying Content Vocabulary

Each of us has faced challenges in our own education when we have been asked to memorize and learn specialized vocabulary for content reading. Baker,

Simmons, and Kameenui's research highlights the impact of *strategic* word study, yet in many classes we were given lists of words and required to define the words and write them in sentences: "One of the best ways to facilitate greater independence in vocabulary growth is through the strategic integration of vocabulary learning opportunities in multiple curricular areas" (14).

In other contexts, we were asked to do the more difficult task of analyzing and applying the definitions with the support of meaningful text. When those key words and concepts were combined with difficult academic language, many of us struggled to make sense of our reading. That same scenario is played out in hundreds of classrooms every day where students struggle (or make no attempt) to learn content vocabulary that would help them be successful in their content reading.

Camille Blachowicz and Peter Fisher remind educators that teaching and learning new words can have many purposes, especially when teaching diverse populations: "These realizations imply that teachers need to be knowledgeable about what they want students to know with respect to both the depth and breadth of learning and the kinds of connections to be made. Teaching vocabulary becomes not a simple process of teaching words but one of teaching particular words to particular students for a particular purpose" (517).

When shared reading becomes a foundation for content literacy, we are able to support word learning at two levels: the incidental word learning that occurs as a natural part of rich reading experiences, and the conspicuous word learning that can occur prior to, during, or after shared reading. In conjunction with a shared reading text, we can support word learning and concept knowledge in the following ways:

- Demonstrate the use of context to figure out meanings.
- Discover key concept words by highlighting repeated or specialized words.
- Connect words to a larger concept.
- Show multiple meanings of words based on text and context.
- Create visuals, webs, or organizers to help students develop memory links for words.
- Help students discriminate between and among common, academic, and specialized vocabulary words.

If we were using the following passage from Kohut and Sweet's *News from the Fringe* in an art, health, or science class, we could demonstrate the integration of several of these word-learning strategies:

Dr. Graziella Magherini, chief of psychiatry at the Santa Maria Nuova Hospital in Florence, Italy, coined the term "The Stendhal Syndrome" to describe the numerous cases she has treated in more than 10 years of observing tourists who have become disoriented in the presence of great works of art in that city. Magherini has collected more than 100 cases in the past decade of tourists who, while visiting the churches and museums of Florence, experience rapid heartbeats, stomach pains, fainting, heavy perspiration, depression, euphoria, feelings of omnipotence, and hallucinations. Although some of those affected were in the presence of religious paintings (one woman was convinced that she could hear angels singing), Magherini said that it is the emotional texture of the artwork that triggers the reactions along with the factor of the subjects traveling in a foreign city. Although subjects recover after a few days of rest, she suggested that tourists do not try to appreciate too much great art in too short a time frame. Those who seem most susceptible to the phenomena tend to be single men and women ages 26 to 40 who travel alone or in small groups and who do not travel often. (64)

Since the word *syndrome* is key to understanding this passage, that word could be explored in terms of what students already knew prior to the shared reading of this information text. Using the graphic organizer Understanding a Concept ABC x 2 (I.17, Appendix I), students could brainstorm what they knew about syndromes before beginning the reading of the text. Following the reading, students could go back to the organizer and the shared text to analyze the word by looking for its critical features as highlighted by this text. This word is introduced prior to reading both to assess current level of knowledge and to build a knowledge base for those who have never seen or heard the word. This word study then provides a foundation for the shared reading.

General vocabulary words, and words related to the key word, *syndrome,* can be discussed after the shared reading. Words like *euphoria, omnipotence, hallucinations, susceptible,* and *phenomena* add to a global understanding of the passage, but readers could gain some meaning even if they had only a vague sense of definitions for these words. These words can be explored using context clues. In this way, these words can be connected to the larger concept of "syndrome" by looking at the relationships between and among the words. For example, we can examine the words to see which words denote characteristics of a syndrome or which would be caused by or descriptive of a syndrome.

When content vocabulary is taught in the context of reading a text with the shared reading approach, students immediately have the opportunity to see and hear the word at the same time. For many students, this helps them place the word in a general context such as, "I now know this word is related to science." By revisiting the shared text to flesh out multiple meanings or deeper connotations of the word, we can ensure that our word study has the three critical characteristics for effectively increasing reading comprehension through increased vocabulary knowledge (Nagy): integration (tying new words to familiar concepts and experiences); repetition (repeated encounters with a word in context, leading to automaticity); and meaningful use (understanding how to apply the word and connect it to other words in the knowledge base).

Extending and Synthesizing Content Knowledge

If we want students to choose to extend their shared reading through research, we have to give them a foundation of interesting information that challenges their assumptions about the world. When I suggested a shared reading of Loewen's *Lies My Teacher Told Me* to a group of high school social studies teachers, one of the teachers asked, "Do we really want to hint that the textbook might not be entirely accurate when they still can't read all the words in the textbook?" I suggested that perhaps there would be no better way to get them to read the words in the textbook than by embarking on a quest for the discovery of misinformation. The Billy Collins poem that follows makes an excellent shared reading for inviting students to look at multiple texts around a single event in order to determine whose voices are heard and whose voices might have been silenced:

> **The History Teacher**
> Trying to protect his students' innocence
> he told them the Ice Age was really just
> the Chilly Age, a period of a million years
> when everyone had to wear sweaters.
>
> And the Stone Age became the Gravel Age,
> named after the long driveways of the time.
>
> The Spanish Inquisition was nothing more
> than an outbreak of questions such as
> "How far is it from here to Madrid?"
> "What do you call the matador's hat?"
>
> The War of the Roses took place in a garden,
> and the Enola Gay dropped one tiny atom
> on Japan.

The children would leave his classroom
for the playground to torment the weak
and the smart,
mussing up their hair and breaking their glasses,

while he gathered up his notes and walked home
past flower beds and white picket fences,
wondering if they would believe that soldiers
in the Boer War told long, rambling stories
designed to make the enemy nod off. (67)

When students are challenged to synthesize information and extend their content knowledge, they have to have what Cris Tovani calls an interacting voice. "An interacting voice encourages the reader to infer, make connections, ask questions, and synthesize information, while a distracting voice pulls the reader away from the text" (45). Given the background knowledge and connections established for knowledge about the internment camps, students should have enough information and word knowledge to partner-read an excerpt from an article by Jim Carnes from *Us and Them: A History of Intolerance in America:*

Home Was a Horse Stall
1942, San Bruno, California
On Dec. 7, 1941, Japan's attack on the U.S. naval station at Pearl Harbor, Hawaii, thrust the United States into World War II and changed the life of every American. Thousands of young men were drafted into the Army and sent halfway around the globe to risk their lives in battle. The long, lean years of the Depression abruptly ended as American industry geared up for wartime. In factories and businesses and government bureaus, women played a more prominent role in the national work force than ever before.

Both the news and entertainment media of the era depicted a nation rallying to the defense of freedom. But one group of Americans faced a struggle all its own. For Americans of Japanese descent, the experience of the war years gave the word "freedom" a whole new meaning.

On Sunday morning, December 7, 1941, Sox, her sister Lillian and their mother were riding in the car. A special bulletin on the radio announced that the Japanese had mounted a surprise air attack on the U.S. Naval base at Pearl Harbor, Hawaii. The girls translated the news for Yumi. "This is terrible," she said to them in Japanese. Because she was an Issei ("first generation" Japanese immigrant), she was not a U.S. citizen. Her native country was now the enemy.

Sox and Lillian knew that their lives were about to change. They were Americans, born on American soil. They listened to the same music, followed the same fashions, pledged allegiance to the same flag as everyone else. But now they wondered how other Americans would treat them. They wondered if the storekeepers would still sell them food. Over the next few weeks, shops in towns around the area began posting signs telling Japanese customers to stay away. Old hostilities found new expression in the name of patriotism. There were scattered incidents of violence against Japanese Americans and their property.

The question about what was going to happen was partially answered on February 19, 1942. Pres. Franklin D. Roosevelt on that day issued Executive Order 9066, establishing "military areas" along the West Coast and limiting the activities of "any or all persons" within them.

Evacuation orders posted on telephone poles and public buildings declared that Japanese Americans had one week to prepare to leave their homes. In the meantime, they had to abide by an 8 p.m. curfew and get permission to travel.

The instructions didn't tell people where they would be going, but they did tell them what to bring: only the bare necessities, like clothing and linens and soap. When someone said they could take what they could carry in two hands, the Kataokas took this literally. They had never owned suitcases, so they got a permit to go to a nearby town and buy two each—flimsy cardboard ones, outrageously priced.

Deciding what to pack was easy; getting rid of the rest was not. Anything obviously Japanese could be interpreted as a sign of collaboration with the enemy. Yumi Kataoka burned her family's Japanese books and letters, advertising calendars from Japanese businesses, even her certificates from a Japanese bank. Many people burned family keepsakes such as photographs and antique kimonos.

As for their other possessions, the evacuees had two choices: either leave them to be stolen or sell them at the going rate. One of Yuma's sons sold two cars, a long-bed truck and a Caterpillar tractor, for a fraction of their worth. The Kataokas got $15 for their piano, and Sox was so happy to see it going home with someone that she gave the buyer all her sheet music and even threw her tennis racquet into the bargain. Some people in the valley refused to trade their brand new stoves or refrigerators for pocket change, so they stored them in the Japanese school building, in hopes of retrieving them when the war was over.

Yumi Kataoka had moved her family many times, but never like this. The bus let them out at Tanforan Racetrack in San Bruno, Calif. No one knew what to expect. None of the Kataokas had ever been to a racetrack before. Inside, military policemen searched each person. All suitcases were opened and ransacked. A nurse peered into every eye and down every throat.

On the infield of the track stood new, army-style barracks. Sox said that she wanted to stay in those, but the officer said they were for mothers with infants. He led the Kataokas around back to the stables: Their new home was a horse stall.

In the dark stall that night, listening to the noises of all the other people, Sox couldn't fall asleep. She couldn't stop wondering what any of them had done to deserve being penned up like animals. She couldn't believe this was happening in America. (93–101)

As students read this text together, they can support each other in taking notes of names, dates, places, and events worth remembering by using the Triple Entry Journal (I.18, Appendix I). They can make connections between the information recorded here and the information they discovered during the shared reading of Mueller's poetry. Finally, they can develop questions for further research and other reading. In their research on brain-based learning, Caine and Caine state that "content is inseparable from context. The primary focus for educators, therefore, should be on expanding the quantity and quality of ways in which a learner is exposed to content and context" (5–6). Shared reading of diverse texts helps students gain multiple perspectives to support their synthesis of information in meaningful and personal ways. Appendix B provides a list of resources for content area shared reading, and Appendix C provides a list of titles for shared reading to support content literacy.

When we use content texts that are meaningful and memorable to support learning content knowledge, we can avoid some (though certainly not all) class scenarios like the one a friend from Long Beach recently shared with me:

We were talking about setting in reading and writing and using Cinderella and Rough-Face Girl as examples of descriptive settings. The first sentence in Rough-Face Girl mentions the shores of Lake Ontario. I thought I would be able to get students to compare Europe and North America so I asked them where Lake Ontario is. No one answered, so I tried again. I reminded the eighth graders of their study of American geography. Still no response, so I gave them a prompt: "Lake Ontario is one of the five, great . . ."

Suddenly, Elias blurted out, "CONTENT STANDARDS!"

It doesn't take long for students to internalize what they believe we think is important. This can be a not-so-gentle reminder to us when we lose our way in the maze of content coverage.

6

Writing Roads: Shared Reading as the Foundation for Integrated Language Arts

If you don't have the time to read, you don't have the time or

the tools to write.

Stephen King, *On Writing*

Whether a school has traditional fifty-minute periods or blocks or modified blocks, time management is almost always an issue. A teacher recently told me, "I've got two hours and I still can't fit it all in. It seems like I can either teach reading or writing but I can't teach both." In fact, on a recent coaching visit at a middle school, I was asked by one of the teachers to look at her schedule (see Figure 6.1) and help her figure out how to get it all to fit. I'm guessing most of us could sympathize with this teacher's frustration.

After I observed her class, it was interesting to note with her that she was actually seeing reading and writing as separate teaching goals and was not using the foundation she had begun with shared reading as a place to start for her teaching of writing. On the day I observed, she did a shared reading from Hinton's *The Outsiders,* followed by a talk show in order to examine the ways questioning could help deepen readers' understanding of characters and motivations. Her shared reading could easily have led her to the alternative of teaching the art of questioning through writing leads. Instead, she chose to teach writing via a photojournalism essay, which was more challenging and took longer because her students brought no reading background to the writing task.

Figure 6.1

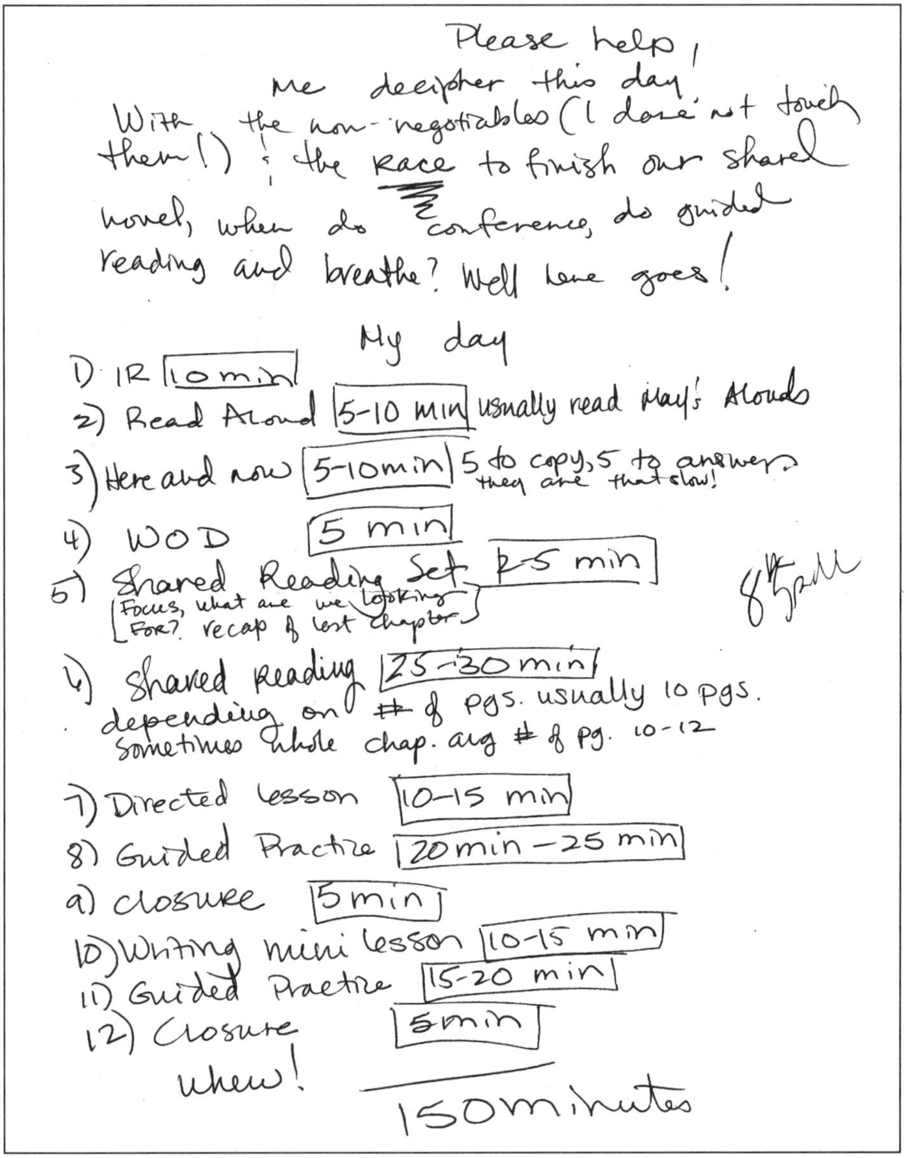

> Please help,
> me decipher this day!
> With the non-negotiables (I dose'nt touch
> them!) ; the race to finish our shared
> novel, when do ~conference, do guided
> reading and breathe? Well here goes!
>
>   My day
>
> 1) IR [10 min]
> 2) Read Aloud [5-10 min] usually read May's Alouds
> 3) Here and now [5-10min] 5 to copy, 5 to answer
>   they are that slow!
> 4) WOD   [5 min]
> 5) Shared Reading Set [~5 min]   8½ spll
>   [Focus, what are we looking]
>   [For? recap of last chapter]
>
> 6) Shared Reading [25-30 min]
>   depending on # of pgs. usually 10 pgs.
>   Sometimes whole chap. avg # of pg. 10-12
>
> 7) Directed Lesson [10-15 min]
> 8) Guided Practice [20 min - 25 min]
> 9) closure [5 min]
> 10) Writing mini lesson [10-15 min]
> 11) Guided Practice [15-20 min]
> 12) Closure [5 min]
>   whew!   _____
>   150 minutes

It has been my experience that well-chosen shared reading texts can offer teachers and students a foundation for integrating the language arts: reading, writing, listening, speaking, thinking, and viewing. In this way, students experience all the language arts as effective communication rather than as isolated activities, methods for covering content, or rules. Shared reading can offer students a mirror in which they can see themselves as readers, writers, and critical thinkers. Our job becomes one of choosing the right mirror and holding the mirror still long enough for students to get an image. With shared reading offering students the opportunity to read a text multiple times, they can return to familiar texts when they encounter various challenges of the language arts.

Building Writing Foundations

There is no doubt about it—teaching writing is difficult work. In our undergraduate classes, most of us learned how to assign writing and grade writing, but we didn't learn many techniques for helping our students become better writers. Many of our students would agree with Melinda, the main character in Laurie Halse Anderson's novel *Speak:*

Word Work
Hairwoman is torturing us with essays. Do English teachers spend their vacations dreaming up these things?

The first essay this semester was a dud: "Why America Is Great" in five hundred words. She gave us three weeks. Only Tiffany Wilson turned it in on time. But the assignment was not a complete failure—Hairwoman runs the drama club and she recruited several new members based on their performances as to why they needed an extension.

She has a warped sense of humor as well as a demented beautician. The next essay was supposed to be fictional: "The Best Lost Homework Excuse Ever" in five hundred words. We had one night. No one was late.

But now Hairwoman is on a roll. "How I Would Change High School," "Lower the Driving Age to 14," "The Perfect Job." Her topics are fun, but she keeps cranking them out, one after the next. First she broke our spirits by overwhelming us with work we couldn't really complain about because the topics are the kind of things we talk about all the time. Recently she's started sneaking grammar (shudder) into the classroom. One day we worked on verb tenses: "I surf the Net, I surfed the Net, I was surfing the Net." Then lively adjectives. Does it sound better to say "Nicole's old lacrosse stick hit me on the head" or "Nicole's barf-yellow, gnarled, bloodstained lacrosse stick hit me on the head"? She even tried to teach us the difference between active voice— "I snarfed the Oreos"—and passive voice—"The Oreos got snarfed."

Words are hard work. I hope they send Hairwoman to a conference or something. I'm ready to help pay for a sub. (84–85)

As students, many of us shared the same writing background that students in Hairwoman's class appear to be experiencing: assignment of topics, little support for understanding how to put ideas into a coherent form, and few effective models of the mode of writing we were to accomplish. Fortunately, we know more about how we can support developing writers in our classrooms today. In *Teaching Writing as Reflective Practice,* George Hillocks describes the kind of support writers need as environmental teaching—"teaching environments to induce and support active learning of complex strategies that students are not capable of using on their own" (55). I believe effective environmental teaching will support students in four broad writing roles and that each of these roles can be supported through shared reading:

- Task reviewer
- Meaning maker
- Code user
- Text crafter

Task Reviewer

Many students find the greatest writing challenge comes from simply getting started. Understanding the audience for the writing, the purpose of the writing task, and how to make writer's choices such as genre and style often leaves writers feeling overwhelmed. Linda Pastan's poem "Whom Do You Visualize as Your Reader?" is an effective shared reading text to begin discussion of audience because many emerging writers imagine that the teacher is the only audience for their writing.

To support writers in this role, we have to help them imagine who might read their writing. One of the ways that I helped my students in this was by choosing several shared readings and asking students to make notes on a Who Is My Audience? form (I.19, Appendix I) about who they thought the intended audience would be for each piece of writing. We examined each text, inferring an audience based on the author's language choices and literary elements such as characters, setting, tone, and organizational structures. In this way, we revisited the strategy of inferring as part of a reader's work, and then we were able to use those inferences to move into our writing lesson.

After inferring the audience for a text, we looked at the piece of writing from the perspective of a writer. We revisited each of the text clues we had used to make our inferences, such as language, tone, characters, and settings, and then tried to determine how the author would have had to change the text to write for a new audience. As a way to illustrate this method of developing audience awareness, I have included here some possible shared readings of diverse examples of writing. Almost any text that has a clear focus could be used as support for understanding this aspect of writing, but I find the more descriptive the writing is, the more effective it is with student writers.

Treacherous Love: The Diary of an Anonymous Teenager
by Beatrice Sparks
September 18th—Wednesday—8:30 p.m.
Today was one of the wondrous days of my life. After lunch Bridget and I sat under the old oak tree in front of school and I told her how I'd written in my diary appreciation part that she was my very nearest and dearest friend. We both started crying then because she said she'd written the very same thing in her diary about me. It's like we truly are sisters. Sometime we pretend to be, and people think we are. We both have long brownish blond hair and sort of greenish eyes but. . . Mother Nature was a little more generous with Bridget in the boob area. Actually, a LOT more generous. I'm as flat in front as I am behind, and I'm short. I hate it! (13)

Amandine
by Adele Griffin
Tuesday, Amandine had saved a place for me in the cafeteria.
    "Delia!" she called, waving me over.
    I felt purposeful and happy as I pushed through the crowd to sit with her. All the previous week, I had been eating lunches with Samantha Blitz, who had been assigned to show me around, and whose patience I was testing. Samantha was the starting center on the freshman girls' soccer team, and at lunch she always sat with her teammates, who had been perfectly nice and had become perfectly indifferent.
    "Hi." I slid my tray opposite hers and sat.
    "Do you smell anything?" She leaned forward.
    "What should I smell?"
    "I forgot to put on deodorant this morning. I can't believe I would ever forget a thing like that, I've been doing it for so long. I have to shave practically twice a day, too. I'm very developed, that way." (25–26)

Reptiles and Children Don't Mix
by Susan Okie
Got a baby or a toddler in the house? Get rid of that iguana.
    Pet reptiles—including all types of lizards, snakes and turtles—can be a source of life-threatening infections and do not belong in house-

holds that have children younger than 5, according to a recommendation issued last week by the federal Centers for Disease Control and Prevention.

Reptiles also shouldn't be handled by small children or by anyone whose immune system doesn't work well, the agency cautioned. In addition, the animals should not be kept as pets in preschools and day-care centers.

With the growing popularity of snakes and lizards as pets, health officials are concerned about a recent increase in reptile-related salmonella infections. Although most cases of salmonella are caused by food contamination, reptiles account for about 93,000 cases of such illness each year, or about 7 percent of the total.

Focus on Physical Science
by David Frank et al.
Amplitude
Some waves are very high, while others are barely noticeable. The distance the water rises depends on the amplitude of the wave that passes through it. *Amplitude* is the maximum distance the particles of the medium carrying the wave move away from their rest positions. The amplitude is a measure of how much a particle in the medium moves when disturbed by the wave. The amplitude of a water wave is the maximum distance a water particle moves above or below the surface level of calm water.

You know that waves are produced by something vibrating. The farther the medium moves as it vibrates, the larger the amplitude of the resulting waves. You can increase the amplitude of the waves on a rope by moving your hand up and down a great distance. To do this, you have to use more energy. This greater amount of energy is then transferred to the rope. Thus, the amplitude of a wave is a direct measure of its energy.

Amplitude of Transverse Waves
Compare the two transverse waves . . . You can see that wave A goes up and down a greater distance than wave B. The amplitude of a transverse wave is the maximum distance the medium moves up or down from its rest position. You can find the amplitude of a transverse wave by measuring the distance from the rest position to a crest or to a trough. (201)

When writing craft lessons are built on helping students see their writing from the perspective of the audience of readers who will interact with that writing, students begin to appreciate the range of choices writers use. Understanding audience is one critical component in clarifying the writing task.

The second essential aspect of task review is understanding the purpose of the writing. In *Teaching Writing as Reflective Practice,* Hillocks suggests that most writing, especially writing in schools, is purposive writing: "Purposive writing includes all writing that is intended to communicate to or have some impact on an audience, even if the only audience is the writer" (81). However, many students come to the task of writing with no personal purposes for writing and unclear about the academic expectations for the writing. In the absence of such purposes, even those students who are writing to meet academic purposes often simply try to meet the formulaic criteria of a piece of writing rather than engaging at the investigative or content levels of writing. The following example from Avi's *Nothing but the Truth* exemplifies this kind of writing (Philip Malloy is the main character):

Excerpt from Margaret Narwin's Winter Term Exam
Question four: What is the significance of Jack London's choice in making Buck, the dog in *The Call of the Wild,* the focus of his novel? Is the dog meant to be symbolic? Explain your answer. Can *people* learn from this portrayal of a dog? Expand on these ideas.

Philip Malloy's Answer to Exam-Question Four
The significance of Buck in Jack London's novel *The Call of the Wild* is that Buck is symbolic of a cat. You might think that cats have nothing to do with the book, but *that* is the point. Dogs are willing to sit around and have writers write about them, which, in my personal opinion, makes them dumb. I think cats are smart. Cats don't like cold. A book that takes up so much time about a dog is pretty dumb. The book itself is a dog. That is what people can learn from Jack London's novel *The Call of the Wild.* (15–16)

A shared reading of Philip's essay response can certainly be used as a foundation for talking about writing for academic purposes. Many developing writers would be well served by clear models of our thinking through ways we challenge ourselves to engage in writing that may not be self-selected. In this process, we can also demonstrate how we use our questions and responses to deepen our connections both to the text being read and to the text we are writing.

As a way to support writers in my classroom, I used a guided response that I completed in collaboration with students so we could determine some common characteristics of writing academic responses to reading. A contemporary example can be illustrated with Cathleen Twomey's moving novel *Charlotte's*

Choice. This story details the life of a young girl named Jesse who is abandoned by her parents in New York City. At this point in the story, readers are beginning to see Jesse's life after she has become one of the children taken west on the orphan trains:

> Ma spotted Mr. and Mrs. Phelps about the same time I did. She poked my father. "What're they doing here? They don't want a child. All they want is a strong body to do their work for them. They're too lazy to do it themselves. You're not lettin' them take in one of those children are you?"
>
> Pa didn't have to answer. Doc Kennett took up the challenge. "The Phelps got as much right to a child as anyone else. Maybe more. They own their own home, and Aaron Phelps makes a might fine livin' off that store of his. Besides," he said, winking at Ma, "they're lookin' for an older boy. I don't see anybody who meets that description, do you?"
>
> It didn't matter who they were looking for, though. Just like Ma, I mistrusted the way Mr. Phelps smiled at people with his mouth even while he stared right through them with those stone-cold eyes.
>
> The storekeeper spotted the skinny girl right off. He tapped his foot impatiently while his wife looked over some of the smaller children. Then he wrinkled his nose and growled something to his wife.
>
> "What about that 'un over there?" he called to the lady in charge of the orphans.
>
> "Why, I'll be right with you, sir. I was just explaining to this nice couple here the responsibilities involved in taking one of these children. In educating them, in bringing them up in the Lord's way . . ."
>
> Mr. Phelps spat, barely missing the woman's skirts. "I got a store to run. Can't waste my time here all day. You want to find homes for these here children or you want to do a lot of fancy preachin'?"
>
> Something about the way Mr. Phelps looked at the girl made my skin crawl.
>
> Mr. Phelps stood there, hands folded across his chest, waiting to talk with that orphan lady. His wife chirped away beside him until he frowned at her. "Why don't you just tighten that jaw of yours," I could hear him say. It made me so mad that I prayed for courage. "Just once, Lord, I'd like to have gumption enough to do something—go over there and warn that poor girl." (15–16)

After our shared reading for that day, we could do shared writing with students to write a response to the reading using a Guided Response form (I.20, Appendix I). In this case, students would highlight their knowledge of how orphan trains worked, that Mr. Phelps was going to be the villain, and that people in the town didn't like him. We could reread sections of the shared reading to find information about Jesse and realize that, at this point, we know only that she was a "skinny girl" and that she stood apart from all the other children by being the last to enter the hall. I would say that this reading had made me realize the incredible risk these children took and that they didn't have any choice in what happened to them, and I would invite students to share what they learned about themselves during the reading. I might talk with them about needing some suspense or finding a way to visualize a scene when I read historical fiction in order to keep my interest. Finally, we could predict together what we think we will find in our next shared reading.

If we were reading *Charlotte's Choice* as a shared novel in order to examine historical aspects of the orphan trains, we could record our responses on the Historical Event Guided Response form (I.21, Appendix I). The first fourteen pages of this book include vivid descriptions of this event in our history. Our guided response can help us solidify new information we have about this event, make personal connections by imagining ourselves living through those times, and make predictions that will help us anticipate upcoming events in the text.

This same kind of Guided Response form can be adapted slightly for different content areas, for instance, scientific or mathematical readings. One of the funniest (and most popular) information books I have read lately is Joy Masoff's *Oh, Yuck! The Encyclopedia of Everything Nasty*. The following excerpt is part of a description of how bacteria can get into our systems and the impact of that invasion:

> Other times sickness starts when bacteria that live aboard one animal make the move to another. A perfectly healthy chicken's guts are crawling with salmonella bacteria that help the chicken digest all that chicken feed. But when that same bacteria gets into our intestines, disaster can strike (see "The Baddest Bacteria in Town!"). "But," you say, "it's not like I'm kissing a chicken." True, but chances are you're eating one! Undercooked chicken can give you salmonella. Even eating the uncooked egg that has been beaten into brownie batter can make you pretty sick, so don't lick that spoon!
>
> Some nonliving things, such as air conditioners, can hide bacteria cities. Certain types of these microbes adore the warm wetness that's created by air conditioner motors. And the air blowing from them propels millions of bacteria into the air—and lungs of whoever happens to be in the room! Before you know what's hit you, you'll be shaking with chills and flushed with a fever from Legionnaires disease (see the box for more grisly details).

Fortunately, other living creatures, named Fungi (fun-guy), can beat the bully bacteria up. That's basically what that nasty pink stuff is that your doctor gives you for ear infections or strep throat—a mess of bigger, meaner critters. Kind of like the principal and the dean of students on the warpath. These ANTIBIOTICS (that's what the pink stuff is called) destroy bacteria. And, boy, are we grateful to them. Their only downside: they wipe out the good bacteria (those that break down food) along with the bad. That's why lots of us end up with the trots when we take antibiotics. But fear not! The good-guy bacteria will be back! And you can even help bring them back faster by eating yogurt that contains active acidophilus cultures (See POOP, page 121, for more on the trots.) (8–9)

After reading this, we can use a Scientific Guided Response form (I.22, Appendix I) to record what we know about the spread of bacteria, what we have learned from general/life observations about bacteria, what we have learned so far from our reading, and what we now believe are facts about the characteristics of bacteria. In this way, students can see that academic response writing often asks us to connect facts from our reading to background knowledge we have gained from life and other reading. We can also stress that scientific processes can be solidified for us if we constantly compare and contrast with other processes we have already learned. Scientific response then becomes one of constantly assimilating new information with previous experiences and prior knowledge.

Similarly, after a shared reading that has a mathematical foundation, we can discuss our cognitive responses to the problem solving required by the reading. For example, in the first chapter of Hans Magnus Enzensberger's delightful mathematical adventure *The Number Devil*, Robert is plagued by the Number Devil's chewing gum problem:

"Tell me, how many pieces of chewing gum do you think have been chewed to this day?"
"I have no idea."
"Guess."
"Billions."
"At least," said the number devil. "Okay, now let's pretend that everyone's gone on a chewing spree and we're down to the last piece of chewing gum. I pull another one out of my pocket, the last one that I've saved for myself, and what have we got?" (16–17)

Using the Mathematical Guided Response form (I.23, Appendix I) we could work through the number devil's ways of illustrating infinity to Robert by determining what the problem is asking readers to do, how we could solve the problem, what difficulties we encountered, what made this kind of problem solving easy or hard, and what we learned as a mathematical pattern as a result of this problem.

After several classes where we wrote collaborative responses based on the synthesis, questions, connections, and predictions invited by the prompts on the guided responses, my students then developed a list of characteristics for effective responses to reading. We formatted the characteristics by noting questions they could ask themselves to make sure they were writing responses and not summaries. In this way, students take with them, either with classroom charting or in their writer's notebooks, a support for writing future responses to literature:

- Have I put the new information into the context of my own life and experiences?
- Have I thought/written about how I'll use this information or why I need to know this?
- Do I have new questions because of my reading?
- What did this reading make me think about in a new or different way?
- How does this reading fit with other reading I've done on the same subject?
- What made this reading easy/difficult for me?

In Jennifer Economos-Green's high school class in Baltimore, she and her students consistently use the same format. After reading multiple texts and discovering the characteristics of the mode of writing, they write a collaborative example on one text, in this case, Mem Fox's *Wilfrid Gordon McDonald Partridge* (see Figure 6.2). They document their discoveries by charting the characteristics of the writing with both essential and optional elements. Finally, they label their collaborative text with the characteristics they have noted as a way for students to own a model for their own writing.

As Jennifer discovers other writing needs, she is able to use the same model of multiple texts, charting defining characteristics, collaborative writing, guided practice, and models for transfer to independent writing. Figures 6.3 and 6.4 show that Jennifer and her students have refined their understanding of how to write a character analysis and a memoir. In both cases, students are able to display their independent writing as examples of the type of writing.

There is no doubt that giving students multiple opportunities for guided support as they internalize a way to review the academic writing tasks they are given will increase their proficiency levels when writing for this purpose. This kind of writing is not intended to take the place of self-selected, personally

Figure 6.2

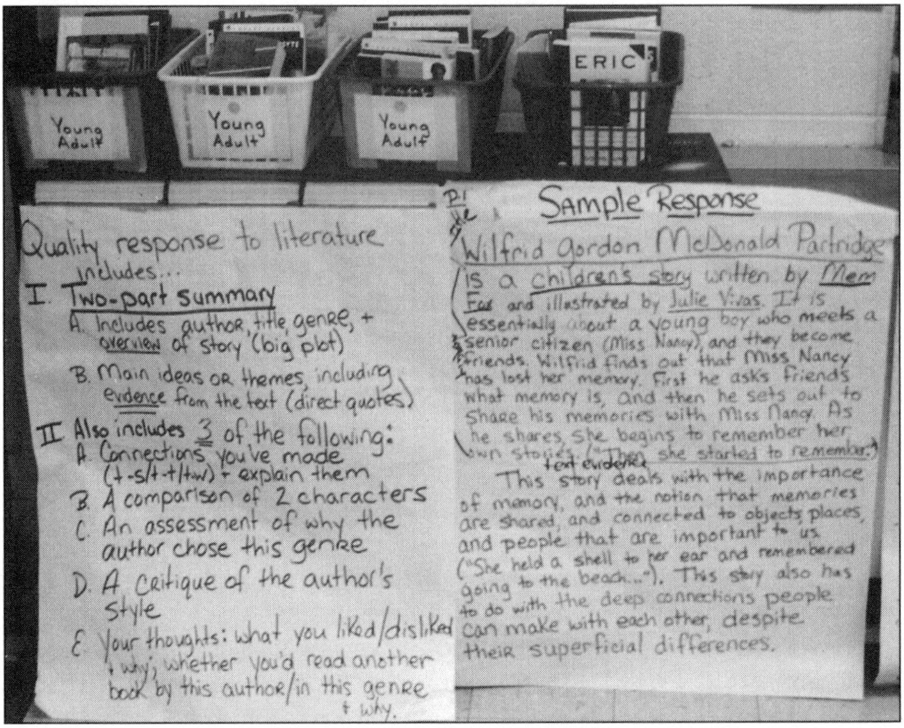
ERIC
Young Adult
Young Adult
Young Adult
Quality response to literature includes...
I. Two-part summary
A. Includes author, title, genre, + overview of story (big plot)
B. Main ideas or themes, including evidence from the text (direct quotes)
II Also includes 3 of the following:
A. Connections you've made (t-s/t-t/t-w) + explain them
B. A comparison of 2 characters
C. An assessment of why the author chose this genre
D. A critique of the author's style
E. Your thoughts: what you liked/disliked + why; whether you'd read another book by this author/in this genre + why.
Sample Response
Wilfrid Gordon McDonald Partridge is a children's story written by Mem Fox and illustrated by Julie Vivas. It is essentially about a young boy who meets a senior citizen (Miss Nancy), and they become friends. Wilfrid finds out that Miss Nancy has lost her memory. First he asks friends what memory is, and then he sets out to share his memories with Miss Nancy. As he shares, she begins to remember her own stories. ("Then she started to remember.")
text evidence
This story deals with the importance of memory, and the notion that memories are shared, and connected to objects, places, and people that are important to us ("She held a shell to her ear and remembered going to the beach..."). This story also has to do with the deep connections people can make with each other, despite their superficial differences.

motivated writing. It is intended to give support in writing for academic purposes. By using shared reading as the foundation for modeling, students are able to read the text several times to refine their thinking and revise their writing. When writers can review and understand the writing task, they become more interested in writing in a way that communicates effectively. This brings us to the meaning-making role in writing.

Meaning Maker

When we have something important to say and we know someone is interested in listening, most of us develop a sense of urgency for making our words make sense. In one of my favorite books, Robert McCammon's *Boy's Life,* Cory is told that a writer must remember everything:

> "Don't you go through a day without remembering something of it, and tucking that memory away like a treasure. When you look at something, don't just look. *See* it. Really, really *see* it. See it so when you write it

Figure 6.3

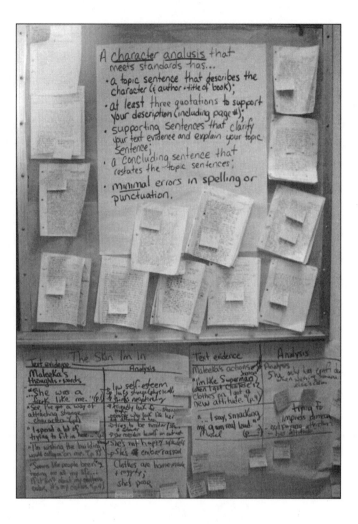

down, somebody else can see it, too. It's easy to walk through life deaf, dumb, and blind, Cory. Most everybody you know or ever meet will. They'll walk through a parade of wonders, and they'll never hear a peep of it. But you can live a thousand lifetimes if you want to. And if you're good and you're lucky and you have something worth saying, then you might have the chance to live on long after—long after." (227)

Our task as teachers in supporting students in the meaning-making role of writing is to help them take the things they have that are worth saying and say them effectively. In this role, I have found that shared reading of students' writing is the most helpful way to support meaning making. In *I Know Why the*

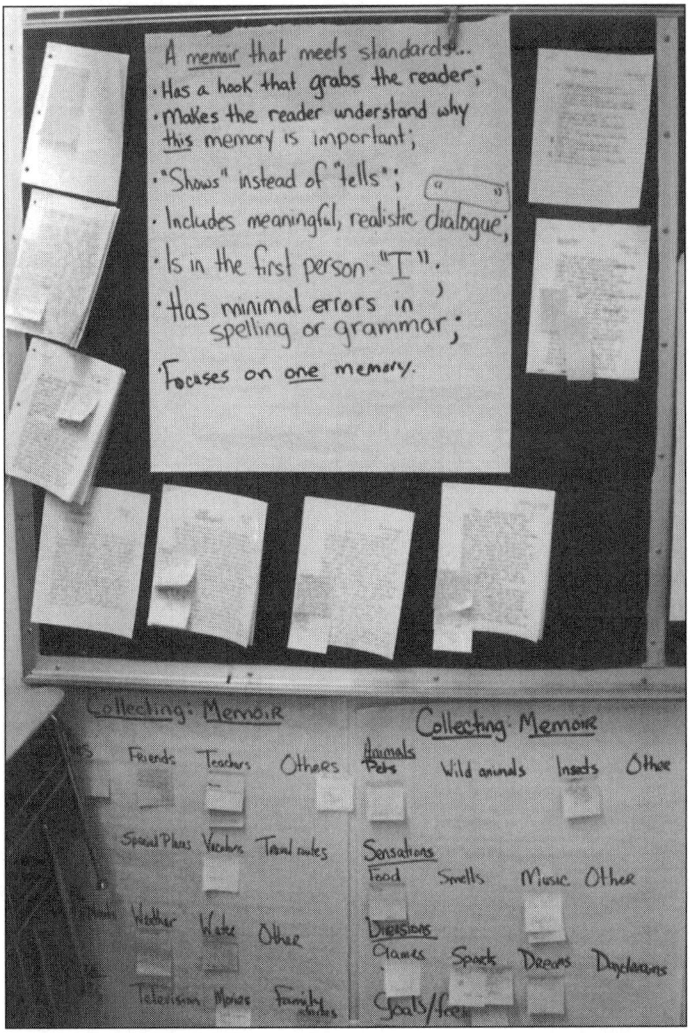

Figure 6.4

Caged Bird Sings, Maya Angelou writes, "Words mean more than what is set down on paper. It takes the human voice to infuse them with the shades of deeper meaning" (82).

A shared reading of a letter by Melvin, one of my students, helped him make his writing more coherent because he could hear natural pauses in the reading, redundancy of ideas, word choices that were inaccurate, and issues of verb tense and subject/verb agreement:

Well I please that you told mrs. Finland that I had a probleme with my reading. And that you care lot to tell me tht you will help with that.

This class is fun in some way and that there's serious time to. And I have not been the honest on in this class, I've been the one that been lazy one. So when Mrs. Finland told me that I need to be honest with you so that you will help me with it buy you cuond't because I would not been honest with you. I hate saying that I have a reading problem, I think it's enbarrancement when peiople nows that you do. So I don't want to go to college and don't understand what they are saying or what they are trying to tell me so I would understand them. Plus I would hate to have a gril that like to study with her, when I do now what they are trying to say to me so I would not be a good help to her in any way. And i would lose a girl and I would be up set, because I would not want help and it thought I could do it by my self and I was wrong, because I was wrong insome way and I thought I was to cool to have help and witch I was wrong and now I have problems with that because I didn't want help before and now I regrite that, I'm gland that I can have a teacher that is willing to help me and also a guidance teacher to that will help em a lot in some ways. I think that my problem was moving to much and I was out of school for a long while, I didn't start school at less 1 or 2 grade, I didn't now as much as the other kids so I was put in the readsours class through out 5,6,7,8,9,10,11 grade and thenthey said that I was doing dood and they kick me out and I was put in the same grade as the other kids where and now I widh that I should of stay in reading class, I geuss I can try very hard in some to read better. thank you for listening to me.

Each of my students had an individual cassette tape so he could read and record completed pieces of writing. In this case, after Melvin recorded his piece and listened to the recording while he followed with his written text, he was able to change many sentence fragments to complete sentences and to separate many run-on sentences. Those sentence changes immediately improved this piece of writing. He was also able to catch some of the spacing issues.

When he had made his revision and editing changes, I read the piece of writing to him. I read it once in its entirety, and then we went back and started again so that Melvin could make revisions and edits with the support of my voice. He was able to make spelling changes because he could hear an accurate pronunciation of a word, word changes, and changes that made his text more coherent, such as getting rid of repetitions.

When students begin to take a closer look at their writing, both the teacher and other students can support the writer by doing a shared reading of the piece for the writer. We can then ask the student where he would like help in making his writing communicate more effectively. This help can occur at four levels:

text, paragraph, sentence, and word. When writers are working with recordings of their writing, they can go back to read and listen with those same four levels in mind by asking themselves questions at each level:

Text Level

Does my writing express what I want to say?

Can I hear my voice?

Does my writing make sense? If not, what is missing?

Have I thought about my audience and purpose?

Is my writing understandable because I have organized it in a way that makes sense?

Paragraph Level

Do I have paragraphs?

Do my paragraphs have topic sentences?

Do I know where to begin a new paragraph?

Do I have details that fit with my topic sentence?

Do I know how to make transitions from one paragraph to the next?

Sentence Level

Do my sentences begin and end, and can the reader tell when that happens?

Are my sentences complete?

Do I have several sentences in one sentence?

Do I vary my sentences? (subject-verb, sentence length)

Is the tense consistent from sentence to sentence?

Word Level

Are my words spelled correctly?

Am I using the word I meant to use?

Am I using the best word to convey my message?

Do I repeat the same words?

Do I use synonyms correctly/effectively?

Am I using descriptive words?

When students are attempting to use these levels to make their writing more effective, they have moved into the writing role of code user.

Code User

Writers who are effective code users know that writers use conventions of print, text, and language as part of how they communicate their message. We can discuss writers such as e. e. cummings, who used the absence of these conventions to support a message, or writers who misuse conventions and this gets in the way of communication for readers. In *On Writing,* Stephen King talks about the importance of a writer's toolbox. He remembers asking his uncle Oren why he didn't just carry the one tool he needed rather than the entire toolbox and being told of the importance of keeping your tools with you. "I didn't know what else I might find to do once I got out here, did I? It's best to have your tools with you. If you don't, you're apt to find something you didn't expect and get discouraged" (114). Codes of text make up the toolbox for writers.

Fortunately, we don't have to buy new shared reading texts in order to fill our writer's toolbox. Any text can offer examples or nonexamples of tools that writers use to communicate. As we encounter these conventions, either intentionally or as a natural part of the shared reading we do, we can reread a text and record how and why the writer used the conventions. Using a graphic organizer (I.24, Appendix I), we can do this for conventions of print such as punctuation, use of boldface or italics, or signs and symbols; conventions of text such as titles, subtitles, cue words, figures, diagrams, and visuals; and conventions of genre such as fairy tales, memoir, nonfiction narrative, or expository text structures.

Students can keep these conventions in a writer's notebook so they have access to them while writing. For example, in the story "A Mouthful," Paul Jennings uses italics for the word *so* as a way to foreshadow the hilarious events that follow:

> Finally we decide to go to bed. Anna takes ages and ages cleaning her teeth. She is one of those kids who is into health. She has a thing about germs. She always places paper on the toilet seat before she sits down. She is *so* clean.
>
> Anyway, she puts on her tracksuit bottoms and gets ready for bed. Then she pulls back the blankets. Suddenly she sees the bit of cat's poo. "Ooh, ooh, ooh," she screams. "Oh, look, disgusting. Foul. Look what the cat's done on my pillow."

After a connected shared reading of this short story, we could return to the story and record why we think Jennings used this convention.

One of my students' favorite books for examining conventions of print as part of our shared reading was Don Marquis's *archy and mehitabel:*

> **mehitabel was once cleopatra**
> boss i am disappointed in
> some of your readers they

are always asking how does
archy work the shift so as to get a
new line or how does archy do
this or do that they
are always interested in technical
details when the main question is
whether the stuff is
literature or not
i wish you would leave
that book of george moore s on
the floor

mehitabel the cat and I want to
read it and I have discovered that
mehitabel s soul formerly inhabited a
human also at least that
is what mehitabel is claiming these
days it may be she got jealous of
my prestige anyhow she and
i have been talking it over in a
friendly way who were you
mehitabel i asked her i was
cleopatra once she said well i said i
suppose you lived in a palace you bet
she said and what lovely fish dinners
we used to have and licked her chops

mehitabel would sell her soul for
a plate of fish any day i told her i thought
you were going to say you were
the favorite wife of the emperor
valerian he was some cat nip eh
mehitabel but she did not get me
    archy (17–18)

On each of our writing days, I would do a shared reading of two or three pages of this book, and then we would go back and reread, inserting punctuation and capitalization that would have made the text easier to read. In spite of the fact that many of my students wrote with the same absence of these conventions, they were quick to point out that without them a book was more difficult to read.

Conventions of text can be analyzed as part of shared reading by looking at the purposes for which writers might choose to use these conventions. For example, if our shared novel is Paul Many's *These Are the Rules,* we could take each of the chapter titles and anticipate the content for prereading purposes. After shared reading of that chapter, we could revisit the title/rule for writing purposes and look at why Many chose that rule as his title for the chapter:

Rule 1: Be prepared for surprises.
Rule 2: Keep your eyes on the stars, but don't be surprised if you step on a banana peel.
Rule 3: You can't always be sure the girl's going to be there when you swim out to the middle.
Rule 4: It's hard to steer when you don't know where you're going.
Rule 5: Everyone has his own life to swim.
Rule 6: Different people are different.
Rule 7: "Mistakes" is the name we give to our experiences.
Rule 8: If you're stuck in a well, feel around for the rope.
Rule 9: Don't look back; your wishes may be gaining on you.
Rule 10: "Things can't get much worse" is often more a wish than a statement of fact.
Rule 11: True friends find you when you need them the most.
Rule 12: There are no rules.

We can revisit a shared reading that we might have taught for content literacy to look at the use of print and text conventions. In Jack Myers's *On the Trail of the Komodo Dragon, and Other Explorations of Science in Action* we find conventions of text such as titles that anticipate content; use of introductory lines to hook the reader ("This lizard is big enough for a storybook"); subheadings (Big Babies, Big Appetites, A Tropical Home); illustrations (map of islands, drawings of Komodo dragons); use of parentheses as aside for readers ("(Oras are scavengers, which means that they eat dead animals. Also, they have a keen sense of smell, which they use in finding food.)"); use of questions to keep reader engaged ("If there is a real animal out there that someone would call a dragon, what is it like?"); and use of quotation marks to set apart specialized vocabulary ("Most big-time predators, like wolves and lions, are 'warm-blooded' and have an automatic temperature control like a human's. Their body machinery is always revved up and ready to go. But lizards are 'cold-blooded.'"). Appendix H provides the complete *Komodo Dragon* text.

Additionally, we can reread a text and examine expository text structures: cause and effect, definition, description, problem/solution, comparison/contrast, sequence. If we looked at all these conventions with a struggling reader and writer, it would be overwhelming. However, for the more mature writers, looking at one piece in its entirety helps them understand the incredible range of content and code choices writers make to communicate information. At this level of writing, students become increasingly interested in the craft of their writing.

Text Crafter

In *Craft Lessons*, Fletcher and Portalupi cite the importance of using shared texts to support the craft of writing: "The writing you get out of your students can only be as good as the classroom literature that surrounds and sustains it" (10). We can use shared reading to introduce and reinforce the crafts of revising and editing. In Jennifer Economos-Green's classroom, as students begin to focus at the text crafter level, she helps them make a distinction between revising and editing in support of both kinds of process writing (see Figure 6.5). Since we focused earlier on aspects of editing, I focus here on lessons for revising.

Figure 6.5

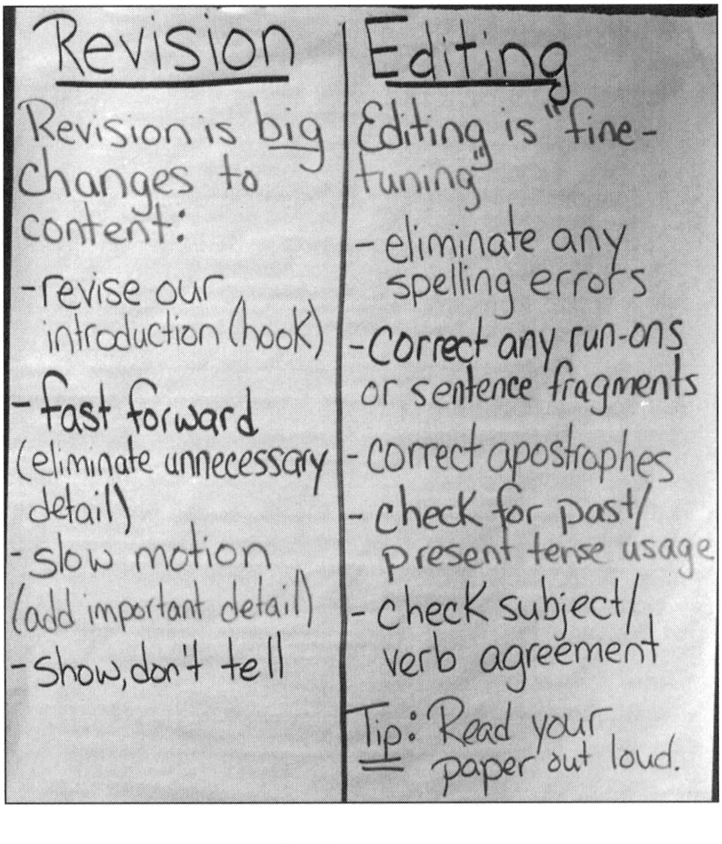

Revision

Revision is big changes to content:
- revise our introduction (hook)
- fast forward (eliminate unnecessary detail)
- slow motion (add important detail)
- show, don't tell

Editing

Editing is "fine-tuning"
- eliminate any spelling errors
- correct any run-ons or sentence fragments
- correct apostrophes
- check for past/present tense usage
- check subject/verb agreement

Tip: Read your paper out loud.

In this context, I have found it helpful to use shared reading as a way to provide examples and nonexamples of effective craft. There is a lot of room for individual opinion in terms of effectiveness of the piece, but students are usually able to draw some patterns from the samples. If my students were struggling with writing description, the following lesson could support them in revising their writing in order to have more effective descriptive passages.

Another shared reading from Stephen King's *On Writing* could introduce the topic of effective description:

> And you probably *have* told your story well enough to believe that when you use *he said,* the reader will know how he said it—fast or slowly, happily or sadly. Your man may be floundering in a swamp, and by all means throw him a rope if he is . . . but there's no need to knock him unconscious with ninety feet of steel cable. (128)

This writing gives us the opportunity to brainstorm reasons why writers attempt to use effective description. Once we have determined its importance, we can move to discovering characteristics of effectiveness. For students to keep track of our shared texts as examples of descriptive writing, I would have them note each shared text in their writer's notebook or on a graphic organizer (I.25, Appendix I). Each shared text is read through once and then read again in order to look at the characteristics of description and the effectiveness of their use.

Bride of Dark and Stormy
by Julie Dean Smith
After playing the final note of her solo, Julia haughtily tossed her flaming auburn curls, emptied her trumpet's spit valve onto the smooth wooden floor, and sauntered proudly off the stage, unaware that Rodney, sitting in the first row of the audience, was rapturously gazing at the glistening pool of saliva she had left behind—the auditorium lights dancing off the soft, foamy bubbles like sunlight on the ocean— and yearned to wipe it up with his handkerchief and take it home, knowing that it would be the only part of her he could ever possess. (40)

A Sudden Silence
by Eve Bunting
I paddled for shore and waded out. Up under the lip of the sandbank, someone moved, stood. I knew who it was OK. Sowbug, our resident beach bum. He sleeps here a lot, curled up under a ratty gray blanket,

hugging a big old jug of wine. Ours is one of Sowbug's three or four private beaches. Everything he owns is in a cardboard box that he stashes behind the big rock by the tunnel entrance when the police throw him into jail for a night or two. The kids get a kick out of playing tricks on old Sowbug. (13)

Lizard
by Dennis Covington

She was so thin that people sometimes mistook her for one of the neighborhood girls. She wore yellow bath slippers that she could hardly keep on her feet, and she carried a straw purse with a pink flamingo painted on top. She had a row of freckles across the top of her nose and a mole the size of a thumbtack stuck at her hairline. I remember now that the flamingo on her purse was chipped where it had hit the radiator. One of Miss Cooley's front teeth was chipped too. The edge of it glistened at night when she laughed. (2–3)

Danger Zone
by David Klass

It's an old gym—it was built just after the Second World War. The bleachers are the same color wood as the hardwood floor, and for some reason it always reminds me of a big cigar box. It even has a sweet, almost tobaccolike, smell. Lights are suspended from a spider web of iron bars just beneath the ceiling. A big American flag dangles down from the center of that network of iron. On either side of the flag hang two league championship banners from a decade or so past, when Granham was a regional powerhouse. (5)

Of Mice and Men
by John Steinbeck

They had walked in single file down the path, and even in the open one stayed behind the other. Both were dressed in denim trousers and in denim coats and both carried tight blanket rolls slung over their shoulders. The first man was small and quick, dark of face, with restless eyes and sharp, strong features. Every part of him was defined: small, strong hands, slender arms, a thin and bony nose. Behind him walked his opposite, a huge man, shapeless of face, with large pale eyes, with wide, sloping shoulders; and he walked heavily, dragging his feet a little, the way a bear drags its paws. His arms did not swing at his sides, but hung loosely. (9)

It Was a Dark and Stormy Night
by Jim Lovering
Toilet bowl rims, not microchips, were the working domain of custo-
dian Bob Johnson, and yet he had been astute enough to salvage that
key piece of software from the trash, and standing in the window of the
seventy-fifth-floor penthouse suite, he realized that his too-good dream
of reward had become reality; the heart of Rita Payne-Webbar, beautiful
heiress to millions and brilliant twenty-four-year-old senior vice-presi-
dent of Software Conglomerate International, was his. (24–25)

With each of these shared texts, we can make notes about the text sample and
talk about the descriptive characteristics the author employs, such as color,
comparison, concrete images, and adjectives. We can decide on the effectiveness of the description and then synthesize our findings in order to support students' transfer of this craft to their own writing.

As students use their discovered patterns in conferring, they can discover
methods for making their own writing more effective. During this conferring,
we can take students back to these patterns by asking them to look critically at
their writing:

- Show me a place in your writing where you feel you have effective
  description. What characteristics of description do you see there that you
  believe adds to its effectiveness?
- If I had been watching you in this situation, would I have seen what you
  were seeing? Have you helped me feel what you were feeling?
- Could you underline any places in your writing where you have used a
  general term like nice or fine? Then, could you take each one and rewrite
  just that line using more specific, descriptive language?
- Listen while I read this to you and see if you feel there is any way you
  could make your description more show and less tell.

Each craft lesson can be organized in the same way: *introduce* the concept
with a shared text; provide opportunities for students to *discover* patterns of the
craft through multiple shared texts; *synthesize* the discoveries into transferable
information; *apply* the craft to an individual's writing; and *provide support* for
students to internalize the craft so that this revision becomes part of their writing repertoire.

Karen Elizabeth Gordon has written several books that make excellent
shared reading for more advanced readers and writers. Each of the brief pieces
of writing elaborates a stylistic issue or a word usage problem. In *The Deluxe
Transitive Vampire: The Ultimate Handbook of Grammar for the Innocent, the*

Eager, and the Doomed, we have grammatical lessons embedded in very engaging text:

Sentences, The Subject
The subject is part of the sentence about which something is divulged; it is what the sentence's other words are gossiping about.

> *My name* is Jean-Pierre.
> *The girl* is squatting under the bridge.
> *The girl squatting under the bridge* is a debutante.
> *The door* opened.
> *The contraption* shut.
> *He* was caught.
> *His huge, calm, intelligent hands* wrestled with her confusion of lace.
> *The werewolf* had a toothache.
> *The afflicted fang* caused him to wince pathetically as he stifled his sobs in his sleeve.
> *The persona non grata* was rebuked.
> *The door* slammed in his flabbergasted face.

The *italicized* words in the above sentences form the complete subject. The simple subject, a noun or pronoun, is the essence lurking at its center, without which the complete subject would be nothing at all. (3)

In an equally engaging book, *Torn Wings and Faux Pas: A Flashbook of Style, a Beastly Guide Through the Writer's Labyrinth,* Gordon takes the reader through a wonderfully imaginative look at grammar, word choice, and style. As you will see from the following passage, these humorous vignettes are not for the most struggling reader nor for younger readers. A shared reading of some with advanced students could certainly make students more aware of usage issues.

All together/altogether
All together means as a group. Altogether means entirely or in all.

> Their teeth still bloody from this unholy repast, the vampires decided all together to comb their mustaches and greet the dawn over a game of poker.

> That fuchsia-hued frock on the grandfather clock is altogether too picturesque for this dolorous occasion.

> Have you gone altogether berserk, or are you certifiably still O.K.?

Altogether there were seventeen impersonators of Incognito VIII during the so-called Cashmere Crisis that muffled the morganatic monarch and discredited his regime.

"We can't proceed with the orgy till we're all together," said the secretary and sergeant-at-arms in unison, looking about for some stragglers, after they'd read the minutes of the last orgy, and the Mardi Gras videotape had aired its buttocks and its bellows and its groans. (7)

Internalizing the Reading/Writing Connection

We don't always have the opportunity for direct feedback from published authors but when we do, it is a very effective way of helping students understand how writers use reading to support their writing. Stephen King writes, "The commonest of all, the bread of writing, is vocabulary. Put your vocabulary on the top shelf of your toolbox, and don't make any conscious effort to improve it. (You'll be doing that as you read, of course . . .)" (117). When personal advice from an author-in-residence isn't available, we can certainly turn to the writing they have in print as a way to get advice from a variety of writers. Appendix D provides a list of titles for shared reading to support independent writing, and Appendix E lists picture books to support the teaching of literacy devices.

I was fortunate to meet the writer Hal W. Lanse in a workshop in New York. He is the author of the wonderfully humorous *Penelope Quagmire and the Lizard Men from Outer Space.* As we talked about writing, I told him how fortunate students would be to hear published writers talking about and working through the same choices they have to make as writers. He generously shared with me the following craft lesson he had done with a group of middle school writers. Their classroom teacher had asked him for help getting her students to write more effective leads. Hal describes a lesson in which he connected the craft of writing to his own novel as a way of helping young writers understand how authors work at their craft.

Hal Lanse on Teaching Writing
Taking my lead from Chapter 11 in *Yellow Brick Roads* [Allen], I realized that if the students were to write effective introductions, they would have to study authentic examples. I pored over the first pages of many

books written for intermediate readers and discovered that a majority of writers (myself included) open their stories in one of the following ways:

A. They put you in the middle of a situation.

B. They create a mood or feeling using descriptive language.

C. They do both of the above.

"As a published author," I explained, "I'm aware that there are certain strategies writers know how to use." I passed around my book, *Penelope Quagmire and the Lizard Men from Outer Space,* and began talking about the real world reasons for creating a good introduction. "When you're in a bookstore or a library," I asked, "what makes you decide to choose one book and leave another behind?"

"I look at the cover," said Tenisha.

"If it's colorful," Dwayne agreed, "I might take it."

"I read the back cover," Carline added.

"What else do readers do when choosing a book?" I asked.

"I might read part of it," Brad answered.

"You're all correct. All of these things are important to readers. Did you know that my publisher made me write a new beginning to the book? I worked a long time on the first chapter." Holding up my wallet I said, "As a published author, I know that I won't get any of this if readers find my opening dull when they browse through it in the bookstore."

After giving groups of students examples of leads, we were able to talk about our discoveries—and they made many. They found that stories with an "A" beginning often include dialogue. They found that dialogue puts the reader in the middle of a conflict and creates suspense. The readers want to know how the conflict started, where it's going, and how it will end.

We were able to use my own book as an example. The story opens with the school bully addressing his gang, the Green Rattlers. They are plotting against their rivals, a group of young geniuses. Suspense is created as the reader gradually uncovers gang leader Fang Finnegan's diabolical plot. The reader's attention is pulled forward by a sense of conflict that may lead to dangerous consequences.

We discovered that sometimes, instead of putting you in the middle of the action, a book begins with a description of the setting. Rashad used my book to argue that my story beginning was a "C" rather than an "A" because I placed readers in the middle of a situation but I did it by creating a mood with the use of an exclamation point. Instead of adjectives, Rashad discovered that punctuation allows readers to feel what the character is feeling. In *Penelope Quagmire,* we find ourselves in the middle of a malicious plot, and the use of an exclamation point in the first sentence ("We can't let those brainiacs win!") clues us in to the intensity of Fang Finnegan's emotions. Rashad helped me become more conscious of what I do as a writer.

Once students had a sense of how an author begins a story, they selected previously written pieces from their portfolios. As they began rewriting the openings of their pieces, they borrowed and adapted language from the literature we just examined. Throughout the lesson, the students and I referred back to the authentic literature we used as a way to energize their writing.

As we can see from the careful design of Hal's lesson, this kind of guided examination of the interconnectedness of reading and writing requires time, resources, and a commitment to teach rather than assign. It also takes careful assessment in order to know which craft lessons will support students as developing writers.

So, how do we know which craft lessons to teach? Hillocks supports the use of student writing to influence our teaching decisions: "We need to look at our students' writing and ask to what extent and in what ways it has improved as a result of our teaching. There is no reason that most students should not show improvement. If they do not, the teaching needs to change" (1995, 207). A careful examination of student writing should show us what students need as writers. These needs can be supported through our choices for shared reading but students can also search for examples of writing that demonstrate the writer's craft.

One of the techniques I used in my own classroom was asking students to collect models of writing from their reading for our craft lessons. I read a chapter Robin Brancato had written for Gallo's *Authors' Insights,* in which she detailed a practice she called Lit-Lib (91–103). I used her idea to create what I called a literacy scavenger hunt. The directions I gave my students are detailed here:

A Writer's Notebook of Resources: A Literacy Scavenger Hunt
During our reading and writing craft lessons, we will be searching for effective models of writing so that we can compare the characteristics those pieces of writing have in common. I'm hoping we can all come to those craft lessons prepared to discover our own best writing selves. The following list is only a beginning. During your independent reading, please try to find examples (at least one for each category) of the following:

- A great beginning (it made you want to read more)
- Ten interesting words you would like to use in your writing
- A poem that speaks to you
- A book you wish you had written
- A description of a character that makes the character seem real to you
- An example of language that uses sensory images
- A newspaper article that convinced you of something
- An ending you would have written differently
- A description of a setting that made you want to go to the place being described
- A piece of writing that is really boring
- Some directions that are so clear you could follow them
- A comparison or contrast
- An example of dialogue so interesting you felt as though you were eavesdropping

Using this as a beginning, we can get students involved in creating the craft lessons that will help all members of the class become more effective writers. For example, in Lynnette Elliott's eighth-grade language arts class, after students completed their literacy scavenger hunts, she had groups of students create instructional lessons for their peers using the collective resources they had discovered. In this way, one group of students worked with those who needed or wanted to write more effective leads. On another day, another group of students worked with peers who were trying to improve their descriptive writing.

When we make the commitment to provide students with opportunities to experience writing lessons with the foundation of strong shared reading and the support of writing strategies embedded in that reading, we begin to see improvement in the craft of their writing. Hillocks's research supports this emphasis. In *Ways of Thinking, Ways of Teaching,* he writes, "Research on the teaching of writing provides very strong evidence, however, that the two are very different: programs focusing on how to investigate and construct content have an effect several times greater than programs focusing exclusively on learning the features of the structures" (76). Student writing is a direct reflection of the range of reading we share with them. As we become more adept at sharing diverse models of effective writing, we will begin to see that range of writing reflected in our students' writing.

7

Shared Reading as a Bridge to Independence

I figured if I crisscrossed Florida from coast to coast as if I were

tying up the laces on a high-top sneaker I would eventually

stumble on something juicy to write about. I was full of hope.

I had been reading constantly. I kept up my daily journal-

writing routine, logging my favorite quotes and building my

vocabulary. And now it was time for me to stop being a chippy

high-school writer and to challenge myself.

Jack Gantos, *Hole in My Life*

As teachers, we would like to believe that read-alouds and shared reading would have the same positive effect for our students' independence as readers and writers as Gantos's reading and journal writing did for him. In the middle school survey I discussed previously, nearly one thousand students (out of twelve hundred) reported they chose books for independent reading for one or more of the following reasons: book read aloud by the teacher, another book by the same author as our shared reading, a book about the same topic as our shared reading, or a sequel to a read-aloud or shared reading book. Many developing readers take their reading cues from us; therefore, it is critical to offer enough variety in the texts we choose for shared reading so that all our students can finding reading that meets their independent reading tastes.

In my classroom, I made it a goal that students sample at least five different texts each day using a read-aloud or shared reading approach. A typical literacy block class might have the following shared experiences with books during a single class period. If beginning a unit on choices and consequences with our students, we could open with a shared reading of Sara Holbrook's "You Promised":

You Promised

I gave you private thoughts
to hold.
You promised not to tell.
You told.
I trusted friendship
like a bank.
Now they know;
I've you to thank.

When secrets have my name on them,
don't pass them out
to her or him.
My secrets are a loan
to be
returned upon request
to me. (39)

This shared reading would certainly be inviting to most students because of their experiences with choosing to tell a friend something personal only to end up living with the consequences of that information's being shared with others.

From our reading of the poem, we could explore the word *consequences* as part of our word study that would tie back to the Holbrook poem and anticipate the whole-class novel we plan to use as the shared core for our unit. There are many great novels from which to choose for the choices and consequences theme, but one that I especially like is Gretchen Olson's *Joyride*.

Chapter 1

Jeff McKenzie untied his shoes and wondered if he'd ever play tennis again. He kicked them onto the hard ground and winced as a sharp twig poked through his sock. What a crummy place to change. The oak knoll was littered with dried leaves, fallen branches, dead weeds, and little brown puffballs. But he wasn't about to change clothes at school. The guys had razzed him enough already. "Goin' to work with the beaners, Kenzie?" "How do ya want your tortillas? Rare or well-done?" Then they'd laughed and punched him in the arm and slapped his back.

146

Now the shade of the tall trees brought a quick chill to his legs as he took off his pants; his thigh muscles tightened. He yanked a navy blue T-shirt over his head and tossed it to the ground. The graphics and letters scrunched together, but he knew the words: *Madrona Hills Fourth of July Invitational.* He grimaced. Slim chance he'd be there this year—he'd be lucky to even practice in the next three weeks.

He shoved his legs into a pair of Levi's and pulled on a long-sleeved denim work shirt. As he began buttoning, his eyes followed a twisted oak limb reaching high into a dense, leafy canopy. He stared and the leaves blurred. The reluctant thought drifted back again . . . he wished he hadn't helped Paul celebrate.

One thing had led to another that night. Soon he and Paul were driving out west of Salem and then down some county back road, Jeff's Bronco II zigging and zagging and skidding on the gravel. It was awesome—until the field. That big, open field, calling to them.

Why not? Windows rolled down, music turned up. It felt great bumping across the rows, swirling in tight turns, digging into the dirt. Great. Until they hit something.

"Jake Hampton's the name," the farmer had said later that night as Jeff's parents stood on the front porch in their bathrobes. "Shall we settle this ourselves? Or shall I call the police?"

Jeff had rolled his eyes. Just what he needed—flashing lights announcing to the neighborhood that such-a-nice boy Jeffery Taylor McKenzie had turned into a rotten vandal.

Jeff's father cleared his throat. "We can take care of it."

"I'd like to see them work it off." The farmer nodded at Jeff and Paul.

Paul shuffled his feet and caught Jeff's eye.

"Oh yeah," said Jeff, "uh, my buddy, here, didn't have anything to do with this. It was my idea."

His father looked over his glasses.

"It was all my idea." Jeff crossed his arms. "He tried to stop me."

"Well, then, young man," said Mr. Hampton, his broad hands on his hips, "in order to replace that irrigation motor, it'll mean three to four weeks' work for you."

"But Jeffery has tennis practice and tournaments," said his mother, stepping to the edge of the porch.

Mr. Hampton stared at her. "Excuse me, ma'am, but starting in a week, I've got forty acres of strawberries to harvest, and perishable crops do not wait for tennis tournaments."

She was about to speak again when Mr. McKenzie grasped her shoulder. "He'll do it." Jeff's father glanced around the group, then at Jeff. "He'll be there—and he'll do the job."

Now wishing it had all been a bad dream, Jeff bent for a boot, crammed in his foot, and pulled out the tongue. He jerked the leather laces through the metal holes, around the hooks, and into a double knot. Three or four weeks away from the courts, he lamented, grabbing the other boot. What a waste. He'd lose his rhythm, his speed—his ranking.

He walked from the shade of the oaks into the bright June sunlight and closed his eyes for a moment. What a way to celebrate the last day of school. Everyone else had gone to BJ's and then to the courts or the club pool. Everyone else was going to have an incredible summer.

"You'll be working with my two daughters and my wife," Mr. Hampton had told Jeff, "running the picking crew, weighing flats, loading trucks."

Wonderful, he thought, retracing his path through the wild grass and thistles. Me and the womenfolk, down on the farm. He climbed over the sagging barbed wire fence and walked in front of his Bronco, ignoring the dented frame.

The gravel road seemed wider now as he drove in a straight line. It dipped and climbed, a low ridge forming on the right and a valley on the left. Green and brown fields spread across the broad valley floor, patched together with bushy fence rows, dotted with old barns, farmhouses, clumps of trees, and an occasional pond.

As the road eased downhill, Jeff spotted a white house next to a lake. A barn stood behind the house and three long buildings lined the far side. According to Mr. Hampton's brief directions, the strawberries were past the grain tanks. "Don't worry," he'd said, "you'll see the cars."

There they were. Pickups, vans, cars, bumper-to-bumper, hugging the ditch. A woman leaned against a gray van. She held a small child in diapers. Two other children peered out the rear door, their dark eyes studying him.

He found a vacant spot, parked, and locked his car. Pausing, he took in the field stretched out before him. Row after row of thick, lush foliage marched in straight lines to the lake. A dirt road cut through the middle and another road crossed precisely at center, creating four equal sections. Tall stacks of yellow containers and two blue outhouses stood along the crossroad.

"NO CARS IN THE FIELD." The sign posted at the field entrance was in English and Spanish. Jeff sucked in a deep breath, let it out slowly, and began walking down the hard dirt drive. Pickers heading to their cars carried buckets, jackets, and grocery sacks. Their shirts hung loose and their pants drug about their tennis shoes. Mud and berry stains padded their knees.

Jeff avoided eye contact. Maybe they'd think he was staring. Maybe they'd say something he wouldn't understand.

They passed him in silence, then broke into chatter and laughter, a sure sign, he figured, they were talking about him and his new *gringo* clothes.

A handful of pickers still crouched over the dark green rows. Others stood in a line at the crossroads, their arms cradling yellow boxes filled with strawberries. Their eyes focused on a girl weighing the boxes and punching white cards. As she punched, a worker whisked the crates to a nearby truck.

"You made it," Mr. Hampton called to Jeff from the rear of the truckbed. "We can use you. Bring over those flats from Alexa's scale."

Here we go, Jeff thought grimly. Farm work at its best. He moved to the scale as a picker set two containers on the metal platform. Alexa shook her head and studied his ticket. "Lorenzo Perez. *Muchas fresas.* Forty-one pounds. Too much. The berries get smashed. *No mucho,* okay?"

"*Si, no mucho.*" He grinned, gave several quick nods, and stuffed his ticket inside his baseball cap.

Alexa sighed and grabbed the flats.

"I'll get 'em." Jeff stopped her.

She stared.

"I'm Jeff—Jeff McKenzie."

Her eyes narrowed. "The one who tore up my bean field?" The corner of her mouth pulled tight.

Jeff swallowed.

She stepped aside.

He reached for the flats. The weight tugged at his arms, and the plastic rims dug into his fingers. God, he panicked, what if I drop these? He held his breath, turned, stepped once, twice, three times, then swung them up to the truck.

The flats barely cleared the steel edge, landing with a thud on the wooden surface. Thank you, he thought with relief.

Mr. Hampton was gone. Now the man who'd been helping Alexa stood on the truck. He snatched up Jeff's flats, swiftly adding them to the load.

"Looks easy, huh?" A girl walked up to the truck holding a single crate.

The man returned and smiled down at her, wrinkles creasing into his dark brown skin. *"Gracias,"* he said, leaning to take her fruit.

The girl was younger and a whole lot friendlier than Alexa. Freckles ran across her nose and cheeks. She studied Jeff. "Are you the one who got in our field?"

He felt his neck heat up. Geezuz. Was everyone going to drill him? "Why'd you do it?"

For fun, Jeff remembered. Even now he felt the exhilaration as he raced into that endless space. Each move was his, each turn, each circle. And Paul, laughing, yelling. For a brief moment, he'd been out of this world, out of himself. Wrong answer. He cleared his throat. "Uh, I don't know." (7–12)

Following our shared reading of the first chapter of *Joyride,* we could move into writers' workshop and a craft lesson on writing persuasive essays. In *Nonfiction Craft Lessons,* Portalupi and Fletcher have two excellent lessons to support persuasive writing: "Listing the Pros and Cons of an Argument" and "Airing the Opposing Point of View" (102–103). In the context of the two lessons described in that book, Portalupi and Fletcher offer a list of pros and cons as well as an article for shared reading on preserving the Alaskan Wilderness. Newspapers and magazines offer a wealth of shared reading resources that could be used as a foundation for teaching strategies for persuasive writing. Regardless of what we chose to read in order to demonstrate strategies for persuasive writing, we could then transfer the strategies we developed to a collaborative persuasive piece based on the shared reading of *Joyride.* We could list the pros and cons of Jeff's father's decision to force Jeff to suffer the consequences of his poor choices and then create a persuasive piece that Jeff or his mother would write to convince Jeff's dad that he should not work to pay for his mistake.

Prior to students' beginning silent reading time, we could fill out a Book Pass form (I.26, Appendix I) with students in order to give them the opportunity to discover other novels and genres that highlight the same theme. Each student receives a book, has a couple of minutes to sample the book to see if it meets the student's interest and readability needs, and passes the book along. After a half hour, students have had the opportunity to see fifteen or more new titles all related to the theme. While some students always opt to continue reading books they had begun before, others might choose to extend the theme of the shared text into their independent reading time. A book pass provides a bridge for students between the shared novel and their independent reading choices. A beginning list of titles I might include in a book pass connected to a choices and consequences unit follows.

Picture Books
The Eye of the Needle (Sloat)
Faithful Elephants (Tsuchiya)
Going Home (Bunting)
Hiroshima No Pika (Maruki)
I Never Knew Your Name (Garland)
It Doesn't Have to Be This Way: A Barrio Story (Rodriguez)
Just a Dream (Van Allsburg)
Just One Flick of a Finger (Lorbiecki)
Listening for Leroy (Hearne)
The Sleeping Lady (Dixon)
The Tower (Evans)

Young Adult Novels
All We Know of Heaven (Bridgers)
Annie's Baby (Sparks)
Blackwater (Bunting)
Breaking Rank (Randle)
The Buffalo Tree (Rapp)
The Chocolate War (Cormier)
A Dance for Three (Plummer)
The Drowning of Stephan Jones (Greene)
fist stick knife gun (Canada)
Give a Boy a Gun (Strasser)
Go Ask Alice (Sparks)
Heroes (Cormier)
Imitate the Tiger (Cheripko)
It Happened to Nancy (Sparks)
Jay's Journal (Sparks)
Killing Mr. Griffin (Duncan)
The Last Payback (VanOosting)
Make Lemonade (Wolff)
Making Up Megaboy (Walter)
Monster (Walter Dean Myers)
Mr. Was (Hautman)
No More Dead Dogs (Korman)
Nothing but the Truth (Avi)
Remembering the Good Times (Peck)
The Rifle (Paulsen)
Scorpions (Walter Dean Myers)
Shabanu (Staples)

Smack (Burgess)
Speak (Anderson)
Staying Fat for Sarah Byrnes (Crutcher)
Stone Water (Gilbert)
Swallowing Stones (McDonald)
Tears of a Tiger (Draper)
Tenderness (Cormier)
Treacherous Love (Sparks)
Trino's Choice (Bertrand)
Turnabout (Haddix)
We All Fall Down (Cormier)
Whirligig (Fleischman)

Nonfiction
Hard Time (Bode and Mack)
Teen Violence: Out of Control (Newton)
Voices from the Streets (Atkin)

Short Stories
Athletic Shorts (collection) (Crutcher)
"Confession" (Miklowitz)
"Moonlight Sonata" (Brooks)
No Easy Answers (collection) (Gallo)
Twelve Shots (collection) (Mazer)

Poetry
CrashBoomLove: A Novel in Verse (Herrera)
Skin Deep and Other Teenage Reflections (Medearis)
The Taking of Room 114 (Glenn)
Who Killed Mr. Chippendale? (Glenn)

After students have chosen texts for independent reading, either from the book pass or from the classroom library, those books can be read in class or as part of a reading homework program. Our class for that day might end with Portia Nelson's poem "Autobiography in Five Short Chapters":

> *"Autobiography in Five Short Chapters"*
> Chapter I
> I walk down the street.
>> There is a deep hole in the sidewalk.
>> I fall in.

I am lost . . . I am helpless.
    It isn't my fault.
It takes forever to find a way out.

Chapter II
I walk down the same street.
    There is a deep hole in the sidewalk.
    I pretend I don't see it.
    I fall in again.
I can't believe I am in this same place.
        But it isn't my fault.
It still takes a long time to get out.

Chapter III
I walk down the same street.
    There is a deep hole in the sidewalk.
    I see it is there.
I still fall in . . . it's a habit . . . but,
        my eyes are open.
I know where I am.
It is my fault.
I get out immediately.

Chapter IV
I walk down the same street.
There is a deep hole in the sidewalk.
    I walk around it.

Chapter V
I walk down another street.

Students take home their copies of the shared poem for that day in order to begin free-writing for a paper to be completed by the end of the unit. Their homework for the first night would be to begin brainstorming ideas for a multi-genre piece of writing (Romano, *Blending Genre, Altering Style*), in which students could explore their own or others' holes in the sidewalk.

This lesson is built on a foundation of shared reading; however, much of the content and process of the texts we read is intended to bridge to students' independent reading and writing lives. In the course of this class period, students would have sampled many texts: nonfiction, poetry, picture books, novels, and informational essays. All of these contribute to a wider range of independent choices for students. For students who have learned to wait for teacher direction for each aspect of class work, moving from this teacher-controlled model to literature circles might be too large a step.

Shared Reading and Literature Circles

I'm guessing that most of you who are reading this book have attempted to use literature circles with students. I'm hoping that you have found enough professional support so that you have been more successful than I was when I first tried them in my classroom. At the time, I could find no professional books written about literature circles. I had not met Karen Smith or Harvey Daniels, or read their writing about how to use literature circles effectively. I had heard one person talk about literature circles at a conference, and it is true that a little information can be a dangerous thing. I returned to my classroom thinking, "This could be a great way for students to have more choice without my focusing their discussion and response to a text." Those words probably should be included in the *Famous Last Words* book we could each write.

I had returned from the conference armed with good intentions and multiple copies of several books. We did a book pass so that students could make choices for the book or book groups they might want to join. In a matter of minutes, these students had figured out a way to get into book groups based not on their needs and interests but on which other kids they liked.

I then gave some of the poorest instructions of my teaching career. I told them to get into their groups and decide how many pages they would read each day. I told them they had four options for getting the pages read: they could take turns reading aloud; they could choose someone in the group to read to them; they could listen to audiotapes and follow along; or they could read silently.

We brainstormed a list of things we had talked about in connection with the shared reading of a novel, and they came up with the following: ask questions, discuss interesting stuff, make sure we understand the book, look at words, write down important or interesting stuff, and do projects. I told them they would be responsible for making sure all of these things happened in their groups, so maybe they would want to give each person in the group a job to do. I then set them loose.

After a couple of days of literature circle chaos, I decided to put a tape recorder with each group so I could figure out what was going wrong. It had all seemed to make so much sense in that one-hour presentation at the conference. The following transcript is a portion of one of the literature circles on the third day of students' being in their groups. This transcript is from a group reading

Caroline Cooney's *Face on the Milk Carton.* There are five students in the group, represented in the transcript in the following way: G1, G2 for the two girls and B1, B2, B3 for the boys.

G1: OK, who's going to read today?

G2: I'll read but I don't want any interruptions.

B1: Who made you queen?

B2: Why do you always get to read?

G2: Because you guys are morons and I'm the only one who can read like Mrs. Allen.

B2: This is a stupid book anyway.

G1: Why did you choose it then?

B2: You told me to!

G1: God, you're dumb.

B3: Shut up and read before we get in trouble. Somebody just read this stupid book.

G2: So, do you guys want me to read or what?

B2: Just read!

(*G2 reads about five pages of the book out loud and the others follow along, occasionally correcting her.*)

G1: OK, that's enough for today.

B1: We said we were going to read fifteen pages on our schedule.

G1: So, we'll add the pages to tomorrow and make it up then.

G2: So, let's talk about some good stuff.

G1: I wonder if there is going to be any sex in the book. I would have had sex by now.

B3: You would have had sex the first day but that isn't what we're supposed to talk about.

G1: Shut up, you pervert!

G2: So, big mouth, have you ever had sex?

B2: You girls are so stupid. Talk about the book.

G1: Did you ever get in any trouble in school?

B2: I can't remember anything.

G1: Are you nuts? You were friggin' always in trouble.

B2: Aw, shut up.

G1: OK, so I'll start. Remember when K had sex in middle school and got crabs?

B3: This is stupid and that's not even true. I knew her.

G1: Oooo . . . I bet you did—everybody did.

B2: This book isn't even about sex. We're supposed to talk about the book.

G1: God, you're so boring. Who remembers when J was out in the hall screamin' her head off at the principal?

B3: This is all on the tape, you know.

G1: Just say something fast. She probably won't even listen to these anyway. Say something.

G2: Who was that seventh grader you used to make fun of all the time? She was so weird.

G1: The one I told to f—— off?

G2: Yeah, didn't you throw hamburger buns at her in the cafeteria?

B3: I'm not doing this. We're going to get in trouble.

G2: Shut up and go tell for all we care.

For those of you who have not read *The Face on the Milk Carton,* don't let this transcript influence your decision of whether to read the book. This "discussion" in no way matches the content of this young adult novel. I had tried to move my students prematurely from an orchestrated class where I explained the purpose of each activity, chose the reading, decided what we would do before, during, and after reading and determined how students would demonstrate their learning to one where students made all the choices. I offered them no support, assuming they could just take what I had done with them and transfer that to student-directed small groups. It was too drastic a change.

It was a year later before I ever thought about doing literature circles again. Every time I heard someone talk about literature circles, I shuddered. When I finally had enough distance from the failure and reread the transcripts of the book groups, I was able to sort out some of the problems:

- Students need more information before making book choices. They needed to rank-order their top three choices, and I then need to assign the groups.
- We need to begin literature circle groups with shorter selections. Novels are too lengthy and require too many decisions on the part of students who aren't used to making decisions.
- Instructions for roles need to be clearer, and students need to practice those roles by taking on one role at a time. We need to flesh out those roles together by using a shared text. For example, I could have read a poem or short story to the entire class, and we could have brainstormed ways individuals in the class could have taken on roles to facilitate learning within a group.
- A way is needed to tie the small groups back to the whole class. The community I had worked hard to build quickly disintegrated because students were spending too much time in their small groups. Students quickly began to see this as time equivalent to a study hall.
- Ways are needed to hold individual group members accountable for their reading and response.

After time and reflection, I was able to see how I could have front-loaded the process in a way that might have led to success. However, as with most learning moments, it took failure to learn what I needed to do differently. When we started literature circles again, I spent the prior three weeks giving students an opportunity to flesh out the roles they had highlighted: ask questions, discuss interesting stuff, make sure we understand the book, look at words, write down important or interesting stuff, and do projects. We then used a short story in each group so that group members could practice asking each other questions. The next day we changed roles, and every person in the group practiced helping keep the discussion going and focused.

At the end of each time period, we came back together as a class and did a shared reading that connected thematically to the story they had read. Each student then had some literacy task I created that required her to connect the reading she had done in her group to the shared text I read to them (learning log, comparison/contrast, character charts, I Am poem, character meetings between two texts). In this way, students felt responsible to their group members and accountable individually. Literature circles improved as I improved in my ability to help students understand the purpose for literature circles and the process for being part of any small-group learning.

I shared this literature circle method with Beth Scanlon at Timber Creek High School in Orlando this year, and she decided to try it as an alternative to what she had done in the past. If we examine Beth's comments on the learning with her students during this time, I think we can see how complex it is to move high school students from a teacher-driven to a student-directed model of learning. They have had many years of someone's telling them what to do, and they often flounder in the absence of that direction.

[Beth:] I decided the theme for our literature circles would be intolerance so students can connect what they are reading to the world. We could also find enough books for all my students around this theme. I had tried literature circles before with my ESOL students and they were successful using the roles that Daniels identified. What made the group successful is that I had varying levels of readers and a definitive leader in each group. We also had been reading together every day for a year using shared, guided, and independent reading. The second time I tried literature circles it was not very successful. It was the first thing I did that year with my intensive reading class. I felt as though that was my only option because I didn't have any class sets of books. Even with books on tapes, these students were not able to do literature circles. They didn't have enough reading mileage to rely on. So, I abandoned lit circles with my intensive readers.

Now I'm teaching tenth graders and thinking again about literature circles. I had planned on using this approach during our Holocaust unit. I teach English II and this is a required subject for this class. Most of the students have read *Night,* and I wanted to use literature circles so they would get a sense that there were other stories out there besides *Anne Frank.*

As Beth considers trying literature circles again with her class, she is thinking about what has worked for her in the past, the reasons why she wants to use literature circles, and how she can overcome some of the pitfalls of the previous experience. Her first step was altering what had happened previously with groups. Students did an extended book pass for all the books available for literature circles and then highlighted their top three choices. They recorded the titles and what they thought the content might be, and then indicated whether each book would be of interest (see Figure 7.1). On the reverse of the card, they wrote whom they would like to work with and what role they would take in the group. Prior to assigning students to their chosen groups, Beth asked them to use their notes from the book pass to figure out some things the literature circle book choices had in common (see Figure 7.2). This allowed them to have a broad picture of what everyone in the class would be reading and established a base for bringing the small groups back together for common discussion.

Figure 7.1

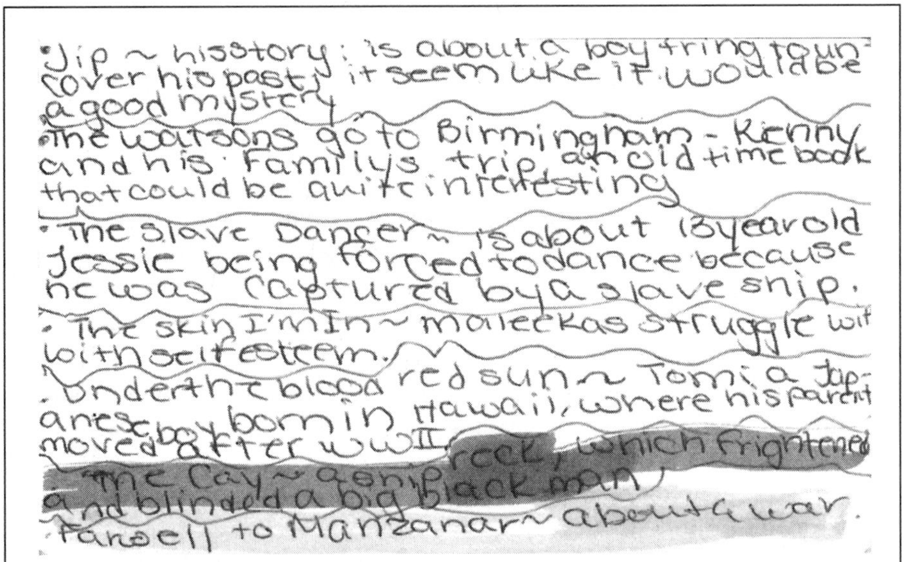

Figure 7.2

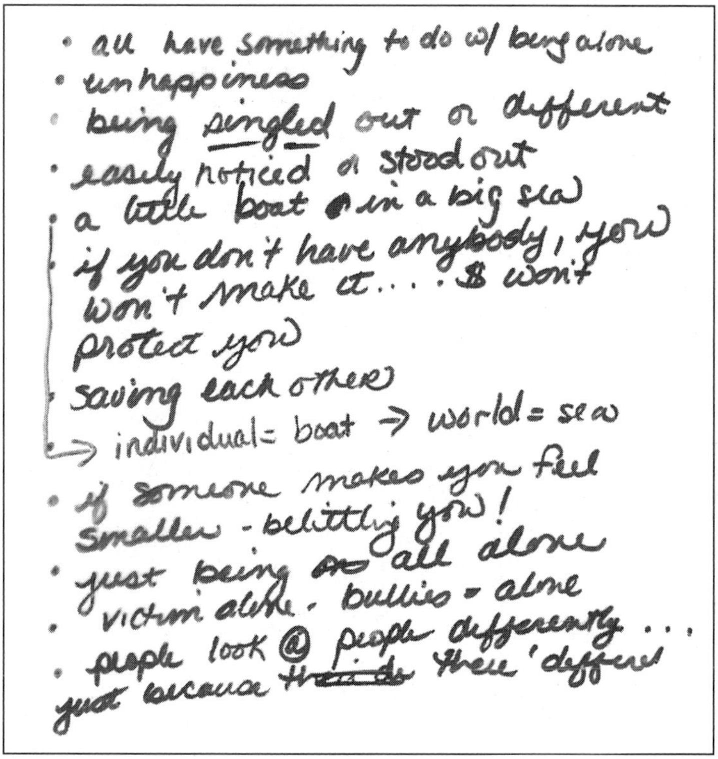

- all have something to do w/ being alone
- unhappiness
- being singled out or different
- easily noticed or stood out
- a little boat ● in a big sea
- if you don't have anybody, you won't make it.... & won't protect you
- saving each other
  → individual = boat → world = sea
- if someone makes you feel smaller - belittling you!
- just being ~ all alone
- victim alone - bullies - alone
- people look @ people differently ... just because they're 'diffent'

Before Beth's students began reading their texts, she wanted to assess their background knowledge. She asked students to free-write on the word *intolerance.*

> [Beth:] Many of them did not know what *intolerant* meant and asked me to break the word down for them. I asked them to break the word into two parts, *in* (not) from our prefix study and *tolerate,* and think about what those parts might mean. I didn't want to give them too much information because I wanted to see their starting points. After writing, I asked students to share a word, sentence, or idea from their papers.

Students used their free-writing as a bridge to completing a Concept Ladder form related to intolerance (see Figure 7.3). After they collaborated about the range of understandings they had about intolerance, they completed a class concept ladder (see Figure 7.4). At this point, Beth and her students had developed a core of understandings about intolerance and the texts they were going to read.

Figure 7.3

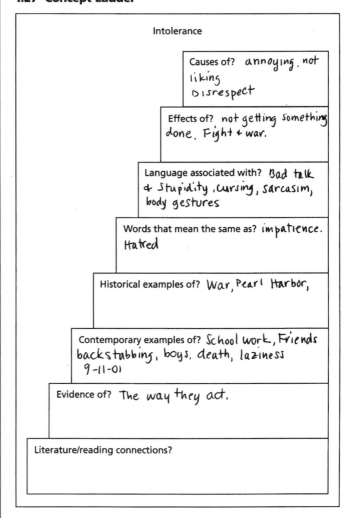

1.27 Concept Ladder

Intolerance

Causes of? annoying, not liking Disrespect

Effects of? not getting something done. Fight + war.

Language associated with? Bad talk + Stupidity, cursing, sarcasim, body gestures

Words that mean the same as? impatience. Hatred

Historical examples of? War, Pearl Harbor,

Contemporary examples of? School work, Friends backstabbing, boys. death, laziness 9-11-01

Evidence of? The way they act.

Literature/reading connections?

One more procedural task remained: How would students learn to work together in groups so that the time there would be productive? They brainstormed a list of elements of a good discussion. They decided that good discussion consisted of maturity, no yelling, talking things out, listening and not just hearing each other, having respect for others' opinions, asking questions, having opinions, giving answers, making eye contact, watching body gestures, knowing the rules, knowing the facts, being prepared, and doing research if

Figure 7.4

Causes of: people acting stupid
Starting fights, short tempers
get mad easily, ignorance,
disrespect, rap ~~on~~ ~~record~~
$money soc\iioeconmic
~~prejudice~~ prejudgism in society
Effects: fights, war, attitudes, trouble
in school, anger, sadness,
jealousy, friends → enemies,
impatience, fear, embaressmt
incompitance,
Lang assoc. - curse words, inflammatory
language, sarcastic lang,
body gestures, disrespectful
offensive or defensive
racial slurs
Words: Low tolerance, impatience,
hatred
Historical Examples: WWII → Japanese, Jewish
assasination
Bill Clinton → Civil War, NAZI
of MLK, - JFK, RFK, + MX, JL.,
Contemporary Example 9-11-01, daily
fights, Kamikazee pilots,
Skinheads, KKK, burning flags,
Evidence of: people honking, yelling, body
gestures, walls, speech,

necessary. I don't think anyone believed that all the students would abide by these all the time, but they had created a foundation for respect.

Beth and I talked about the value of using a shared reading each day as a way to pull the groups back into a whole class. She found several texts that she felt would be excellent for comparison so that students could bring their developing understandings from their literature circle novels to another work of literature. This gave the class some common ground as a basis for discussion. The other texts Beth chose included the following:

"Priscilla and the Wimps," a short story by Richard Peck
"Guilty Until Proven Innocent," a poem by Angela Shelf Medearis

"Alone," a poem by Maya Angelou
The Shadow of Hate, a video from the Teaching Tolerance kit
A Time for Justice, articles from the Teaching Tolerance kit
"Ballad of Birmingham," a poem by Dudley Randall
"Sunday School Bombing," a news article
An excerpt on Birmingham from the textbook *History of a Free People*

Beth also carefully planned ways to help students stay focused with their reading and group responsibilities. She knew from experience that keeping students together would be difficult, and this class of students was no exception.

[Beth:] I thought my students could set reading deadlines for themselves. What I found was most of the groups could set realistic deadlines but not keep them. Only one group decided they were going to finish the book in three days! I think the key here is that you make sure the right students are put together. I tried to make groups based on book interest and people tolerability. I think I need to make sure that I have a strong leader. I might change when I do independent reading. Maybe if I have IR on Monday instead of Thursday, the students who have fallen behind can use IR to get caught up.

Beth developed several ways of helping students stay focused. Each day, she asked students to complete a literature circle checklist (see Figure 7.5). When she combined these with the anecdotal notes she took as she visited each group, she could get a sense of what was working in the group and where the group was having problems. She also invited students to keep track of what was happening in the groups from an individual perspective. As you can see from this student's comment (see Figure 7.6), some of the groups still struggled.

Figure 7.5

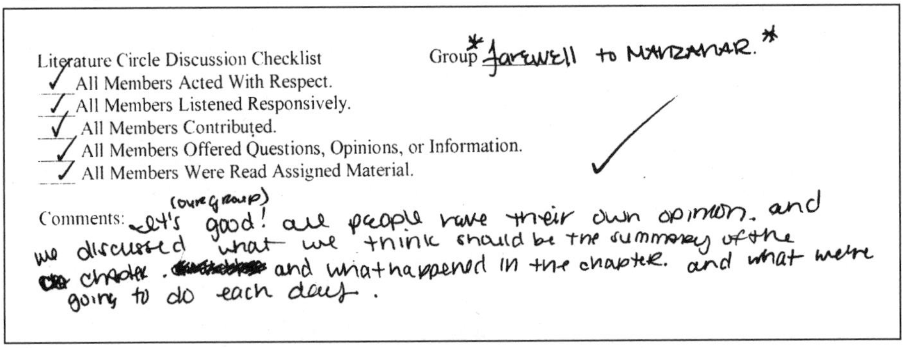

Literature Circle Discussion Checklist   Group *Farewell to Manzanar.*
✓ All Members Acted With Respect.
✓ All Members Listened Responsively.
✓ All Members Contributed.
✓ All Members Offered Questions, Opinions, or Information.
✓ All Members Were Read Assigned Material.

(our group)
Comments: Let's good! all people have their own opinion. and we discussed what we think should be the summary of the chapter. and what happened in the chapter. and what we're going to do each day.

Figure 7.6

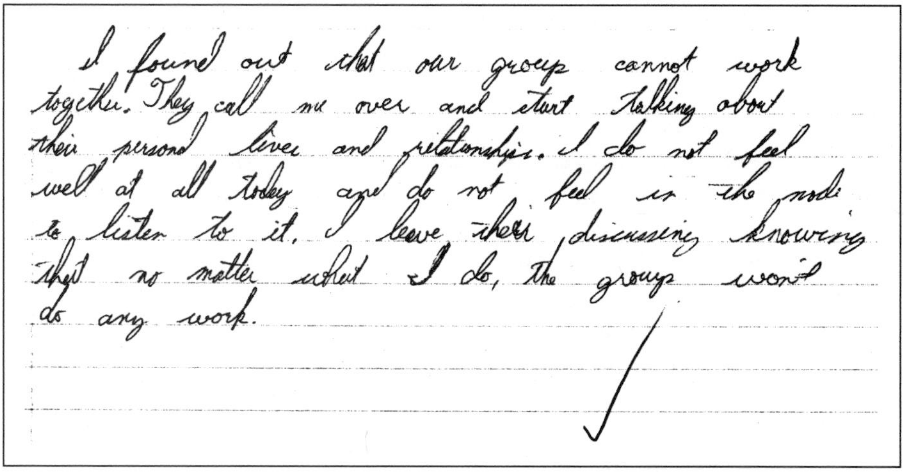

> I found out that our group cannot work together. They call me over and start talking about their personal lives and relationships. I do not feel well at all today and do not feel in the mood to listen to it. I leave there discussing knowing that no matter what I do, the group won't do any work.

Once again, Beth saw that the group functioned reasonably well if there was a strong leader but struggled if there was not.

Each day during the course of the literature circles, Beth began and ended the class with a common activity. Students discussed art, literature, nonfiction, and personal experiences in relation to the common shared reading/viewing and their own experiences. They free-wrote, were part of inner and outer circles following the reading of Peck's "Priscilla and the Wimps," did word studies, wrote personification poetry, wrote personal responses, and took part in discussions as a way to invite the text-to-text, text-to-world, and text-to-self connections (Keene and Zimmerman 1997; Harvey and Goudvis 2000) so critical for deep response to literature.

Beth created a generic exam that would fit all books and give students flexibility in what they chose to provide as evidence of learning from their literature circle novel and the class readings/discussions. The test asked students to highlight their learning about intolerance by completing the following tasks:

- Choose ten words significant to your learning and discuss what makes those words important to your book and your understandings of intolerance.
- Discuss some critical aspect of your main character.
- Write about three causes and effects in the context of your novel and the impact of those on your novel.
- Discuss three facts and opinions that make a critical connection to what you learned.

Students also produced an individual project to provide evidence of what they had learned from their reading. One of my favorite examples from this class is a poem written by Crystal Whiteaker based on Sharon Flake's book of the same name:

The Skin I'm In
Every day she's teased,
With her skin, no one is pleased;
It's dark as chocolate and
her soul is golden like the sun,
Yet, she's still an outcast to almost everyone.
She's constantly pushed around,
but when she screams there is no sound.
She cries secret tears
hoping no one will find her fears.
She puts up with so much day in and day out,
but she never raises her voice to shout.
In the end, she opens her eyes,
To see that their taunts were nothing but lies.
Her lesson was learned and
The bully was burned.
She finally loved the skin
    that her body was in.

So, what did Beth learn from this experience that she will take into her next attempt to bridge the gap between shared reading and independence? She discovered that her students did not have enough reading supports in place to be truly independent with a novel-length text. She had not read a whole-class novel with students at this point in the year, and so her students did not have that model of discussion and making deeper connections to take with them as they approached a substantial text. She was also reminded of the fine balance between giving choices and total independence.

[Beth:] I wanted/needed a tape recorder so that I could tape each group's discussion session. I think it is essential to be able to listen . . . so they can listen . . . do more inner and outer circle discussions . . . maybe require a log or journal. There is such an intricate balance between letting them make independent decisions and establishing boundaries and support where they still need them.

I believe we can all acknowledge the truth of Beth's statement about balance. I believe shared reading of a common text or shared viewing of a film can help support independence for students in their literature circle groups. As you take part in students' groups and read their responses about the challenges they are experiencing, you can use the common shared texts as a way to teach or reinforce effective reading strategies. Beth and I learned similar lessons: students need our support in learning how to become independent with academic tasks. Part of being an effective teacher is knowing when and how to provide support and when to move out of the way so we can see students putting those supports into place.

It is important to remember that, for the most part, teachers are still choosing the texts for literature circle groups. Our choices will not always be their choices and so can offer some challenges. In "Choices for Children: Why and How to Let Students Decide," Alfie Kohn reminds us of the importance of learning how to let go in places where students are prepared to take on the challenges of a task. "For decades, prescriptions have been offered to enhance student motivation and achievement. But these ideas are unlikely to make much of a difference so long as students are controlled and silenced" (19).

Just as shared reading is an incremental bridge toward some independence with literature circles, literature circles are a bridge to more extensive independence. Our goal for sharing a wide variety of texts with students is not that they would stay dependent on our choices forever but that they would use the skills and strategies developed in the course of our reading as a way to support their own questions, interests, and reading paths. If we spend from three to five weeks on a theme that is built out from a common novel, and several students can't get engaged in the novel or the theme, those students will not have the same impetus for related reading and research. As interesting and engaging as we try to make our choices, they are still our choices.

Each time I see a teacher trying to get students interested in something she finds thoroughly engaging, I think of James Beane's essay "Re-Entry Blues," detailing his day with students when he described his plan for a community-based unit they would study together:

> I planned what was undoubtedly one of the finest lessons in the history of education. First I would show these young people the "J curve" of world population growth, growing so slowly for centuries and then accelerating in the twentieth to make a J. Next I would show the population projections for Madison, not only growing sharply but also involving that peristalsis-like bulge of middle-aged baby boomers moving inexorably toward their elder years. Then we would work in cooperative groups to figure out some of the implications and effects of these shifts on our world and city. Finally, after debriefing the small-group work and just at the end of our time, I would pull all of this

together with a breathtaking concept that would stay with these seventh graders for all the days of their lives.

And so it went, through the presentation and the small-group work. As the debriefing proceeded with the students' excellent insights about health care, transportation, taxes, and so on, I kept one eye on the clock, counting down to the perfect timing for my unforgettable concept. Finally, the moment! As I ascended into the breathtaking beauty for the big idea, a front-row student who had begun to teeter in her chair sat bold upright and threw up her lunch on me and two others. Now the bell rang and the class dutifully stood and left the room, leaving behind a messy floor, one sick student, two spattered others, a stunned teacher, and a great concept only half spoken.

Two things stay with me from this. One is that for the life of me I cannot remember what that unforgettable concept was. The other is the terrifying thought that in the middle of that sentence, one student, I hope not speaking for others, had offered up her evaluation of my curriculum. (2)

James Beane has it right, doesn't he? It was *his* curriculum. As our education system moves toward standardization, this becomes a critical distinction for us in thinking about our reading plans with students. At what point in this standardization do we take away all of students' reading choices and, in so doing, take away much of their motivation?

In *The Tipping Point,* Malcolm Gladwell reminds us that "epidemics tip because of the extraordinary efforts of a few select carriers" (22). When all the hours of a day are filled with the things we have to cover, when is the time we model for students how to make choices for text, and time to continue our habit of lifelong reading? I think shared reading of diverse texts should be a protected zone—an isolation ward—where we let the epidemic spread. In the absence of that time and supportive approach, we will never have the country of independent, lifelong readers we are trying so desperately to create.

8

"But What About Grades?" Assessing the "Value" of Shared Reading

"Poor, poor, little Alice!" bemoaned G. K. "She has not only been caught and made to do lessons; she has been forced to inflict lessons on others. Alice is now not only a schoolgirl but a schoolmistress. The holiday is over and Dodgson is again a don. There will be lots and lots of examination papers, with questions like: (1) What do you know of the following: mimsy, gimble, haddocks' eyes, treacle-wells, beautiful soup? (2) Record all the moves in the chess game in Through the Looking-Glass, *and give diagram. (3) Outline the practical policy of the White Knight for dealing with the social problem of green whiskers. (4) Distinguish between Tweedledum and Tweedledee."*

Lewis Carroll, *The Annotated Alice*

$\mathbf{M}$any lovers of reading and literature have been as distressed as G. K. Chesterton at the thought of a beloved text's being used as a vehicle for hundreds of lessons and exams. And we *should be* distressed. Study guides, graphic organizers, lists of vocabulary words, and Post-its fill so many hours of students' days that I sometimes wonder if there is a time or place left for students to enjoy the magic of a good book. I know that it was an awakening for me when I interviewed my students and asked them to tell me what they thought my goals were for them as readers. Only seven students out of ninety told me they thought I wanted them to enjoy reading. After observing a teacher confer with her tenth-grade students about their independent reading, I know my students weren't the only ones confused about our goals.

The classroom was filled with charts and student writing—evidence of active learning covered even the windows. It was early on Monday morning, yet a quick glance around the room showed me that most students had located their books for independent reading and were engaged. As the less-motivated and less-organized finally settled in, the teacher sat behind a small conferring table and began to talk with one of the young women in the class about her reading. The work of the class appeared to be a model for what we would like to see in an effective reading-writing workshop class. Then, I started to really listen to the dialogue of the conference.

Miss M: So, do you want to tell me about your book.

Selena: Miss, this was the best book.

Miss M: Which one? I see you have three books there.

Selena: I do. I read them all this weekend.

Miss M: Wow, that's great. Let's look at one of them at a time. Oh, they're all by
    Lurlene McDaniel. You've discovered an author you like?

Selena: I love her books! I read three of them this weekend. These weren't my
    independent reading books for class. I went to the library and got them.

(*There is a lengthy summary here of each of the novels as the young woman
    details the events of each book by comparing and contrasting with the other
    McDaniel books she has read. She also talks about how much better these
    books are than the one they are reading for a class novel. When the reader
    pauses, the teacher tries to focus the conference.*)

Miss M: So, let's look at your Post-its and see what you were thinking about
    while you were reading.

Selena: Miss, I don't have any Post-its in these books. You don't understand—I
    read these on my own—these aren't my class books.

Miss M: Oh, I know, but I need to see the evidence of your thinking when you
    read independently so I can give you credit for reading the books.

Selena: I thought we only had to do that for what we read in class. I read these
    on my own. I can't get credit for reading them?

Miss M: I have to have evidence that you read them.

Selena: I told you about the books, so what else can I do?

Miss M: Well, you can go back and put Post-its where you would have put them
    if you had read them in class or you can read another book and put the
    Post-its in as you read.

Selena: If I go back, how many Post-its do I need in each?
Miss M: 37.
Selena: This sucks—I read the books.

It was heartbreaking to listen to the conference, yet this teacher's confusion over how to monitor, assess, and evaluate was honest (and common) confusion. I struggled with the same dilemma, and I'm guessing many of you do as well. We are responsible for giving students multiple opportunities to demonstrate learning so that the grade accurately reflects student learning. If reading forms the foundation for your curriculum, then the assessments and evaluations you do will be tied to those shared experiences. Assessment and evaluation should extend the value of a shared reading experience, not diminish it. So, how do we effectively assess and evaluate student learning without taking away from the experience of reading?

Defining Assessment and Evaluation

I define *assessment* as identifying starting points (for teachers and learners) and *evaluation* as assigning value (such as points and grades) to the work. In terms of evaluation, or assigning grades, I believe that how to give value to the work students produce as evidence of learning has to be a professional decision for each teacher. Some teachers use points that translate to grades, and others rely on scoring guides and rubrics to determine grades. I'm guessing we've all been challenged to stay calm when students say, "What grade did you give me?" Regardless of the types of tools you use to come up with an honest evaluation, there are some general guidelines that can make evaluation more learner-centered. I certainly didn't discover all these guidelines at once nor on my own. I do know that as evaluation became more collaborative and less a mystery, students began to own some of the responsibility for their grades.

- Reasonable deadlines should be created with students, and *they* should generate the consequences of missed deadlines. This avoids the comment, "No wonder he got an A, you always let him pass his work in after we have ours back."
- Use ongoing assessments that lead to intermittent evaluation rather than putting too much weight on a single product.
- Correct for a limited number of errors and ignore the rest. Give students an opportunity to re-do work based on the feedback you have given.

- Give students specifics on what you are grading. If you are looking for all the elements of a complete paragraph, grade for that.
- When possible, generate a range of options for students to demonstrate learning, and let students know if you value one option over any other.
- Vary the evaluation techniques you use for the task, but let students know how each fits with other evaluations they have experienced. If using + and −, how do those translate to letter or number grades? If using scoring guides or rubrics, how does a 4 translate to a number or letter grade?
- Whenever possible, conduct grading conferences a few weeks before grades are due. This is especially critical in the first quarter when students are trying to establish what the norms are for your class.
- Allow some assignments to be graded by students in collaboration with other students. This gives them the opportunity to see how difficult it is to actually measure learning.

If we make evaluation and grading more collaborative, we are less likely to have students caught by surprise with their grades. We certainly do not want our students to mirror the feelings of one of the characters in Robb Thomas's *Doing Time: Notes from the Undergrad:*

> English is my worst subject. I usually make A's, but I make A's in everything. English is just tougher. I don't think it's really me, though. I think it's English teachers. They assume that because they teach English, they can just invent answers. In math, if the answer is 256, that's the answer. You never hear a math teacher saying, "Two hundred fifty-six was intended as irony." Or, "What is the underlying meaning of the equation two to the eighth power?"
>
> I like it when the answer is the answer. All the fuzzy stuff just makes me mad.
>
> *How can the ghost of his father compel Hamlet to such desperate measures?*
>
> I don't know. It doesn't say. The teachers don't know either. They just think they know the answer, and they're so sure about it that they figure they can mark my answers wrong and get me sent off to prep school. On this last test, Mrs. Paulson asked us her standard question after we finish a book: *Did you like* Hamlet? *Please explain why or why not.*
>
> Here's what I would have liked to have written.
>
> *No.*
>
> *I just don't.*
>
> I *never* know why.

But the question was worth ten points, so I put down that I liked it, even though I didn't, because I figured that's what she wanted to hear.

I liked Hamlet *because it was written by William Shakespeare (1564–1616), considered by many to be the greatest English dramatist and poet. Shakespeare, born in Stratford-upon-Avon, is best known for his great tragedies, including* Julius Caesar, Romeo and Juliet, Othello, *and* Macbeth. *Most of his plays were performed in London at the Globe Theatre.*

She gave me two points.

That's why I hate English. (135–137)

Assessment differs from evaluation in that it can be a source of learning for teachers and students without having grades attached to it. While any assessment tool that is used could produce a grade, the purpose for assessment should be one of informing next teaching and learning steps. I believe assessment should occur every day in order to give students the opportunity to demonstrate their progress toward independence as readers, writers, listeners, speakers, thinkers, and learners. This gives us information we need in order to know where our teaching may have missed the mark and what we need to teach next. These assessments can range from quick checks to see where students are in their daily work to elaborate tools used throughout the year to document student progress. Regardless of the design or use of the assessment tool, the goal remains the same—gaining information that informs instruction and continued learning. Knowing the kinds of assessment and evaluation tools that will extend the learning experience and inform your next teaching decisions without taking away the pleasure of the shared texts is often the most difficult aspect of the shared reading experience.

Assessing Fluency and Foundations of Reading

Throughout this book I have discussed ways I believe shared reading builds foundations for reading fluency. In the absence of these foundations, it is difficult for students to examine and learn from more complex texts requiring sophisticated use of strategies. When these reading foundations are combined with a repertoire of strategies, students have moved into the role of experienced and knowledgeable readers.

Many children develop the foundations of reading long before they enter school. For those children, teaching adds to those early reading strengths by providing increasingly sophisticated texts and supports to help readers overcome the challenges of new texts. For other children, they come to school and discover for the first time the things that readers do with automaticity in order to make sense out of the printed word. Over the past few years, I have found that some teachers are spending the bulk of their reading time trying to teach children strategies for reading long before these children have solid foundations on which to add those structural supports.

When trying to determine whether readers are at a point where the teaching of reading strategies would make sense to them, we can look for evidence that they have knowledge of several important aspects of reading. There are at least eight knowledge areas I believe form the foundations of reading:

- Text can provide enjoyment.
- Text is spoken word and has meaning.
- Text has predictable features, codes, and conventions.
- Text has words that can be decoded.
- Readers make connections to text.
- Readers have responses to their reading.
- Text has a purpose: authors write with a purpose, and readers are supported when they think about the author's purpose.
- Readers monitor their reading and have fix-up strategies to help them when reading stops making sense.

For each of these eight knowledge areas, there are critical indicators we could look for to assess student progress in developing solid elements of a reading foundation. (See I.29, Appendix I.) As we look for this evidence, we might see that some students are at a basic awareness level while others are moving toward a skill level of competence.

A1. Enjoyment
1.1 like words and word play
1.2 see humor and emotion in events or characters
1.3 mimic interesting words or rhyming patterns
1.4 express choices for texts
1.5 find favorite authors

A2. Text has meaning
2.1 know that oral language can be written down for reading by self and others
2.2 understand that letters form words, and words form phrases or sentences

2.3 see connection between background knowledge and understanding of language

2.4 discover or infer author intentions or purpose of text

2.5 know that writers use predictable patterns or support to help readers

A3. Conventions of text/print

3.1 recognize predictable patterns of language (syntax) in text

3.2 recognize predictable characteristics of genre

3.3 punctuate to support readers

3.4 use surface features of text (boldface, italics, highlights, underlines) to support readers

3.5 use pictures, graphs, headings, paragraphs to support readers

A4. Decoding

4.1 use sight words to increase fluency

4.2 build bank of sight words by connecting words with similar meanings and patterns

4.3 use phonetic knowledge to support word predictions

4.4 use known prefixes, root words, suffixes to analyze unknown words (structural analysis)

A5. Connections

5.1 make personal connections to text

5.2 see connections between and among texts (genre, author, style, topic)

5.3 discover similarities and differences between and among texts

5.4 see connections between world events and text

A6. Responses

6.1 move from "seeing" the words to "living" the words on the page

6.2 understand that language can produce emotional or physical responses while reading

6.3 see their spoken responses as support for written responses

6.4 imagine themselves in the book (character, events)

6.5 find comfort, enjoyment, and new ways of thinking through reading

A7. Purpose of text

7.1 establish purpose for reading a text (information, enjoyment)

7.2 infer the author's purpose for writing the text

7.3 use text supports to help obtain information from the text (table of contents, glossary, index, references, footnotes, visuals)

7.4 understand patterns of informational text organization (sequence/
directions, cause/effect, problem/solution, listing/description,
comparison/contrast)

7.5 discover cue words that indicate type of informational text structures (sequence: first, then, next, finally)

7.6 use cue words as a support for reading, remembering, and recounting information from text

A8. Monitor reading

8.1 recognize when text stops making sense and loses meaning

8.2 develop strategies for maintaining focus during reading

8.3 make notes or use aids (Post-its, markers, charts) to keep track of
information

8.4 establish self-questioning strategies in order to support, anticipate,
and remember significant ideas from the text (What should I
remember from this paragraph? How will I remember it? What is
the connection between this chapter and the last one I read?)

8.5 identify areas in text causing confusion (word meaning, sentence
structures, insufficient/inappropriate background knowledge, readability, literary devices, plot-character confusion)

8.6 see that readers use a repertoire of strategies for overcoming text
confusion and maintaining reading focus

I believe these elements provide evidence of effective reading habits. As we
observe and assess students during our shared reading experiences, we are able
to see readers move through this continuum as they develop fluency and competence. Typically, readers will not move through the chart from one knowledge
level to the next, and I would hope that teachers wouldn't try to "teach" each of
these indicators in a hierarchical manner. These reading foundations will
develop fairly simultaneously in a classroom or home where language use is
rich and varied and children are introduced to a wide range of reading. To support continued development, we choose shared texts that introduce incremen-
tally more challenging material and give students more opportunities to take
responsibility for holding themselves and their classmates responsible for learning from those texts.

The assessment tool we have just discussed is analytic in nature. Perhaps
the real test of whether students have solid foundations for reading is whether
they want to read. Do they ask for time in class to read? Do they ask for other
books like the one you just read? Are they like Rick, the main character in Will
Hobbs's novel *The Maze*?

Rick hadn't been a reader before. That had come with taking refuge in the library. But he's discovered that he liked reading, liked it a lot. It enabled him to go places in his head, places very far from Blue Canyon.

He still couldn't sit down and just start reading. It usually took him five or ten minutes. He'd let his mind wander, thinking about things. As soon as he got bored doing that, he started reading. (12–13)

In Allan Wigfield's summary report of findings related to children's reading motivations, he highlights the importance of taking the time and giving support in order to develop intrinsic motivation for reading. "Although both kinds of motivation [extrinsic, intrinsic] can increase children's reading, a great deal of evidence now shows that intrinsic motivations lead to more sustained involvement in different activities, including reading" (1). Taking the time and providing the support necessary for building strong reading foundations enables students to add new learning to solid beginnings. Shared reading provides a safe approach for getting those foundations in place.

Assessing the Value of Shared Reading for Language Acquisition

Another area where we would expect to see evidence that students had internalized strategies is in the ability to understand new and difficult words they encounter in their reading. After years of looking words up in a dictionary, writing them in sentences, and memorizing definitions for tests, becoming independent word learners is often difficult for older students. Assessment of progress toward independence in word learning should include determining whether students have multiple word-learning strategies. I think many students have come to believe that word lists grow on trees, just as the earl tells Milo in *The Phantom Tollbooth* (Juster):

"Dictionopolis is the place where all the words in the world come from. They're grown right here in our orchards."

"I didn't know that words grew on trees," said Milo timidly.

"Where did you think they grew?" shouted the earl irritably. A small crowd began to gather to see the little boy who didn't know that letters grew on trees.

"I didn't know they grew at all," admitted Milo even more timidly. Several people shook their heads sadly.

"Well, money doesn't grow on trees, does it?" demanded the count.

"I've heard not," said Milo.

"Then something must. Why not words?" exclaimed the undersec-retary triumphantly. The crowd cheered his display of logic and contin-ued about its business.

"To continue," continued the minister impatiently. "Once a week by royal proclamation the word market is held here in the great square and people come from everywhere to buy the words they need or trade in the words they haven't used."

"Our job," said the count, "is to see that all the words sold are proper ones, for it wouldn't do to sell someone a word that had no meaning or didn't exist at all . . ." (42)

Assessment for evidence of growth in word learning would include any or all of the following knowledge and strategy elements:

- Knowledge that fluent readers make choices about whether an individual word needs to be known in order to make sense of the reading.
- If a reader deems a word unnecessary, he may skip over the word.
- Readers sometimes skip an unknown word, read to the end of the sen-tence to gain context, and then begin the sentence again to see if they can now figure out what the word means.
- Readers can use structural analysis to figure out some words. They know word parts (prefixes, root words, suffixes) and are able to combine the knowledge of the parts to predict word meaning.
- Readers use local context to figure out the meaning of unknown words (the surrounding words in a sentence).
- Readers use global context to figure out the meaning or get a sense of meaning for an unknown word (glossary, tone, parentheticals, visual sup-port, footnotes/endnotes, author's purpose).
- Readers use background knowledge to create associations that might help them figure out the unknown word.
- Readers can remember words by making conscious connections to a larger context (words like *bigotry, stereotyping, bias* can all be stored under the concept of prejudice).
- Readers use resources to help them figure out words (other people, dic-tionary, thesaurus, reference materials).
- Readers know that the more they read, the more new words they will know.

Assessment of these elements of knowledge and strategy can occur in a variety of ways. If using tests to check for meaning, students can be asked to apply the word rather than simply define it. The student exam from Ann Bailey's eighth-grade class in Long Beach, California (see Figure 8.1) provides students with an opportunity to demonstrate their knowledge of word meanings. However, they do this not by matching the meaning to a definition but by

Figure 8.1

CONNECTIONS

Read each question and think. Answer each question completely. You will probably need to use more than one sentence for your answer. 1.) The vocabulary word must be used in your response. 2.) Write with complete sentences. 3.) Use proper punctuation and capitalization. 4.) Your handwriting must be legible. (Each response is worth four points.)

1. Describe a situation which required you to be **somber**. Where were you? Why were you **somber**?

I was somber when they play a mean joke on me and I didn't like it. We where at my aunts house playing and I was somber for the whole day.

2. Write about why a person might appear **sallow**? What would cause someone to look **sallow**?

A person might appear sallow when they find out about something bad, like if some body they knew die.

3. What **chaos** have you ever created? What did you do to create the **chaos**?

The chaos I created was a big one because I throw Games, toys, clothes all over my room but at the end I clean it up.

4. What sort of books **intrigue** you? What about them do you find **intriguing**?

The sorts of books that intrigue me are Mystery. I get all into the book and I can stop reading because it's really good.

5. What should our school do to prevent public areas like the restrooms and the cafeteria from becoming **filthy**?

Cur school should recycle and make students receive a punishment if they dont throw the trash were they have to so this won't be a filthy place.

6. Describe something you **exaggerated** about when talking to a friend.

... when I was talking to my friends was when I saw some movie and I say it was the book and then they could go see it it had alot of action and the movie wasn't to good.

7. When have you acted **hastily**? What did you do? Why did you act in **haste**?

I acted hastily when I was going to school because I didn't look at the time and I lookedat it it was really late so I went to school.

8. Most people have one behavior they **loathe**. What behavior do you see in yourself or in others that you **loathe**?

The behavior I see in my self or loathe is that I dont like ... and look bad at them. I als see that other people do that to.

9. Think of someone you know who is **docile**. What does that person do that makes you think he or she is **docile**?

my neice is really docile she wants to go with me everyday and she would do what I ask her to do.

10. Why would the crew in The True Confessions of Charlotte Doyle want to **avenge** Cranick's injury? Why would they seek revenge on Captain Jaggery?

They wanted to take avenge for cranick's injury because captain Jaggery caute his hand of.

transferring their word knowledge to a new context or discussing the word in relation to a character or event in a previously shared text.

Shared reading often provides you with a quick assessment of language students may never have encountered. Their puzzled expressions and questions can quickly tell you that you have uncovered a word-learning opportunity. During a shared reading of Yep's *Child of the Owl*, Ann realized her students had only a vague sense of idiomatic expressions. The expressions either made no sense because they sounded like nonsense, or students had a skewed sense of the word because their interpretations were concrete rather than symbolic. After a study of idioms, Ann asked her students to apply some of the idioms

Figure 8.2

Idioms   Child of the Owl   39/40 5 good

Answer the following questions with thoughtful, sensible responses making sure the underlined expression is written in your response. (1) Write with complete sentences. (2) Hint: use the question in your response. Use proper punctuation and capitalization.(3) Write legibly. (4) Each response is worth four points based on the above directions.

1. Who is your bosom buddy? What makes him or her your bosom buddy?

4   Jessica is my bosom buddy what makes her my bosom buddy is that she is nice and I could trust her in everything.

2. Describe a time you would have liked to tell someone to get off your back.

4   I will tell someone to get off my back will I'm in a bad mood.

3. Think of a time when you were a real pill. Write about what you did.

3   I was a pill last time when wanted my cousin to let me borrow her pans I was really pilling her with that. ??

4. What situation causes (or has caused) you to push the panic button. Describe the cause.

4   The thing that made me push the panic bottom was when They through away my favorite shirt.

5. Which of your belongings would you like to chuck out? Why would you choose those objects to chuck?   pants?

4   I would like to chuck out my pans because they are old and I dont like them any no more so I want to chuck them out.

6. Do you have good taste in clothing? Why do you think so?

4   I think I have good taste because all the clothing I buy my cousin and every one likes it.

they had discovered in their shared text to their own lives (see Figure 8.2). Shared reading provided the opportunity for the assessment, and Ann created an evaluation tool to measure and grade their understanding of what she had taught.

Independent word learners extend their knowledge of words beyond the parameters of an exam in order to use the word in their writing and talk. In Jennifer Economos-Green's class, her students collect words from their independent and shared reading. The words they collect are words they believe everyone should know. These words are displayed on a "Words (we need to know) Wall" (see Figure 8.3).

In Lori Benitiz's class at Washington Intensive Learning Center in Long Beach, California, students in her drama class always connect word learning as part of the work they do together. For example, when her students were doing a choral reading with "The Song of the Centipede" from Dahl's *James and the Giant Peach,* Lori discovered her students didn't understand many of the words. When she could see that it was lack of understanding of language that was causing the difficulty, she helped them develop a strategy for remembering a new word by creating a visual image connected to the word. The example from

Figure 8.3

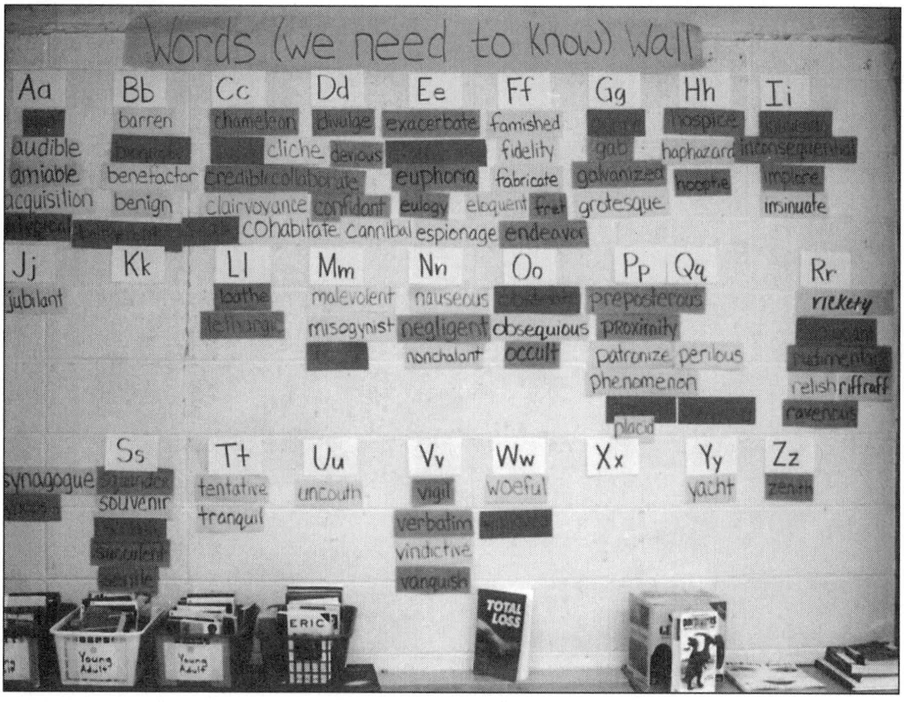

one group of students for the word *gnat* is certainly a memorable image (see Figure 8.4). Over time, Lori will be able to assess her students' use of this strategy by asking them what they see when they hear a word and what clues in the text made them see that.

In *Reading for Meaning,* van den Broek and Kremer cite the critical role that assessment plays in comprehension: "Teachers can explicitly influence goal formation through the specific instructions or rationale that they provide for a reading activity. They can also implicitly affect reading goals, such as by the methods they select to assess comprehension" (15). When our goal for students is that they have internalized a range of strategies for making sense of text, we should assess in ways that ask students to apply those strategies in the act of meaning making. In all the classrooms mentioned previously, teachers were assessing word knowledge; in two of the examples (Bailey and Benitiz), those assessments produced grades.

Figure 8.4

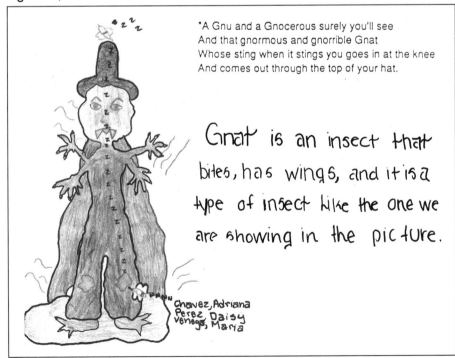

Assessing Reading Paths to Content Literacy

For content literacy, there are two broad assessment goals: assessing students' abilities to access the texts that contain content knowledge, and assessing the breadth and depth of their content knowledge together with their ability to make that knowledge personally meaningful.

When using texts that contain content reading, I would want to assess whether students knew how to judge the considerateness of the text. If a text is considerate, it contains reading supports that are predictable, consistent, and coherent, and that make the text readable and interesting. If a text is inconsiderate, it lacks obvious text supports and has text that is not engaging or has extreme variations in readability. Giving students the opportunity to compare and contrast texts helps them develop a barometer for the supports they might need to depend on in order to make the text coherent.

Using as an example Joy Hakim's series of social studies texts, *A History of US*, we can explore the level of considerateness of the text. This series is simply the best social studies series I have ever seen in terms of considerate text. It is readable, consistent, coherent, and engaging. In one of the middle schools where we are using this series, the students ask to read the books during independent reading time—a first in my experience as an educator! By examining the first two pages of Chapter 33 in Book 9 (see Figure 8.5), we can elicit from students the elements that are there to support their reading:

- It begins with a story of one person affected by this historical event.
- The language is interesting and readable.
- It uses conventions such as parentheses for asides to readers: "Reports of Japanese atrocities in Nanking, China, and elsewhere are horrible (and turn out to be true)" (145).
- The chapter title is intriguing: "Forgetting the Constitution." It makes us wonder about these events.
- The chapter uses poignant photographs. The photographs invite readers to imagine themselves in the situation.
- The author of the text talks to the reader:
  "What had they done? Just a minute, and I'll get to that. But first, imagine that you are Haruko. You have some hard decisions to make, and you need to make them quickly. What will you choose to take with you? Sorry your dog can't go. You'll have to give her away. Books? Games? Toys? Not if they are heavy" (144–145).

Figure 8.5

When students use this text as well as others available to them, they are able to demonstrate their knowledge of how to use text supports when the text is interesting, and how to use them to overcome texts that are challenging. As an assessment, you could offer reading partners the opportunity to use the Content Brainstorming form (I.28, Appendix I) prior to reading a chapter of their textbooks. In this form, students are asked to use the chapter title, key words, headings and subheadings, pictures, and captions in order to anticipate chapter content by developing predictions and connections and asking questions to focus their reading. For the next chapter of reading, students could make their own graphic maps illustrating the supports that helped them make sense of the content. By giving students the opportunity to assess text supports during a shared reading, they are able to focus on the cognitive task of strategic reading with the voice support of another reader. This provides you with the opportunity to see if they are struggling with understanding the supports or with decoding the text.

Another way to assess content literacy is through the use of Costa's Questioning Strategy (Costa and Kallick 2000). Costa's strategy highlights the importance of asking questions at three different levels: gathering and recalling information, making sense of gathered information, and applying and evaluating actions in novel situations. He suggests asking students to gather the knowledge they have related to a concept or event prior to asking them to apply that information to new concepts or situations. As a way to clarify for students what they are asked to do, Costa suggests the use of cue words as we model thinking and questioning at each level:

- Gathering and recalling information—name, define, observe, match, select, or describe
- Making sense of information—summarize, identify, classify, organize, or form an analogy
- Apply and evaluate information—predict, plan, hypothesize, and evaluate new situations

After teacher modeling of these levels of thinking and questioning, students can create guides for themselves and their classmates. In the process of creating the guide, students are recalling information, analyzing information, determining importance, and synthesizing knowledge as they also review their reading. Students can design a guide that would anticipate the questions they believe teachers might ask in order to determine if students had learned the essential information from a reading. The level of questions they create will provide you with an assessment of their knowledge base as well as their ability to sort through the wealth of information included in a single chapter of a textbook. If we look inside Christine Landaker's social studies classroom at Liberty Middle School in Orlando, Florida, we can see that when she used Costa's strategy with her students, she found she learned as much about her teaching as she did about her students' learning:

> We began our work by looking at literal-level questioning and why answering those questions doesn't require a lot of thought. I shared some of the thinking/questioning terms from Costa's Questioning Strategy and asked them to think about the kinds of questions I could ask that would show me that a student was reading and thinking about the reading. "What kinds of questions, if a student could answer them, would show me they had read, understood, and thought about the chapter?" As you will see, each of them wrote two questions, and these sparked more discussion on higher-level questioning.
>
> Summarize the chapter.
>
> Compare Eisenhower and Nixon.
>
> Contrast Eisenhower's domestic policies with George W. Bush's domestic policies.
>
> Organize by date the most important events in the chapter.

Predict what might have happened if Adlai Stevenson had won the election.

If Eisenhower were president now, how might he handle America's "War on Terrorism"?

Prepare a speech Eisenhower might have made promoting his social policies.

I asked them to go deeper and got some interesting results. Some of them asked good questions, and some of them simply tried to use the terminology without having any idea what it meant. This was a classic example of "If we give her what she wants, maybe she'll shut up." Except that in some cases, the questions were so garbled and nonsensical that it was scary, so we talked some more. Then, after students had read a chapter about the decade they were studying, they came up with five questions about the chapter. Same kind of issue. So, to drive home the point that the questions have to make sense, tomorrow they're trading them with their group members and trying to answer them. The range of questions is represented by the following ones:

1910s: Describe what a family's life would be like if they were following a policy of "rationing" like the one in WWI.

1920s: How did parents/the older generation feel about the "flapper" style of the younger generation? Compare this with how parents/the older generation feel about the younger generation's styles today.

Draw a map of Lindbergh's solo flight across the Atlantic.

1930s: Compare/contrast life for white people and life for African-Americans during the Depression.

What made life more difficult for African-Americans than for white people during the Depression?

It was a good lesson for me about the kinds of language that I *haven't* been using with them this year (though I can think of other language I haven't used with them, and that has been a good thing). So Costa's questioning is a great teacher evaluation tool as well, I think. Are we teaching the kids the language to go along with the higher-order thinking we want them to use? In my case, sadly, it appears not.

Christine's reflection on her teaching and learning is probably more significant than what the students learned at this point. As she is finding her way through an assessment that will ultimately lead to evaluation in her classroom, she is refining her thinking about language, the tasks she asks of students, and how to help students move to deeper understandings of what they read. For her students, there is the safety net of shared reading in all of this. They are able to explore these ideas with others reading the same text.

We can also assess students' developing understandings of content literacy by asking them to demonstrate their knowledge and processes at five levels:

- Activate prior knowledge by asking, "What do I already know?"
- Build content knowledge by asking, "What do I need to know?"
- Check for understanding by asking, "What am I learning?"
- Make connections to reading by asking, "What does this mean to me?"
- Apply knowledge by asking, "How will I use what I've learned?

We can immediately assess whether students have internalized the reading strategies we teach by using exit slips after a lesson. Exit slips ask students to respond to the learning and the learning conditions that take place for them on a given day in class. Teachers create an exit slip prompt, which students complete at the end of class. The slips can contain a single question such as, "What did you learn today?" or more detailed prompts such as, "List the five steps to reporting a scientific process." In all cases, the exit slips can be used by teachers as they plan instruction for the next day because they are able to see what students still need to learn.

In Mary McDaniel's seventh-grade class at Gompers Secondary School in San Diego, she uses the following generic prompts, and students respond to the one they need for that day (see Figure 8.6). Each student can write about the one he chooses, and Mary responds to those needing a response. She can also form study groups based on areas of common need.

- Write about something new you learned today.
- What made learning easy/difficult for you today?
- What questions were left unanswered?
- How did what we learned today connect to the work we did yesterday/last week/previously?
- How will I know when you have mastered this concept?
- What new questions do you have?

These quick assessments are extremely efficient in making sure we don't move on and leave students behind. In my own classroom, I used only one of these prompts each day, and all students responded to the same prompt. Some days, the exit slip prompt simply stated, "Tell me something you need to tell me about

Figure 8.6

Exit Slip

Date 11-28-01

Name Anthony Sauritamangkol

Respond to one or more of the following prompts:

- Write about something new you learned today.
- What made learning easy/difficult for you today?
- What was left unanswered?
- How did what we learned today connect to the work we did yesterday/last week/previously?
- How will I know when you have mastered this concept?
- What new questions do you have?

I have a question, how do you put the response on the reading log.

Please read the instruction sheet I gave you - It has heading information, what to include + how to start

class as I plan for tomorrow." As you can see from Figure 8.6, Mary's students have taken this assessment tool and found a way to get the support they need to continue learning.

If the shared reading we have done with students has been meaningful and memorable, there will be noticeable changes in their content knowledge, their spirit of inquiry, the range of strategies in their independent learning repertoires, and their ability to demonstrate new learning. In *Learning to Read,* Margaret Meek writes, "But no exercise, however well ordered, will have the effect of a genuine reading task that encourages the reader to learn what he wants to know as a result of his own initiative" (207). The first and most important assessment is whether students want to extend their content knowledge through further reading.

All these questions and learning processes are incorporated when teachers work with students to design performances that demonstrate new understandings of content. I had the opportunity to see some wonderful evidence of the value of shared reading forming the basis for acquisition of content knowledge and the effect of both on students' abilities to demonstrate new understandings of content from Jenny Orr, a middle school science teacher in Macon, Georgia.

When Jenny decided to study spiders with her students at Miller Middle School, she discovered there were only a couple of pertinent paragraphs in her textbook. She had received a pamphlet on spiders from Callaway Gardens and that began their collaborative pursuit for understanding spiders. On some days, their shared reading came from the Internet; on other days, they used pamphlets and articles they had found in their research.

Each student chose a spider that was particularly interesting to him, which led to student writing and creation of models of spiders. These were displayed in the hallway "In the Garden of Good and Evil Spiders." Spiders were displayed with "spider specs," which included information on habitat, location, method of food getting as well as unusual or interesting facts about the spiders. Students then worked together to create a newspaper spiders would want to read. Figure 8.7 shows the range of learning Jenny could assess with this tool. Using the newspaper as a performance, Jenny was able to assess students' knowledge of content about spiders and use of specialized content vocabulary. However, the real value of both the shared reading and the assessment came as her students continued to read, research, and share the excitement long after the unit was completed:

My students learned so many interesting things about spiders. For many weeks after the unit, students would come rushing into my room from time to time with a jar containing one of the spiders we had studied or an egg case or a beautiful web they were able to preserve. It's really easy for me to get excited about these kinds of things because it is my passion. Seeing my seventh graders get excited about what they initially thought to be such an uncool subject and seeing them take an interest in the world around them creates an exhilaration that nothing else can match.

Figure 8.7

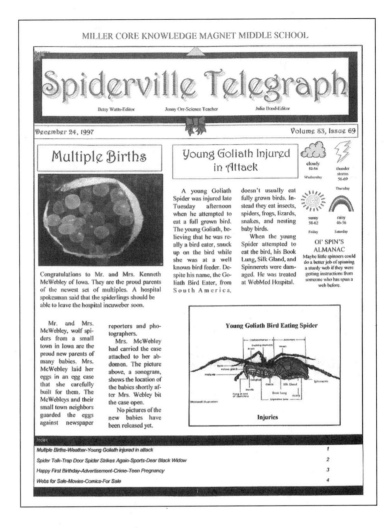

If students want to read more content texts, know how to overcome challenging texts, see personal relevance for reading, and are able to make connections between and among multiple texts, you will know that the use of shared reading has helped create a solid content and strategic reading foundation for your students. When students begin to think like scientists, mathematicians, artists, and historians, you will know they have begun to see themselves in the texts you have shared.

In *The Well,* Mildred Taylor recalls the role of a good story in her development as a literate adult: "Wherever the family gathered, in our northern home where I grew up or in the south where I was born, the stories were told. Some of the stories were humorous, some were tragic, but all taught me a history not then written in textbooks. They taught me a history about myself" (7). Content literacy is life literacy. Providing opportunities for students to see themselves as part of all that has gone before and critical to all that is to come requires us to use texts and assessment/evaluation approaches that make those life lessons real—especially in our content classrooms.

The Exponential Effect of Being on the Same Page

When shared reading is used as an approach to create classrooms and schools filled with engaged readers, we begin to see the impact of that reading throughout the school. At Los Nietos Middle School, when the principal, Dr. John Bailey, got excited about shared reading at his school, he began reading young adult literature. Each week he wrote a book review of his pick of the week, and teachers read the review to their students (see samples in Figure 8.8). Soon students

Figure 8.8

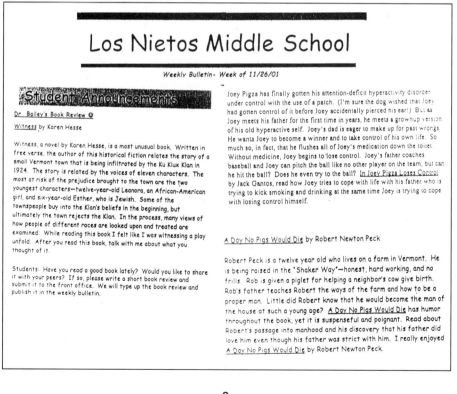

Figure 8.9

began coming to his office and talking with him in the hallways about the books he was reading. When I first visited that school, the hallways were bare; the last time I was there, the hallways were lined with student-created advertisements of the books they were enjoying during shared reading (see Figure 8.9).

Effective shared reading programs are infectious; the broad value of that reading is often obvious in classrooms. In Lynnette Elliott's eighth-grade classroom at Odyssey Middle School, the impact of their shared reading is seen all over the classroom. There are charts that synthesize their developing understandings of the way our cultural values get passed along through the picture books we share with children. Student writing is displayed along with the shared reading that inspired the writing. Two of my favorites were written by students who internalized the concept of not wanting to lose something after a

Figure 8.10

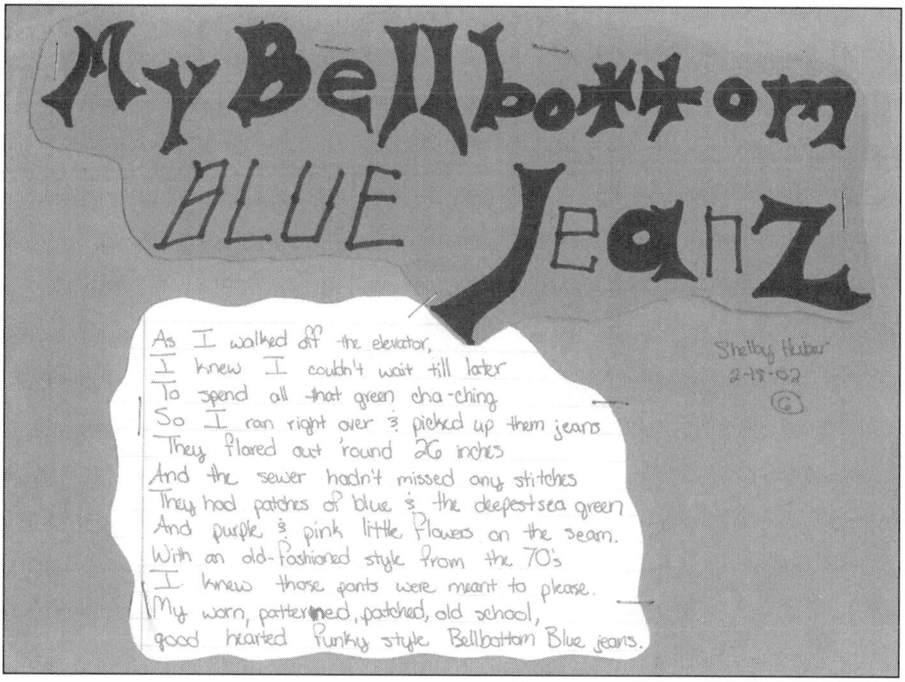

shared reading of Maya Angelou's poem "No Losers No Weepers." The writer of the poem in Figure 8.10 doesn't want to lose her bell-bottom blue jeans, and the writer of the poem in Figure 8.11 doesn't want to lose her home girlz—both valuable when you are in the eighth grade.

At Gompers Secondary School, all the windows surrounding the principal's office are filled with new books that are available for teachers and students to read. As teachers became avid readers of these books, the principal established a budget for teachers to buy individual copies or sets of books they wanted for shared reading in their classrooms. Soon, evidence of that emphasis on shared reading spread throughout the school. The walls outside Elizabeth Trude's classroom are lined with "Guess Who I Am" posters based on their shared reading of Jean Ferris's novel *Bad*. In this book the main character says that what she shows on the outside isn't who she is on the inside. Students created their own versions of what they show and what they hide (see Figures 8.12a and 8.12b), and those posters prompted other students to ask for copies of the book. While such displays are common in elementary schools, it is a rare high school where students advertise their reading in the hallways and offices. I am never on this school campus that I don't see students stopping to see the posters and

Figure 8.11

books displayed in the windows. Every day I'm there, students stop the principal and the staff developer to ask if they can order specific book titles just for
them and their friends.

One of the best assessments of the value of shared reading is documenting
students' personal connections to the reading you do. When students begin to
make personal connections to shared reading, they develop confidence in giving
voice to their opinions. In Elaine Coulson's class in Tampa, Florida, her students
documented their reader response voices by giving advice to Curtis and
Lateesha, characters in Paul Fleischman's *Seedfolks,* after a shared reading of
the book (see Figure 8.13). Students don't always agree with the responses of
their classmates, but in assessing the value of shared reading one of the things
we would want to see is that students have developed the ability to connect,
respond, and support their opinions.

Figure 8.12a

Figure 8.12b

Figure 8.13

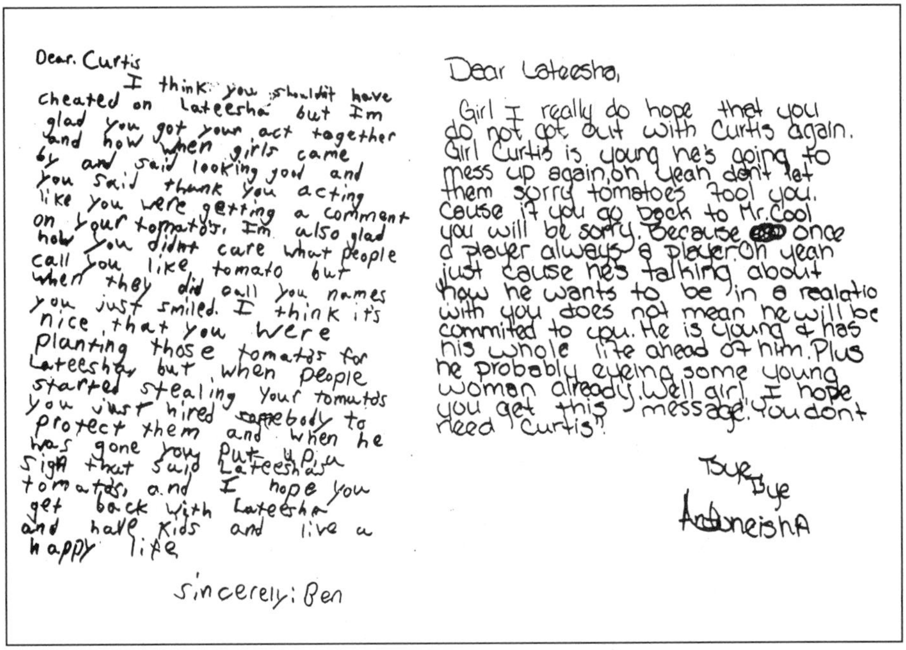

Dear. Curtis
        I think you shuldn't have
cheated on Lateesha but Im
glad you got your act together
and how when girls came
by and said looking good and
you said thank you acting
like you were getting a comment
on your tomatos. Im also glad
how you didnt care what people
call you like tomato but
when they did call you names
you just smiled. I think it's
nice that you were
planting those tomatos for
Lateesha but when people
started stealing your tomatos
you just hired somebody to
protect them and when he
has gone you put up your
sign that said Lateesha's
tomatos, and I hope you
get back with Lateesha
and have kids and live a
happy life

                sincerely; Ben

Dear Lateesha,

Girl I really do hope that you
do not got out with Curtis again.
Girl Curtis is young he's going to
mess up again, oh yeah dont let
them sorry tomatoes fool you.
Cause if you go back to Mr.Cool
you will be sorry. Because and once
a player always a player.Oh yeah
just cause he's talking about
how he wants to be in a realatio
with you does not mean he will be
commited to you. He is young & has
his whole life ahead of him.Plus
he probably eyeing some young
woman already.Well girl I hope
you get this message. You dont
need Curtis".

                        Bye Bye
                        Antoneisha

A Word or Two About Test Preparation

Would a chapter on assessment and evaluation be complete without a word about standardized testing? In a time of high-stakes testing, it is important that students understand what will be expected of them as readers when they take part in mandated testing. When we read with our students and when they read independently, we assess and evaluate their progress with multiple measures ranging from learning logs and academic journals to essays and content-specific tests. We factor in variables such as talk, interest, motivation, participation, and behavior.

When students come to a standardized test, they are asked to demonstrate learning in ways that may seem foreign to them. In a test situation, students are being asked to demonstrate background knowledge and learning that may have occurred over many years. They are often asked to apply both in novel ways, such as figuring out the humor and literary allusion in the Mark Stivers cartoon in Figure 8.14. Very few high-stakes tests are actually matched to a prescribed curriculum for all schools within that state, so how do we prepare students for information they *might* need to know?

My first and best answer to that question is always to err on the side of reading too much. Read with students every day and challenge them to read a

Figure 8.14

lot on their own. In the course of the shared reading, point out language that is unique and interesting. Read informational texts that build background knowledge for other reading they will do outside of school. As students see and hear words in a meaningful context, they acquire language and knowledge that will serve as a foundation for any test. However, there is one other element that is often left to chance or osmosis but that would help students transfer their knowledge to a test-taking situation—familiarity with typical test questions.

We can explain to students that the test is only assessing their knowledge and understanding of reading as we do on a daily basis, but in this case the format for assessment will be different than what we would typically use. Throughout the year, we can revisit shared texts we have read and enjoyed. The students can recall the ways they showed us they learned something from those texts. As a contrast, we can then show that even if test makers used the same text, they would ask students to demonstrate their learning by asking different kinds of questions than we would ask. Point out that the reading part is not something new to them; understanding the language and format of the questions may be the part that is new.

In one of the schools where I work and learn, teachers revisited shared texts from the reading they had done during the school year as a way to demonstrate test questions and specialized language. Familiarity with the texts gave students the opportunity to focus just on the questions and the language of the questions that they might encounter during testing. As is evident from the following questions related to S. E. Hinton's *The Outsiders,* we would not want to reduce shared reading to this type of questioning very often:

Reading

We all had money to get in, but Dally hated to do things the legal way. He liked to show that he didn't care whether there was a law or not. He went around trying to break laws. We went to the rows of seats in front of the concession stand to sit down. Nobody was there except two girls who were sitting down front. Dally eyed them coolly, then walked down the aisle and sat right behind them. I had a sick feeling that Dally was up to his usual tricks, and I was right. He started talking, loud enough for the two girls to hear. He started out bad and got worse. Dallas could talk awful dirty if he wanted to and I guess he wanted to then. I felt my ears get hot. Two-Bit or Steve or even Soda would have gone right along with him, just to see if they could embarrass the girls, but that kind of kicks just doesn't appeal to me. I sat there, struck dumb, and Johnny left hastily to get a Coke. (21)

1. The passage *mainly* tells that—
   a. The Greasers like movies
   b. Dallas can be very rude
   c. Ponyboy is different than most of the other Greasers
   d. Two-Bit and Soda go along with Dally's tricks
2. In this selection, Dally shows that he is all of these *except*—
   a. A loud talker
   b. A respectful person
   c. A law breaker
   d. A user of bad language
3. There is enough information in this article to *show* that—
   a. Ponyboy likes to be with Dally
   b. Johnny doesn't give him any money
   c. Dally treats girls courteously
   d. Ponyboy does not approve of Dally's behavior.

Then he walked down the aisle and sat right *behind them.*

4. In which sentence does the word *right* mean the same thing as in the sentence above?
   a. Turn *right* at the corner.
   b. You have the *right* to an education.
   c. I had the *right* answer on the test.
   d. He was *right* there when I needed him.

Language Arts

Directions: Read the sentence in the box. Choose the sentence that best corrects the·underlined portion of the sentence.

5. *They're shirt was* madras.
    a. There shirts are
    b. Their shirt were
    c. Their shirts were
    d. Correct as is
6. Johnny *and me is greasers.*
    a. and I are greasers.
    b. and I are Greasers.
    c. and me are Greasers.
    d. Correct as is
7. Mine shoe are blue.
    a. My shoe are blue.
    b. Mine shoes are blue.
    c. My shoe is blue.
    d. Correct as is
8. Ponyboy and Johnny *ran away the church was* on a hill.
    a. ran away, the church was on a hill.
    b. ran away. the church was on a hill.
    c. ran away. The church was on a hill.
    d. Correct as is
9. Steve was accused of being a lookout for *the crime King was also* on trial for the same crime.
    a. the crime. King was also
    b. the crime, King was also
    c. the crime. And King was also
    d. Correct as is

When test preparation questions concern familiar texts, it is easier to support students in how they would transfer their knowledge of test-taking strategies to unfamiliar texts. Shared reading is a significant support for students in this process as they develop strategies and skills for taking challenging tests. As students become more confident in both their reading and abilities to understand a task, we can focus on the real value of shared reading for lifelong learning.

Shared Reading and a Passion for Teaching

When I think of the value of shared reading in my own classroom, I don't always think of its value in terms of what happened with students when I used that approach. I sometimes think of the many times shared reading made me feel accomplished as a teacher. With each positive experience I had in choosing a text that was just right for my students, I knew I was providing students with the skills and strategies they needed for the rest of their lives. Each time a student asked if I had any more books like the one I read that day, I knew I had helped make another reader.

These are difficult times for students and teachers. If we use the media and politicians rather than individual signs of improvement as a barometer of our success with students, the art and craft of teaching turn into work that is not very satisfying. A ninth-grade teacher recently e-mailed me: "I feel as if I just have so much to accomplish that no matter how much we do, I go home at the end of the day feeling like a failure. I watch the news and hear about ineffective teachers and think, 'That's me they're talking about.'"

As with all learning, success breeds success. As teachers feel successful with the improvement they see from shared reading, they become even more dedicated to finding ways to help all students unlock the printed word. Alice Hoffman knows about locked doors. In her novel *The River King,* she writes, "Throughout his life, Gus had been taught that for every illusion there was a practical explanation, and such an education can prove worthwhile. After an upbringing such as this, Gus was aware of possibilities someone else might have overlooked, or taken for granted, or simply ignored. This much he knew for certain: for every locked trunk, there was sure to be a key" (60).

In an information age, language is the key to opening locked doors. Those who are deprived of language suffer in school and in life. In Miguel Angel Ruiz's book *The Four Agreements: A Practical Guide to Personal Freedom,* he reminds us of the importance of words: "The word is not just a sound or a written symbol. The word is a force; it is the power you have to express and communicate, to think, and thereby to create the events in your life" (26). During shared reading, when we are all on the same page, *all* children have access to information and knowledge—*all* children have the opportunity to develop skills and strategies to create and shape the events of their own lives. Could shared reading have any greater value?

Appendix A

Shared Reading to Support Word Study

Grammar and Style

Disch, Thomas. 1997. *A Child's Garden of Grammar.*

Gordon, Karen Elizabeth. 1997. *Torn Wings and Faux Pas.*

———. 1993a. *The Deluxe Transitive Vampire.*

———. 1993b. *The New Well-Tempered Sentence.*

Hale, Constance. 1999. *Sin and Syntax.*

Lederer, Richard. 1987. *Anguished English.*

Maizels, Jennie, and Kate Petty. 1996. *The Amazing Pop-Up Grammar Book.*

Morris, Evan. 2000. *The Word Detective: Solving the Mysteries Behind Those Pesky Words and Phrases.*

Wallraff, Barbara. 2000. *Word Court.*

Parts of Speech

Cleary, Brian. 2000. *A Mink, A Fink, A Skating Rink: What Is a Noun?*

Heller, Ruth. 1987. *A Cache of Jewels and Other Collective Nouns.*

———. 1989a. *Many Luscious Lollipops: A Book About Adjectives.*

———. 1989b. *Merry-Go-Round: A Book About Nouns.*

———. 1991a. *Kites Sail High: A Book About Verbs.*

———. 1991b. *Up, Up, and Away: A Book About Adverbs.*

———. 1995. *Behind the Mask: A Book About Prepositions.*

———. 1997. *Mine, All Mine: A Book About Pronouns.*

———. 1998. *Fantastic! Wow! And Unreal! A Book About Interjections and Conjunctions.*

Terban, Marvin. 1986. *Your Foot's on My Feet, and Other Tricky Nouns.*

Vocabulary

Amato, Mary. 2000. *The Word Eater.*

Bryson, Bill. 1995. *Made in America: An Informal History of the English Language in the United States.*

DeGross, Monalisa. 1994. *Donovan's Word Jar.*

Ehrlich, Eugene. 1995. *Veni, Vidi, Vici.*

Frasier, Debra. 2000. *Miss Alaineus: A Vocabulary Disaster.*

Funk, Charles Earle. 1985. *A Hog on Ice and Other Curious Expressions.*

Gordon, Karen Elizabeth. 1998. *Out of the Loud Hound of Darkness.*

Hepworth, Catherine. 1992. *Antics! An Alphabetical Anthology.*

Jacobson, John D. 1993. *Eatioms.*

Juster, Norton. 1961. *The Phantom Tollbooth.*

Konigsberg, E. L. 2000. *Silent to the Bone.*

Lederer, Richard. 1989. *Crazy English.*

Maestro, Giulio. 1983. *Riddle Romp.*

———. 1986. *What's Mite Might?*

Rees, Nigel. 1991. *The Phrase That Launched 1,000 Ships.*

Rice, Scott, ed. 1996. *It Was a Dark and Stormy Night.*

Soukhanov, Anne H. 1995. *Word Watch: The Stories Behind the Words of Our Lives.*

Stevenson, Victor. 1999. *The World of Words: An Illustrated History of Western Languages.*

Word Play

Agee, Jon. 1992. *Go Hang a Salami! I'm a Lasagna Hog!*

Charlton, James, ed. 1986. *Bred Any Good Rooks Lately?*

Eckler, Ross. 1995. *Making the Alphabet Dance.*

Falwell, Cathryn. 1998. *Word Wizard.*

Ginns, Russell. 1994. *Go Figure: Puzzles, Games and Funny Figures of Speech.*

Gwynne, Fred. 1988. *A Little Pigeon Toad.*

Janeczko, Paul. 1984. *Loads of Codes and Secret Ciphers.*

Juster, Norton. 1900. *Otter Nonsense.*

Lederer, Richard. 1988. *Get Thee to a Punnery.*

———. 1990. *The Play of Words.*

Levitt, Paul M., Douglas Burger, and Elissa Guralnick. 1989. *The Weighty Word Book.*

Maestro, Giulio. 1985. *Razzle-Dazzle Riddles.*

———. 1984. *What's a Frank Frank?*

McMillan, Bruce, and Brett McMillan. 1982. *Puniddles.*

Morice, Dave. 2001. *The Dictionary of Wordplay.*

Norr, Rita. 1994. *The Literate Puzzler.*

Suid, Murray. 1981. *Demonic Mnemonics.*

Terban, Marvin. 1982. *Eight Ate: A Feast of Homonym Riddles.*

———. 1985. *Too Hot to Hoot.*

Treat, Lawrence. 1988. *Crime and Puzzlement.*

Turner, Priscilla. 1996. *The War Between the Vowels and the Consonants.*

Tyler, Jenny. 1987. *Brain Puzzles.*

Appendix B

Resources for Content Area Shared Reading

Magazines and Newspapers

Boy's Life Magazine
P.O. Box 152350
Irving, TX 75015-2350
972-580-2088; fax 972-589-2079
http://www.bsa.scouting.org/mags/boyslife/
12 issues/$18.00

Boy's Life is published by the Boy Scouts of America for boys ages 7–17. Includes articles on nature, science, sports, and hobbies that cater to the needs and interests of young men.

Cicada Magazine
P.O. Box 300
Peru, IL 61354
http://www.musemag.com/
6 issues/$35.97

A literary magazine written by adults and young adults for children ages 14 and older. Includes poetry, novellas, fiction, nonfiction, and artwork.

Cobblestone Magazines
30 Grove Street, Suite C
Peterborough, NH 03458
800-821-0115; fax 603-924-7380
http://www.cobblestonepub.com/

Cobblestone produces a variety of nonfiction magazines for young readers dealing with American or world history, world cultures, archaeology, and science. Their publications vary in age and skill level from pre-K through secondary.

Discover Magazine
http://www.discover.com/
12 issues/$24.95

The print companion to the Discovery Channel covers space, biology, health, medicine, AIDS, computers, new technology, the environment, astronomy, ancient life, archeology, evolution, physics, mathematics, and ecology. There is also a special program for educators that includes monthly lesson plans, quizzes, and activities based on current articles and features.

Explore Magazine
P.O. Box 37590
Boone, IA 50037-0590
877-817-4395
10 issues/$21.95 (bulk orders less)

Magazine for 9–13-year-olds based on the scientific premise of how the world works. Includes behind-the-scenes stories on technology and science.

Muse Magazine
http://www.musemag.com/
10 issues/$32.97

Muse is the children's version of *Smithsonian* magazine, containing illustrated science and discovery articles for children ages 10 and up.

National Geographic World
P.O. Box 63002
Tampa, FL 33663-3002
800-647-5463
http://www.nationalgeographic.com/world/
10 issues/$17.95

Magazine for children in grades 3–6 includes articles, photos, and projects.

The Prehistoric Times
145 Bayline Circle
Folsom, CA 95630-8077
916-985-7986
http://www.prehistorictimes.com/
6 issues/$28.00

Each issue includes interviews with scientists and artists, reviews of new books, and prehistoric animal figures, plus great color illustrations and beautiful artwork.

Scholastic Classroom Magazines
2931 East McCarty Street
Jefferson City, MO 65101
800-724-6527
http://teacher.scholastic.com/products/classmags/
Scholastic produces a variety of publications at the pre-K, elementary, and secondary levels. There are magazines on current events, math, science, literature, social studies, and the fine arts. All levels include publications in a variety of languages, including Spanish, German, and French. A teacher edition is included with every order of 10 or more copies.

Sports Illustrated for Kids
P.O. Box 60001
Tampa, FL 33660-0001
800-992-0196
http://www.sikids.com/
13 issues/$29.95
Includes colorful photography and insightful, easy-to-read articles for kids. www.sikids.com is the online counterpart to *Sports Illustrated for Kids* magazine.

Stone Soup
P.O. Box 83
Santa Cruz, CA 95063
800-447-4569; fax 831-426-1161
http://www.stonesoup.com/
6 issues/$33.00
A literary magazine containing poems, essays, artwork, and stories created by 8–13-year-olds from all over the world.

Teen Ink: VOYA
Box 30
Newton, MA 02461
617-964-6800
http://www.teenink.com/nonfiction/
10 issues/$25.00
Published by the Young Authors Foundation, a nonprofit educational organization. Includes a fine collection of poetry, nonfiction, essays, book reviews, and artwork written by teens for teens.

Time for Kids
1271 6th Avenue, 25th floor
New York, NY 10020
800-777-8600
http://www.timeforkids.com/TFK/
Time for Kids, the student version of *Time* magazine, comes in three different levels: the Big Picture edition for grades K–1, the News Scoop edition for grades 2–3, and the World Report edition for grades 4–6. Each edition provides facts, stories, and games, and includes a teacher's edition. The activities contained in *Time for Kids* fulfill state and national standards.

US News & World Report for the Classroom
U.S. News Classroom Program
33 South Delaware Avenue #102
Yardley, PA 19067-9508
800-736-9623; fax 215-321-4249
http://www.usnewsclassroom.com/
49 cents per issue
Teachers can find all levels of articles and activities in subject areas such as economics, English, and social studies in each weekly issue of *US News & World Report.* Each subscription provides teachers with access to a lesson plan library, resource kits, and interactive activities.

USA Today Education
800-757-TEACH, ext. 650; fax 800-242-4595
http://www.usatoday.com/educate/home.htm
30 cents per copy/20-copy minimum
Copies of *USA Today* can be delivered daily to your classroom with a teachers' study guide for that day's paper, including lesson plans and monthly project guides.

Weekly Reader
P.O. Box 120023
Stamford, CT 06912
203-705-3500
http://www.weeklyreader.com
Weekly Reader is a four-color newspaper with an accompanying teacher's guide for students in each grade of elementary school. The company also publishes educational products for middle and high school students, including *Teen Newsweek, Current Science, Current Events, Read, Know Your World Extra, Writing!, Current Health 1 & 2,* and *Career World.*

Other Media

A & E Classroom Pages
http://www.aande.com/class/teach/index.html
Teachers can download free printable materials to accompany television programs that appear on the A&E channel.

C-Span in the Classroom
http://www.c-span.org/classroom/
Provides free teacher guides and materials for that week's programs on the C-Span channel as well as archives for previous programs.

CNN FYI
http://fyi.cnn.com/fyi/index.html
Teachers can download and print daily top stories written by CNN journalists, working in collaboration with teachers, that are appropriate in vocabulary and content for junior and senior high school students. Each story is accompanied by a full lesson plan, discussion, or activity.

Children's Lit Web Guide (lists)
http://www.ucalgary.ca/ ~ dkbrown/index.html

Kathy Schrock's Guide for Educators (list of journals, magazines, newspapers, and Web sites)
http://school.discovery.com/schrockguide/news/nsp.html

List and links of online newspapers
http://www.tesol.org/pubs/magz/wanweb/1997/wanweb9710.html

Appendix C

Shared Reading to Support Content Literacy

Art

Agee, John. 1988. *Incredible Painting of Felix Clousseau.* New York: Farrar, Straus and Giroux.
A painter becomes famous when his paintings come to life.

Anholt, Laurence. 1994. *Camille and the Sunflowers: A Story About Vincent Van Gogh.* Hauppauge, NY: Barron's.
Despite the derision of their neighbors, a young French boy and his family befriend the lonely painter who comes to their town and begin to admire his unusual paintings.

———. 1996. *Degas and the Little Dancer: A Story About Edgar Degas.* Hauppauge, NY: Barron's.
Because Marie helps her poor parents by modeling for an ill-tempered artist, she becomes a famous ballerina, but not in the way she had dreamed.

———. 1998. *Picasso and the Girl with a Ponytail: A Story About Pablo Picasso.* Hauppauge, NY: Barron's.
Sylvette gradually begins to gain self-confidence during the summer she models for the renowned artist Pablo Picasso in the French village of Vallauris.

Bjork, Christina. 1987. *Linnea: In Monet's Garden.* New York: Farrar, Straus and Giroux.
A little girl visits the home and garden of Claude Monet at Giverny, France, and learns about the artist's paintings and his life. The illustrations include photographs of the painter and his family as well as examples of his work.

Cummings, Pat. 1992. *Talking with Artists*. New York: Bradbury.
Fourteen noted children's book illustrators answer frequently asked questions. Supplies biographical information about how they became artists.

Hart, Tony. 1994. *Michelangelo*. Hauppauge, NY: Barron's.
Focuses on the childhood of the noted artist Michelangelo.

Krull, Kathleen. 1995. *Lives of the Artists: Masterpieces, Messes (and What the Neighbors Thought)*. San Diego: Harcourt Brace.
Presents the humor and the tragedies in twenty artists' lives. Includes bibliographic references and index.

Mayhew, James. 1998. *Katie and the Mona Lisa*. New York: Orchard.
At the art museum, while her grandmother dozes, Katie steps into the painting of the Mona Lisa and together they have adventures with the characters from four other well-known Renaissance paintings. Includes information about the artists.

———. 1999. *Katie Meets the Impressionists*. New York: Orchard.
On a visit to the museum, Katie climbs into five impressionist paintings and has wonderful adventures. Includes information about impressionism, the paintings shown, and their artists.

Stanley, Diane. 1994. *The Gentleman and the Kitchen Maid*. New York: Dial.
When two paintings hanging across from each other in a museum fall in love, a resourceful art student finds a way to unite the lovers. Pictures reflect the styles and elements commonly attributed to nineteen master artists, from Rembrandt to Picasso.

———. 1996. *Leonardo Da Vinci*. New York: Morrow Junior Books.
A biography of the Italian Renaissance artist and inventor who, at about age thirty, began writing his famous notebooks, which contain the outpourings of his amazing mind.

Sweeney, Joan. 1998. *Bijou, Bonbon and Beau: The Kittens Who Danced for Degas*. San Francisco: Chronicle Books.
Three little kittens create a sensation when they join dancers onstage of a Parisian theater known for its ballet and for the artist who paints there.

Willard, Nancy. 1991. *Pish, Posh, Said Hieronymus Bosch*. San Diego: Harcourt Brace.
The weird creatures that inhabit a medieval painter's home drive his housekeeper away, until a change of heart sends her back to the beasts and to Bosch in a new and loving relationship.

English

Classic Retellings

Coville, Bruce. 1994. *William Shakespeare's The Tempest, Retold by Bruce Coville.* New York: Delacorte.
A simplified prose retelling of Shakespeare's play about the exiled duke of Milan, who uses his magical powers to confront his enemies on an enchanted island.

———. 1996. *William Shakespeare's A Midsummer Night's Dream, Retold by Bruce Coville.* New York: Dial.
A simplified prose retelling of Shakespeare's play about the strange events that take place in a forest inhabited by fairies who magically transform the romantic fate of two young couples.

———. 1997. *William Shakespeare's Macbeth, Retold by Bruce Coville.* New York: Dial.
A simplified prose retelling of Shakespeare's play about a man who kills his king after hearing the prophesies of three witches.

———. 1999. *William Shakespeare's Romeo and Juliet, Retold by Bruce Coville.* New York: Dial.
A simplified prose retelling of Shakespeare's play about two young people who defy their warring families' prejudices and dare to fall in love.

Cummings, E. E. 1989. *Hist Whist.* New York: Crown.
Presents with illustrations the celebrated author's poem of scary, ghostly things.

Cutts, David E. 1982. *Edgar Allan Poe's Cask of Amontillado.* Mahwah, NJ: Troll.
After enduring many injuries of the noble Fortunato, Montresor executes the perfect revenge. Uses full color illustrations to support text.

Deary, Terry. 1999. *Top 10 Shakespeare Stories.* New York: Scholastic.
In language kids can understand, this book explores the Bard's ten best-known plays. Included is a biography of Shakespeare and a discussion of theater in his day.

Johnson, D. B. 2000. *Henry Hikes to Fitchberg.* Boston: Houghton Mifflin.
While his friend works hard to earn the train fare to Fitchburg, young Henry Thoreau walks the thirty miles through woods and fields, enjoying nature and the time to think great thoughts. Includes biographical information about Thoreau.

Loewen, Nancy. 1994. *Walt Whitman.* Mankato, MN: Creative Editions.
Examines the life of the American poet and presents some of his poems.
Can serve as a preamble to *Leaves of Grass.*

McCarty, Nick. 2000. *The Iliad.* New York: Kingfisher.
Retells the story of The Iliad in modern language with illustrations.

Nye, Robert. 1968. *Beowulf: A New Telling by Robert Nye.* New York: Hill and
Wang.
A retelling of the exploits of the Anglo-Saxon warrior Beowulf and how he
came to defeat the monster Grendel.

Osborne, Mary Pope. 1998. *Favorite Medieval Tales.* New York: Scholastic.
A collection of well-known tales from medieval Europe, including *Beowulf,
The Sword in the Stone, The Song of Roland,* and *The Island of the Lost
Children.*

Thoreau, Henry David. 1990. *Walden.* New York: Philomel Books.
In this illustrated adaptation of Thoreau's famous work, a man retreats
into the woods and discovers the joys of solitude and nature.

Vande Velde, Vivian. 2000. *The Rumpelstiltskin Problem.* Boston: Houghton
Mifflin.
A collection of variations on the familiar story of a boastful miller and the
daughter he claims can spin straw into gold.

Williams, Marcia. 1998. *Tales from Shakespeare: Seven Plays.* Cambridge, MA:
Candlewick Press.
Retells seven of Shakespeare's plays—*Romeo and Juliet, Hamlet, A
Midsummer Night's Dream, Macbeth, The Winter's Tale, Julius Caesar,* and
The Tempest—in comic book format.

Mythology

D'Aulaire, Ingri, and Edgar Parin D'Aulaire. 1962. *D'Aulaires' Book of Greek
Myths.* New York: Doubleday.
Mighty Zeus, with his fistful of thunderbolts, Athena, goddess of wisdom,
Helios the sun, greedy King Midas—here are gods, goddesses, and leg-
endary figures of ancient Greece brought to life in the myths that have
inspired great literature and art throughout the ages.

Deary, Terry. 1999. *Top 10 Greek Legends.* New York: Scholastic.
This whimsical guide explains the figures and themes of ten major Greek
myths. Readers also get a glimpse of everyday life in Ancient Greece.

Fleischman, Paul. 1996. *Dateline: Troy.* Cambridge, MA: Candlewick Press.
A retelling of the story of the Trojan War illustrated with collages featuring newspaper clippings of modern events from World War I through the Persian gulf war.

Macrone, Michael. 1992. *By Jove.* New York: HarperCollins.
A concise review of classical mythology recounts the greatest stories and reveals discoveries and twists to some of the world's most commonly held ideas about mythological figures.

Newham, Paul, and Elaine Cox. 1994. *The Outlandish Adventures of Orpheus in the Underworld.* New York: Random House.
Recreates the myth of the Greek poet-musician who charmed the whole world with the power and beauty of his song.

Osborne, Mary Pope. 1989. *Favorite Greek Myths.* New York: Scholastic.
Retells twelve tales from Greek mythology, including the stories of King Midas, Echo and Narcissus, the Golden Apples, and Cupid and Psyche.

———. 1996. *Favorite Norse Myths.* New York: Scholastic.
A collection of rarely retold tales from the Elder Edda and the Younger Edda, two six-hundred-year-old Norse manuscripts.

Wang, Dorothea DePrisco. 2002. *Myth Madness: Tales of Ancient Greece.* New York: Scholastic.
Illustrations and stories about the moods and attitudes of the ancient Greeks.

Yolen, Jane. 1991. *Wings.* San Diego: Harcourt Brace.
The story of Daedalus, the Greek master craftsman, who murdered his nephew because of envy, fled to Crete, and then, with his son, tried to fly away from Crete like a bird.

Math

Anno, Mitsumasa, and Masaichiro Anno. 1983. *Anno's Mysterious Multiplying Jar.* New York: Philomel.
Simple text and pictures introduce the mathematical concept of factorials.

———. 1987. *Anno's Math Games.* New York: Philomel.
Introduces the concept of ratio by comparing what humans would be able to do if they had bodies like different animals.

———. 1995. *Anno's Magic Seeds.* New York: Philomel.

The reader is asked to perform a series of mathematical operations integrated into the story of a lazy man who plants magic seeds and reaps an increasingly abundant harvest.

Liatsos, Sandra. 1995. *Poems to Count On.* New York: Scholastic.
Thirty-two poems and activities to help teach math concepts such as measuring, counting, money, shapes, patterns, etc.

Neuschwander, Cindy. 1997a. *Sir Cumference and the Dragon of Pi: A Math Adventure.* Watertown, MA: Charlesbridge.
When Sir Cumference drinks a potion that turns him into a dragon, his son Radius searches for the magic number known as pi, which will restore him to his former shape.

———. 1997b. *Sir Cumference and the First Round Table.* Watertown, MA: Charlesbridge.
Assisted by his knight, Sir Cumference, and using ideas offered by his wife and son, King Arthur finds the perfect shape for his table.

Pappas, Theoni. 1989. *The Joy of Mathematics: Discovering Mathematics All Around You.* San Carlos, CA: Tetra.
Designed to help the reader become aware of the inseparable relation between mathematics and the world by presenting glimpses and images of mathematics in the many facets of our lives.

———. 1991. *Math Talk: Mathematical Ideas in Poems for Two Voices.* San Carlos, CA: Tetra.
Presents mathematical ideas through poetic dialogues intended to be read by two people.

———. 1993. *Fractals, Googols and Other Mathematical Tales.* San Carlos, CA: Tetra.
Includes short stories and discussions that present such mathematical concepts as decimals, tangrams, number lines, and fractals.

———. 1997. *Mathematical Scandals.* San Carlos, CA: World Wide Publications.
Presents a new vision for exploring math, examining deceptions and math problems that take the form of challenging vignettes and examples.

Pinczes, Elinor J. 1993. *One Hundred Hungry Ants.* Boston: Houghton Mifflin.
One hundred hungry ants head toward a picnic to get yummies for their tummies but stop to change their line formation, showing different divisions of one hundred, causing them to lose both time and food.

Schmandt-Besserat, Denise. 1997. *The History of Counting*. New York: Morrow.
Describes the evolution of counting and the many ways to count and write numbers.

Schwartz, David M. 1998. *G Is for Googol: A Math Alphabet Book*. Berkeley, CA: Tricycle Press.
Explains the meaning of mathematical terms that begin with the different letters of the alphabet from abacus, binary, and cubit to zillion.

———. 1999a. *If You Hopped Like a Frog*. New York: Scholastic.
Picture puzzles, games, and simple activities introduce the mathematical concepts of multiplication, sequence and ordinal numbering, measurement, and direction.

———. 1999b. *On Beyond a Million: An Amazing Math Journey*. New York: Random House.
Explores counting by powers of ten all the way up to the largest numbers.

Scieszka, Jon. 1995. *Math Curse*. New York: Viking.
When the teacher tells her class that they can think of almost everything as a math problem, one student acquires a math anxiety that becomes a real curse.

Wise, Bill. 2001. *Whodunit: Math Puzzles*. New York: Sterling.
In these puzzles the facts are presented and the clues left behind are analyzed to determine "whodunit."

Music

Claverie, Jean. 1990. *Little Lou*. Mankato, MN: Creative Editions.
As a result of spending a lot of his time in a neighborhood bar where he likes the piano music, talented young musician Lou has an exciting brush with organized crime.

Clement, Claude. 1989. *The Voice of the Wood*. New York: Dial.
An incomparable magical cello, made from a Venetian instrument maker's beloved tree, is played during the Grand Carnival only after a famous young musician lets down his public facade and faces the instrument with honesty and heartfelt desire.

Hacker, Carlotta. 1997. *Great African Americans in Jazz*. New York: Crabtree.
Profiles of thirteen African American jazz musicians, including Miles Davis, Duke Ellington, and Billie Holiday.

Haskins, Jim. 1992. *Amazing Grace: The Story Behind the Song.* Brookfield, CT: Millbrook Press.
Relates the story of the British slave trader who rejected his calling, became a minister, and wrote the words to the popular hymn "Amazing Grace."

Igus, Toyomi. 1998. *I See the Rhythm.* San Francisco: Children's Book Press.
Includes song lyrics and an informational time line and history of African American music.

Krull, Kathleen. 1993. *Lives of the Musicians: Good Times, Bad Times (and What the Neighbors Thought).* San Diego: Harcourt Brace.
Fascinating and humorous stories of the private lives of twenty famous musicians.

Moss, Lloyd. 1995. *Zin! Zin! Zin! A Violin.* New York: Simon and Schuster.
Ten instruments take their parts one by one in a musical performance.

Mour, Stanley I. 1998. *American Jazz Musicians.* Springfield, NJ: Enslow Publishers.
Profiles ten notable jazz musicians, including Louis Armstrong, John Coltrane, and Miles Davis.

Rachlin, Ann. 1992a. *Bach.* Hauppauge, NY: Barron's.
Focuses on the childhood and early musical training of the prolific eighteenth-century German composer Johann Sebastian Bach.

———. 1992b. *Handel.* Hauppauge, NY: Barron's.
Focuses on the childhood and early musical training of the eighteenth-century Baroque composer George Frideric Handel.

———. 1992c. *Haydn.* Hauppauge, NY: Barron's.
Focuses on the childhood and early musical training of the eighteenth-century Austrian composer Joseph Haydn.

———. 1993a. *Brahms.* Hauppauge, NY: Barron's.
A biography of the nineteenth-century German composer with emphasis on his childhood and early musical training.

———. 1993b. *Chopin.* Hauppauge, NY: Barron's.
Examines the childhood and early musical training of the nineteenth-century Polish composer.

———. 1994. *Beethoven.* Hauppauge, NY: Barron's.
Focuses on the childhood and early musical training of the eighteenth-century Austrian composer, Ludwig van Beethoven.

Raschka, Chris. 1992. *Charlie Parker Played Be Bop*. New York: Orchard.
Introduces the famous saxophonist and his style of jazz, known as bebop.

Rosenberg, Jane. 1989. *Sing Me a Story: The Metropolitan Opera's Book of Opera Stories for Children*. New York: Thames and Hudson.
An illustrated retelling of the plots of fifteen well-known operas.

Schroeder, Alan. 1989. *Ragtime Tumpie*. Boston: Joy Street Books.
Tumpie, a young black girl who will later become famous as the singer Josephine Baker, longs to find the opportunity to dance amid the poverty and vivacious street life of St. Louis in the early 1900s.

Science

The Animal World

Brooks, Bruce. 1993. *Making Sense: Animal Perception and Communication*. New York: Farrar, Straus and Giroux.
Explores the five senses and how animals use them to perceive potential danger. Encourages inquiry, class discussion, hypothesis formulation, and further research.

Cannon, Janell. 1993. *Stellaluna*. San Diego: Harcourt Brace.
After she falls headfirst into a bird's nest, a baby bat is raised like a bird until she is reunited with her mother.

———. 1997. *Verdi*. San Diego: Harcourt Brace.
A young python does not want to grow slow and boring like the older snakes he sees in the tropical jungle where he lives.

Fleischman, Paul. 1998. *Joyful Noise: Poems for Two Voices*. New York: Harper and Row.
A collection of poems describing the characteristics and activities of a variety of insects.

Florian, Douglas. 1998. *Insectlopedia*. San Diego: Harcourt Brace.
Presents twenty-one short poems about such insects as the inchworm, termite, cricket, and ladybug.

George, Kristine O'Connell. 1997. *The Great Frog Race and Other Poems*. New York: Clarion.
A collection of poems about frogs and dragonflies, wind and rain, a visit to the tree farm, the garden hose, and other familiar parts of indoor and outdoor life.

Moss, Jeff. 1997. *Bone Poems.* New York: Workman Publications.
A collection of poems about dinosaurs, Ice Age mammals, prehistoric people, and other ancient creatures.

Pallotta, Jerry. 1986. *The Ocean Alphabet Book.* Boston: Quinlan Press.
Introduces the letters A–Z by describing fish and other creatures living in the North Atlantic Ocean.

———. 1990. *The Frog Alphabet Book.* Watertown, MA: Charlesbridge.
Introduces the letters of the alphabet by describing a frog or other amphibian for each letter, from the Amazon horned frog to the zig zag salamander.

———. 1991. *The Dinosaur Alphabet Book.* Watertown, MA: Charlesbridge.
Presents a dinosaur for each letter of the alphabet.

———. 1992. *The Icky Bug Counting Book.* Watertown, MA: Charlesbridge.
Fact-filled collection: new and interesting bugs, how butterflies taste with their feet, why gardeners love millipedes, and so on.

———. 1993. *The Extinct Alphabet Book.* Watertown, MA: Charlesbridge.
Each letter of the alphabet features information about a creature that no longer exists.

Astronomy/Astrology

Couper, Heather, and Nigel Henbest. 1996. *Black Holes.* Boston: Houghton Mifflin.
An informational book about the constellations.

Fradin, Dennis Brindell. 1997. *The Planet Hunters: The Search for Other Worlds.* New York: Margaret K. McElderry.
Provides a good explanation of the discoveries of planets orbiting other stars, along with failed searches.

Hall, Calvin. 2001. *Northern Lights: The Science, Myth and Wonder of the Aurora Borealis.* Seattle: Sasquatch Books.
Includes beautiful pictures of the aurora borealis, and the supporting text brings to life the legends, myths, and theories surrounding the lights.

Lurie, Alison. 1989. *Heavenly Zoo.* New York: Farrar, Straus and Giroux.
Sixteen legends of the constellations and how they got their names, taken from such varied sources as ancient Greece, Babylon, Egypt, Sumeria, the Bible, Norway, the Balkans, Indonesia, and the Native Americans.

Experimenting

Cobb, Vicki. 1993a. *Light Action: Amazing Experiments with Optics.* New York: HarperCollins.
Teaches the properties of light (prisms, lenses, shadows, colors, and reflections) through hands-on experience.

———. 1993b. *Wanna Bet? Science Challenges to Fool You.* New York: Lothrop, Lee and Shepard.
A book of "magic" science tricks based on sound scientific principles. All steps are explained in careful detail.

Saunders, Ian. 1999. *Bill Nye the Science Guy's Big Blue Ocean.* New York: Hyperion.
Gives ideas for experiments, research related to the ocean.

Wick, Walter. 1997. *A Drop of Water: A Book of Science and Wonder.* New York: Scholastic.
Photographs help readers explore the properties of water. Includes experiments.

Inventions

Jones, Charlotte Foltz. 1991. *Mistakes That Worked.* New York: Doubleday.
Presents the stories behind forty things that were invented or named by accident, including aspirin, X-rays, Frisbees, Silly Putty, and Velcro.

Petroski, Henry. 1992. *The Evolution of Useful Things.* New York: Knopf.
Takes a look at everyday objects we count on but rarely contemplate how they came to be, such as Post-its and pins.

Sutton, Caroline. 1981. *How Do They Do That? Wonders of the Modern World Explained.* New York: Morrow.
Describes scientific questions and technological wonders such as how archeologists know where to dig, and how they remove tar from cigarettes.

———. 1993. *More How Do They Do That? Wonders of the Modern World Explained.* New York: Morrow.
Offers solutions to the riddles of everyday science that are often taken for granted.

Woods, Michael, and Mary Woods. 2000a. *Ancient Machines: From Wedges to Waterwheels.* Minneapolis, MN: Runestone Press.
Uses photos and reproductions of maps to describe how all modern machines are based upon the six simple machines invented in ancient times.

———. 2000b. *Ancient Medicine: From Sorcery to Surgery.* Minneapolis, MN: Runestone Press.
Describes modern medical accomplishments and ancient surgical techniques. Appropriate for science, global studies, or world history.

———. 2000c. *Ancient Transportation: From Camels to Canals.* Minneapolis, MN: Runestone Press.
Describes how the knowledge, inventions, and discoveries of technology have made life easier in the modes of transportation.

Scientists

Atkins, Jeannine. 1999. *Mary Anning and the Sea Dragon.* New York: Farrar, Straus and Giroux.
Describes Mary Anning's true adventure in paleontology as she discovers fossils of sea dragons in nineteenth-century England.

Martin, Jacqueline Briggs. 1998. *Snowflake Bentley.* Boston: Houghton Mifflin.
A biography of a self-taught scientist who photographed thousands of individual snowflakes in order to study their unique formations.

Sis, Peter. 1996. *Starry Messenger: Galileo Galilei.* New York: Farrar, Straus and Giroux.
A biography of the scientist. Includes symbolic illustrations and many visual references to Galileo's time.

Stanley, Diane. 1996. *Leonardo Da Vinci.* New York: Morrow Junior Books.
A biography of the Italian Renaissance artist and inventor who, at about age thirty, began writing his famous notebooks, which contain the outpourings of his amazing mind.

Social Studies

Geography

Ballard, Robert D. *The Lost Wreck of the Isis.* New York: Scholastic.
Dr. Ballard visits the Mediterranean to explore a Roman shipwreck site and investigate an active underwater volcano.

Cherry, Lynne. 1992. *A River Ran Wild: An Environmental History.* San Diego: Harcourt Brace.
Historical nonfiction. Traces the history of the Nashua River from its earliest settlement by Native Americans, through logging activities of early settlers, to its pollution in the Industrial Age.

Deary, Terry. 1997a. *Horrible Histories: The Groovy Greeks.* New York: Scholastic.
A lively portrait of life in Greece more than two thousand years ago describes the origins of the Greek Olympic games, the highly revered god who ate his own children, the people who had the first flushing toilet, and more.

———. 1997b. *Horrible Histories: The Rotten Romans.* New York: Scholastic.
A fact-filled treasury on ancient Rome celebrates the lesser-known daily realities of the period, such as what the Britons used to make their hair spiky and why rich Romans needed vomitoriums.

———. 1997c. *Horrible Histories: The Vicious Vikings.* New York: Scholastic.
Packed with frightening facts about the vile invaders from the North and their savage enemies, including such legendary warriors as Fat-thighs, Oaf, and Stinking.

Dunphy, Madeleine. 1993. *Here Is the Arctic Winter.* New York: Hyperion.
Using cumulative children's rhyme, this text describes the diversity and vitality of Arctic life and landscape.

Ekoomiak, Normee. 1988. *Arctic Memories.* New York: Holt.
A bilingual Inuit and English text that describes life in the Canadian Arctic.

Fisher, Leonard Everett. 1986. *The Great Wall of China.* New York: Macmillan.
Traces the story of China's Great Wall. Chinese characters describe each page, and the English translation is in the back of the book.

Harrison, Ted. 1982. *A Northern Alphabet.* Plattsburgh, NY: Tundra Books.
Introduces through brief text and illustrations, the letters of the alphabet and various aspects of life in the Arctic.

Hopkins, Lee Bennett, ed. 2000. *My America: A Poetry Atlas of the United States.* New York: Simon and Schuster.
A collection of poems evocative of seven geographical regions of the United States, including the Northeast, Southeast, Great Lakes, Plains, Mountain, Southwest, and Pacific Coast states.

Jenkins, Steve. 1999. *The Top of the World: Climbing Mount Everest.* Boston: Houghton Mifflin.
Presents climate, geography, history, and mountaineering. Includes information about frostbite, avalanches, and pollution.

Pallotta, Jerry. 1986. *The Ocean Alphabet.* Boston: Quinlan Press.
Introduces the letters A-Z by describing fish and other creatures living in the North Atlantic Ocean.

Sis, Peter. 1994. *The Three Golden Keys.* New York: Doubleday.
Led by a cat on a magical journey through the deserted streets of Prague, a man comes upon some of the city's landmarks and finds the keys to his childhood home, in three traditional Czech tales.

Talbott, Hudson. 1996. *Amazon Diary: Property of Alex Winters.* New York: Putnam.
Twelve-year-old Alex is rescued from a plane crash by the Yanomami Indians of Venezuela and spends several weeks in the Amazon jungle with them, learning and appreciating their way of life.

Wisniewski, David. 1996. *Golem.* New York: Clarion.
Caldecott Medal Winner. A saintly rabbi miraculously brings to life a clay giant who helps him watch over the Jews of sixteenth-century Prague.

People Across Time and Place

Adler, David A. 1989. *We Remember the Holocaust.* New York: Holt.
Discusses the events of the Holocaust and includes personal accounts from survivors of their experiences of the persecution and the death camps.

———. 1993a. *A Picture Book of Anne Frank.* New York: Holiday House.
Traces the life of the young Jewish girl whose diary chronicles the years she and her family hid from the Nazis in an Amsterdam attic.

———. 1993b. *A Picture Book of Rosa Parks.* New York: Holiday House.
Details Rosa Parks's commitment to the civil rights movement and her pivotal role in the 1955 Montgomery bus boycott as well as the contributions of other civil rights activists.

Anderson, Laurie Halse. 2000. *Fever, 1793.* New York: Scholastic.
Philadelphia in 1793: capital of the United States and home to a fever that kills thousands. Witness the struggle through Mattie Cook's eyes.

Ayres, Katherine. 1998. *North by Night: A Story of the Underground Railroad.* New York: Random House.
While helping slaves to freedom, Lucy Spencer learns about life and sacrifice.

Bachrach, Susan D. 2000. *The Nazi Olympics: Berlin 1936.* Boston: Little, Brown.
Details events surrounding the 1936 Olympics in Berlin.

Beatty, Patricia. 1992. *Who Comes with Cannons?* New York: Scholastic.
A Quaker family becomes entangled in the Civil War, trying to live by their beliefs while the Confederacy expects them to join the cause.

Bolotin, Norman, and Angela Herb. 1995. *For Home and Country: A Civil War Scrapbook.* New York: Dutton.
A panoramic pictorial and verbal overview of the War Between the States draws on period photographs, diaries, letters, news clippings, and other items.

Bridges, Ruby. 1999. *Through My Eyes.* New York: Scholastic.
Pictures, news clippings, and family quotes tell Ruby Bridges' tale of her days being escorted by federal marshals as she became the first black student at an all-white school in New Orleans in 1960.

Buchanan, Jane. 1997. *Gratefully Yours.* New York: Scholastic.
An orphan train brings Hattie west to Nebraska from New York. Hattie must learn to live in her new home with the two people who have chosen to be her parents.

Burleigh, Robert. 1991. *Flight: The Journey of Charles Lindbergh.* New York: Philomel.
Uses beautiful paintings and exciting text to draw readers into Lindbergh's flight activities during his solo flight across the Atlantic.

Calabro, Marian. 1999. *The Perilous Journey of the Donner Party.* New York: Clarion.
Using newspaper clippings and survivor stories, it depicts the journey of the Donners as they travel across the country in a covered wagon and meet with terrible danger.

Chang, Ina. 1991. *A Separate Battle: Women and the Civil War.* New York: Lodestar.
Documents how women of every color participated in the war in every capacity. Includes historical anecdotes, excerpts from journals, quotations, and other first-person sources.

Coerr, Eleanor. 1977. *Sadako and the Thousand Paper Cranes.* New York: Bantam Doubleday Dell.
Sadako Sasaki, afflicted with leukemia from radiation from the bombing of Hiroshima, becomes a voice of hope and a strong argument for peace.

Coles, Robert. 1995. *The Story of Ruby Bridges.* New York: Scholastic.
Detailed picture book tells Ruby Bridges' story.

Collier, James Lincoln, and Christopher Collier. 1974. *My Brother Sam Is Dead.* New York: Scholastic.
Tim Meeker and his family are divided by their loyalties as his father remains staunchly British and his brother joins the Continental Army.

———. 1981. *Jump Ship to Freedom.* New York: Bantam Doubleday Dell.
Daniel Arabus is separated from his mother and forced to sail to a West Indies plantation. How will he survive if he is able to jump ship in New York?

———. 1984. *Who Is Carrie?* New York: Bantam Doubleday Dell.
Carrie is a kitchen slave in Sam Fraunces's tavern. As she begins to learn the truth of her own family, she becomes involved with the leaders of the American Revolution.

Cormier, Robert. 1998. *Heroes.* New York: Delacorte.
After serving in the United States Army in World War II and having his face blown off by a grenade, Francis, a young soldier, returns home hoping to find—and kill—the former childhood hero he feels betrayed him.

Crist-Evans, Craig. 1999. *Moon Over Tennessee: A Boy's Civil War Journal.* Boston: Houghton Mifflin.
Using free verse poetry, this story gives voice to a thirteen-year-old boy who describes his sense of fear, numbness, and loss as he accompanies his father into the Civil War.

Crossley-Holland, Kevin. 1998. *The World of King Arthur and His Court: People, Places, Legend, and Lore.* New York: Dutton/Lodestar.
Illuminates the essential aspects of King Arthur's chivalrous world.

Curtis, Christopher Paul. 1995. *The Watsons Go to Birmingham—1963.* New York: Delacorte.
Ten-year-old Kenny is growing up in America at the time of some of the worst desegregation battles. We see the Birmingham church bombing through his eyes.

———. 1999. *Bud, Not Buddy.* New York: Delacorte.
A young boy goes on a journey during the Great Depression. Encourages following maps and discusses jazz music.

Cushman, Karen. 1995. *The Midwife's Apprentice.* New York: HarperCollins.
Alyce struggles to find her place in a medieval village.

Davis, Ossie. 1978. *Escape to Freedom: A Play About Young Frederick Douglass.* New York: Viking.
Dramatically portrays events from Douglass's early life, which leaves students to interpret how those events shaped his adult life. Includes a cast of seven characters, but can be expanded to involve the entire class.

Denenberg, Barry. 1996. *An American Hero: The True Story of Charles A. Lindbergh.* New York: Scholastic.
A biography of Charles Lindbergh's life and accomplishments.

———. 1999. *My Name Is America: The Journal of Ben Uchida.* New York: Scholastic.
Ben and his family are interned at Mirror Lake after the Japanese bomb Pearl Harbor.

dePaola, Tomie. 1983. *The Legend of the Bluebonnet.* New York: Putnam.
A retelling of the Comanche Indian legend of how a little girl's sacrifice brought the flower called bluebonnet to Texas.

Durbin, William. 1999. *Wintering.* New York: Random House.
Surviving in the French Canadian wilderness as a fur trapper and trader, Pierre befriends and learns from an Ojibwe brave whom he encounters.

Edelman, Bernard. 1985. *Dear America: Letters Home from Vietnam.* New York: Norton.
A reliving of the war in Vietnam through actual letters from American G.I.s in Vietnam to their families, friends, and loved ones.

Ellis, Deborah. 2000. *The Breadwinner.* Ontario: Groundwood Books/Douglas and McIntyre.
Parvana is forced to become a boy so that her family can survive under the Taliban in Kabul, Afghanistan.

Erdrich, Louise. 1999. *The Birchbark House.* New York: Hyperion.
Depicts everyday life of an Ojibwa girl.

Fleischman, Paul. 1991. *The Borning Room.* New York: HarperCollins.
Lying at the end of her life in the room where she was born in 1851, Georgina remembers what it was like to grow up on the Ohio frontier.

———. 1993. *Bull Run.* New York: HarperCollins.
Uses the first-person accounts of sixteen Northern and Southern characters to show readers what the beginning of the Civil War was like.

———. 1996. *Dateline: Troy.* Cambridge, MA: Candlewick Press.
A retelling of the story of the Trojan War illustrated with collages featuring newspaper clippings of modern events from World War I through the Persian gulf war.

Fletcher, Susan. 1998. *Shadow Spinner.* New York: Simon and Schuster.
Marjan joins the Sultan's harem and helps save Shahrazad's life.

Francis, Lee. 1999. *When the Rain Sings: Poems by Young Native Americans.* New York: Simon and Schuster.
Poetry collection from 37 Native Americans detailing their history and their lives.

Frazee, Charles A. 1999. *World History: Original and Secondary Source Readings.* Vols. 1 and 2. San Diego: Greenhaven.
Contains both primary and secondary source materials covering the Stone Age to present times. Includes questions at the end of each selection that can be incorporated into lesson plans.

Freedman, Russell. 1996. *The Life and Death of Crazy Horse.* New York: Holiday House.
A biography of the Oglala leader who relentlessly resisted the white man's attempt to take over Indian lands.

———. 1998. *Buffalo Hunt.* New York: Holiday House.
Examines the importance of the buffalo in the lore and day-to-day life of the Indian tribes of the Great Plains, and describes hunting methods and the uses found for each part of the animal that could not be eaten.

Gallo, Donald R., ed. 1999. *Time Capsule: Short Stories About Teenagers Throughout the Twentieth Century.* New York: Random House.
Short stories that capture the flavor of each decade of the twentieth century in America.

George, Jean Craighead. 1989. *Shark Beneath the Reef.* New York: HarperCollins.
A great book about choice and confrontation, and a wonderful look at the history and ecology of Baja, California.

Gregory, Kristiana. 1997. *Dear America: Across the Wide and Lonesome Prairie.* New York: Scholastic.
Hattie Campbell's diary chronicles her family's move west on the Oregon Trail in 1847.

Hansen, Joyce. 1999. *The Heart Calls Home.* New York: Walker and Co.
Details the journey of three young runaway slaves during the Civil War, and their adult lives during the Reconstruction era.

Hurmence, Belinda. 1997. *Slavery Time When I Was Chillun.* New York: Putnam.
Twelve oral histories of former slaves selected from the more than 2,000 interviewed as part of the Slave Narratives of the Library of Congress for the Works Progress Administration in 1936.

Innocenti, Roberto. 1985. *Rose Blanche.* Mankato, MN: Creative Editions.
During World War II, a young German girl's curiosity leads her to discover something far more terrible than the day-to-day hardships and privations that she and her neighbors have experienced.

Kay, Verla. 1999. *Iron Horses*. New York: Putnam.
Uses rhythmic verse to depict the great railroad race between the Central Pacific Railroad and the Union Pacific Railroad between 1862 and 1869.

Koller, Jackie French. 1992. *The Primrose Way*. Orlando, FL: Harcourt Brace and Company.
Rebekah has to choose between her missionary culture and the Pawtucket world of which she has become a part.

Kurtz, Jane. 1998. *The Storyteller's Beads*. New York: Scholastic.
Two girls facing the Ethiopian famine of the 1980s overcome prejudices to try to survive.

Lawson, Robert. 1939. *Ben and Me: An Astonishing Life of Benjamin Franklin by His Good Mouse Amos*. New York: Bantam Doubleday Dell.
A quirky look at one of America's heroes and his contributions to history.

Lenski, Lois. 1969. *Indian Captive: The Story of Mary Jemison*. New York: HarperCollins.
Based on a true story. Mary Jemison is captured by the Seneca and learns the ways of her new people.

Lester, Julius. 1994. *John Henry*. New York: Dial.
Retells the life of the legendary African American hero who raced against a steam drill to cut through a mountain.

McKissack, Patricia, and Frederick McKissack. 1997. *Run Away Home*. New York: Scholastic.
Sarah Jane watches as an Apache boy escapes a train taking him to a reservation. She and her family have to decide whether to turn him over to authorities or help him keep his freedom.

———. 1999. *Black Hands, White Sails: The Story of African-American Whalers*. New York: Scholastic.
Details the social, political, and economic context of the whaling industry and the abolitionist movement.

Meyer, Carolyn. 1999. *Mary, Bloody Mary*. San Diego: Harcourt Brace.
A fictionalized account of Mary Tudor's banishment by her father, King Henry VIII.

Mooney, Bel. 1997. *The Voices of Silence*. New York: Bantam Doubleday Dell.
Thirteen-year-old Flora experiences the Romanian Revolution of 1989. How will she save her father?

Moss, Jeff. 1997. *Bone Poems*. New York: Workman Publications.

A collection of poems about dinosaurs, Ice Age mammals, prehistoric people, and other ancient creatures.

Moss, Marissa. 1998. *Rachel's Journal.* San Diego: Harcourt Brace.
In her journal, Rachel chronicles her family's adventures traveling by covered wagon on the Oregon Trail in 1850.

Murphy, Jim. 1995. *The Great Fire.* New York: Scholastic.
A young reader's account of the Great Chicago Fire combines archival photographs and drawings with personal accounts by its survivors and carefully researched historical documents.

———. 1998. *Dear America: West to a Land of Plenty.* New York: Scholastic.
Traveling west from New York to Idaho Territory in 1883, Teresa records her journey.

Naidoo, Beverly. 1986. *Journey to Jo'Burg: A South African Story.* New York: HarperCollins.
A brother and sister encounter the system of apartheid as they travel to Johannesburg to find their mother.

Nixon, Joan Lowery. 1996. *Search for the Shadowman.* New York: Bantam Doubleday Dell.
While working on a class assignment to explore his family tree, Andy Thomas discovers that not all history is as it seems.

Partridge, Elizabeth. 1998. *Restless Spirit: The Life and Work of Dorothea Lange.* New York: Viking.
A biography of Dorothea Lange, whose photographs of migrant workers, Japanese American internees, and rural poverty helped bring about important social reforms.

Paulsen, Gary. 1998. *Soldier's Heart.* New York: Delacorte.
Eager to enlist, fifteen-year-old Charley has a change of heart after experiencing both the physical horrors and mental anguish of Civil War combat.

Perl, Lila, and Marion Blumenthal Lazan. 1996. *Four Perfect Pebbles: A Holocaust Story.* New York: Greenwillow Books.
This story is a factual presentation of the life of a young girl and her family during the Holocaust and the struggles they endured to survive and stay together.

Reeder, Carolyn. 1989. *Shades of Gray.* New York: Avon Books.
Orphaned by the Yanks, Will is forced to live with his uncle, a man who refused to fight for the Confederacy.

———. 1997. *Across the Lines.* New York: Avon Books.
Edward and Simon, master and servant, are separated by the coming of the Yankees. Both boys have to learn to survive in a world that is completely changed.

Rinaldi, Ann. 1993. *In My Father's House.* New York: Scholastic.
Oscie Mason and her family move to Appomattox to escape the war, but what will they do when the war follows them?

———. 1995. *The Secret Life of Sarah Revere.* San Diego: Harcourt Brace.
As the daughter of Paul Revere, Sarah struggles to grow up during the American Revolution.

Ryan, Pam Munoz. 1999. *Amelia and Eleanor Go for a Ride.* New York: Scholastic.
A recreation of Eleanor Roosevelt's and Amelia Earhart's historic flight together on April 20, 1933.

———. 2000. *Esperanza Rising.* New York: Scholastic.
Set during the 1920s in Mexico and the United States, the book shows Esperanza's transition from a Mexican rancher's daughter to a California field worker.

Scieszka, Jon. 2001. *Sam Samurai.* New York: Viking.
Joe, Fred, and Sam are transported to seventeenth-century Japan, where they infuriate a Samurai warrior, encounter their great-granddaughters, and save their lives by reciting an ancient form of poetry.

Shura, Mary Francis. 1989. *Kate's Book.* New York: Scholastic.
Follow Kate and Tildy on a wagon train west in 1843.

Spiegelman, Art. 1986. *Maus: A Survivor's Tale.* New York: Pantheon.
A story of a Jewish survivor of Hitler's Europe and his son, a cartoonist who tries to come to terms with his father's story and history itself.

———. 1991. Maus II: *A Survivor's Tale: And Here My Troubles Began.* New York: Pantheon.
Maus was the first half of the tale of survival of the author's parents, charting their desperate progress from prewar Poland to Auschwitz. Here is the continuation, in which the father survives the camp and is at last reunited with his wife.

Stanley, Diane. 1994. *Cleopatra.* New York: Morrow Junior Books.
A beautifully illustrated and meticulously researched portrait of a courageous and intelligent woman chronicles Cleopatra's Egyptian rule, as she persuades the Romans Julius Caesar and Mark Antony to help her try to make Egypt powerful.

Stanley, Jerry. 1992. *Children of the Dust Bowl: The True Story of the School at Weedpatch Camp.* New York: Crown.
Describes the plight of the migrant workers who traveled from the Dust Bowl to California during the Depression and were forced to live in a federal labor camp, and discusses the school that was built for their children.

Steedman, Scott. 1997. *The Egyptian News.* Cambridge, MA: Candlewick Press.
Uses a newspaper format to present articles about the history, politics, fashion, food, daily life, and afterlife of the ancient Egyptians.

Sterne, Emma Gelders. 1953. *The Slave Ship.* New York: Scholastic.
The story of the *Amistad* revolt.

Tsuchiya, Yukio. 1998. *Faithful Elephants.* Boston: Houghton Mifflin.
Recounts how three elephants in a Tokyo zoo were put to death because of the war, focusing on the pain shared by the elephants and the keepers who must starve them.

Volavkova, Hana, ed. 1993. *I Never Saw Another Butterfly: Children's Drawings and Poems from Terezín Concentration Camp, 1942–1944.* New York: Schocken Books.
A selection of children's poems and drawings reflecting their surroundings in Terezín concentration camp in Czechoslovakia from 1942 to 1944.

Wallis, Velma. 1993. *Two Old Women: An Alaska Legend of Betrayal, Courage and Survival.* New York: HarperCollins.
Two old women are abandoned by their tribe during a winter famine and have to try to survive.

Whelan, Gloria. 2000. *Homeless Bird.* New York: HarperCollins.
Through Koly's arranged marriage and subsequent abandonment, we learn about aspects of life in modern India.

Wolff, Virginia Euwer. 1998. *Bat 6.* New York: Scholastic.
With Shazam and Aki on opposing teams, this year's annual sixth-grade girls' softball game is going to be different. A book that proves that war affects everyone.

Woodruff, Elvira. 1991. *George Washington's Socks.* New York: Scholastic.
A trip back in time plunges five friends into the battle at Trenton.

———. 1994. *Dear Levi: Letters from the Overland Trail.* New York: Scholastic.
Austin Ives records his wagon train journey to Oregon through letters to his brother Levi.

The Places We Live

Bial, Raymond. 1993. *Frontier Home.* Boston: Houghton Mifflin.
Describes the pioneer life of the early 1800s, with emphasis on building log cabins and their furnishings. Challenges of daily life also discussed.

Biesty, Stephen. 1994. *Cross-Sections: Castle.* New York: Dorling Kindersley.
Detailed illustrations revealing the construction of a medieval castle and the daily life within its walls.

Jackson, Ellen. 1998. *Turn of the Century.* Watertown, MA: Charlesbridge.
Children living in Great Britain and the United States at the beginning of each century between A.D. 1000 and 2000 describe their lifestyle at the time.

Macaulay, David. 1977. *Castle.* Boston: Houghton Mifflin.
Text and detailed drawings follow the planning and construction of a typical castle and adjoining town in thirteenth-century Wales.

Wilson, Laura. 1993. *Daily Life in a Victorian House.* Washington, DC: National Trust for Historic Preservation.
Provides a unique glimpse into the Smith house and the lives of the family and servants who live there. Includes over 100 color photographs and drawings.

Appendix D

Writers on Writing:
Shared Reading to Support
Independent Writing

Books

Allen, Paula Gunn, ed. 1996. *Song of the Turtle: American Indian Literature, 1974–1994.* New York: Ballantine Books.

Asher, Sandy, ed. 1996. *But That's Another Story: Famous Authors Introduce Popular Genres.* New York: Walker and Co.

Bloom, Susan P., and Cathryn M. Mercier. 1997. *Presenting Avi.* New York: Twayne Publishers.

Blume, Judy, ed. 1999. *Places I Never Meant to Be: Original Stories by Censored Writers.* New York: Simon and Schuster.

Brown, Joanne. 1998. *Presenting Kathryn Lasky.* New York: Twayne Publishers.

Christ, Henry I., and Jerome Shostak. 1948. *Short Stories: A Collection for High School Students.* New York: Oxford Book Co.

Cleary, Beverly. 1988. *A Girl from Yamhill: A Memoir.* New York: Morrow.

———. 1995. *My Own Two Feet: A Memoir.* New York: Morrow.

Cormier, Robert. 1991. *I Have Words to Spend: Reflections of a Small Town Editor.* New York: Delacorte.

Craven, Margaret. 1980. *Again Calls the Owl.* Boston: G. K. Hall.

Crowe, Chris. 1999. *Presenting Mildred Taylor.* New York: Twayne Publishers.

Dahl, Roald. 1984. *Boy: Tales of Childhood.* New York: Farrar, Straus and Giroux.

Dorris, Michael, and Emilie Buchwald, eds. 1997. *The Most Wonderful Books: Writers on the Pleasures of Reading.* Minneapolis, MN: Milkweed Editions.

Duncan, Lois. 1982. *Chapters: My Growth as a Writer.* Boston: Little, Brown.

Duncan, Lois, ed. 1998. *Trapped! Cages of Mind and Body.* New York: Simon and Schuster.

Ehrlich, Amy, ed. 1996. *When I Was Your Age: Original Stories About Growing Up.* Cambridge, MA: Candlewick Press.

Fox, Mem. 1992. *Dear Mem Fox, I Have Read All Your Books Even the Pathetic Ones: And Other Incidents in the Life of a Children's Book Author.* San Diego: Harcourt Brace.

Fritz, Jean. 1992. *Surprising Myself.* Katonah, NY: Richard C. Owen.

———. 2002. *Homesick: My Own Story.* Waterville, ME: Thorndike Press.

Gallo, Donald R., ed. 1984. *Sixteen: Short Stories by Outstanding Writers for Young Adults.* New York: Delacorte.

———. 1987. *Visions: Nineteen Short Stories by Outstanding Writers for Young Adults.* New York: Delacorte.

———. 1989a. *Connections: Short Stories by Outstanding Writers for Young Adults.* New York: Delacorte.

———. 1989b. *Presenting Richard Peck.* Boston: Twayne Publishers.

———. 1990. *Speaking for Ourselves: Autobiographical Sketches by Notable Authors of Books for Young Adults.* Urbana, IL: National Council of Teachers of English.

———. 1992a. *Authors' Insights: Turning Teenagers into Readers and Writers.* Portsmouth, NH: Heinemann-Boynton/Cook.

———. 1992b. *Short Circuits: Thirteen Shocking Stories by Outstanding Writers for Young Adults.* New York: Delacorte.

———. 1993a. *Join In: Multiethnic Short Stories by Outstanding Writers for Young Adults.* New York: Delacorte.

———. 1993b. *Speaking for Ourselves, Too: More Autobiographical Sketches by Notable Authors of Books for Young Adults.* Urbana, IL: National Council of Teachers of English.

———. 1993c. *Within Reach: Ten Stories.* New York: HarperCollins.

———. 1995. *Ultimate Sports: Short Stories by Outstanding Writers for Young Adults.* New York: Delacorte.

Gantos, Jack. 2002. *Hole in My Life.* New York: Farrar, Straus and Giroux.

Gonzales, Doreen. 1991. *Madeleine L'Engle: Author of A Wrinkle in Time.* New York: Macmillan.

Hambleton, Vicki, and Cathleen Greenwood. 2001. *So, You Wanna Be a Writer?* Hillsboro, OR: Beyond Words Publishing.

Hentoff, Nat. 1986. *Boston Boy.* New York: Knopf.

Konigsburg, E. L. 1995. *TalkTalk: A Children's Book Author Speaks to Grown-Ups.* New York: Atheneum.

Lasky, Kathryn. 1994. *Memoirs of a Bookbat.* San Diego: Harcourt Brace.

Little, Jean. 1987. *Little by Little: A Writer's Education.* Ontario: Viking.

Lowry, Lois. 1998. *Looking Back: A Book of Memories.* Boston: Houghton Mifflin.

Marcus, Leonard S. 2000. *Author Talk: Conversations with Judy Blume.* New York: Simon and Schuster.

Mazer, Harry, ed. 1997. *Twelve Shots: Outstanding Short Stories About Guns.* New York: Delacorte.

Meltzer, Milton. 1991. *Starting from Home: A Writer's Beginnings: A Memoir.* New York: Puffin.

Monseau, Virginia. 1995. *Presenting Ouida Sebestyen.* New York: Twayne Publishers.

Myers, Walter Dean. 2001. *Bad Boy: A Memoir.* New York: HarperCollins.

Naylor, Phyllis Reynolds. 2001. *How I Came to Be a Writer.* New York: Aladdin.

Nilsen, Alleen Pace. 1997. *Presenting M. E. Kerr, Updated.* New York: Twayne Publishers.

Nixon, Joan Lowery. 1988. *If You Were a Writer.* New York: Four Winds Press.

Paulsen, Gary. 2001. *Guts: The True Story Behind Hatchet and the Brian Books.* New York: Delacorte.

Peck, Richard. 1995. *Anonymously Yours.* New York: Beech Tree Books.

Reid, Suzanne Elizabeth. 1997. *Presenting Ursula K. LeGuin.* New York: Twayne Publishers.

Rylant, Cynthia. 1993. *But I'll Be Back Again.* New York: Beech Tree Books.

Spinelli, Jerry. 1998. *Knots in My Yo-Yo String: The Autobiography of a Kid.* New York: Knopf.

Stover, Lois Thomas. 1997. *Presenting Phyllis Reynolds Naylor.* New York: Twayne Publishers.

Sutcliff, Rosemary. 1992. *Blue Remembered Hills.* New York: Farrar, Straus and Giroux.

Weiss, Jerry M., and Helen S. Weiss, ed. 1997. *From One Experience to Another: Award-Winning Authors Share Real-life Experiences Through Fiction.* New York: Tor.

Yolen, Jane. 1992. *A Letter from a Phoenix Farm.* Katonah, NY: Richard C. Owen.

Other Resources

ALAN Review—Young adult authors frequently write articles about their books and respond to critics. http://scholar.lib.vt.edu/ejournals/ALAN/alan-review.html.

Teenreads.com—Young adult authors respond to teen readers about their books. http://www.teenreads.com/authors/index.asp.

VOYA—Often contains interviews with young adult authors about their writing. http://www.voya.com/.

Writing!—This publication of Weekly Reader contains writing tips and articles often written by writers about their writing. http://www.weeklyreader.com/.

Appendix E

Picture Books to Support the Teaching of Literary Devices

Alliteration

Angelou, Maya. 1993. *Life Doesn't Frighten Me.*
Bond, Rebecca. 2000. *Bravo, Maurice!*
Cha, Dia. 1996. *Dia's Story Cloth: The Hmong People's Journey of Freedom.*
Clements, Andrew. 1998. *Workshop.*
Cole, Babette. 1988. *Prince Cinders.*
Fox, Mem. 1996. *Feathers and Fools.*
Gray, Libba Moore. 1995. *My Mama Had a Dancing Heart.*
Kellogg, Steven. 1985. *Chicken Little.*
Lobel, Anita. 1996. *Alison's Zinnia.*
Nixon, Joan Lowery. 1988. *If You Were a Writer.*
Willard, Nancy. 1994. *The Voyage of Ludgate Hill.*

Dialogue

Allard, Harry. 1981. *The Stupids Die.*
Day, Alexandra. 1994. *Frank and Ernest on the Road.*
Duke, Kate. 1992. *Aunt Isabel Tells a Good One.*
Simmons, Jane. 1998. *Come Along, Daisy.*
Starbird, Kaye. 1966. *Snail's a Failure Socially, and Other Poems.*

Flashback

Baylor, Byrd. 1992. *One Small Blue Bead.*
Cooney, Barbara. 1982. *Miss Rumphius.*
Lyon, George E. 1992. *Who Came Down That Road?*
Macaulay, David. 1987. *Why the Chicken Crossed the Road.*
Noble, Trinka. 1980. *The Day Jimmy's Boa Ate the Wash.*
Pryor, Bonnie. 1987. *House on Maple Street.*

Say, Allen. 1993. *Grandfather's Journey.*
Van Allsburg, Chris. 1983. *The Wreck of the Zephyr.*

Foreshadowing

Agee, Jon. 1988. *The Incredible Painting of Felix Clousseau.*
Bunting, Eve. 1988. *How Many Days to America.*
dePaola, Tomie. 1987. *An Early American Christmas.*
Flournoy, Valerie. 1985. *The Patchwork Quilt.*
Johnson, Angela. 1997. *The Rolling Store.*
Kasza, Keiko. 1997. *The Rat and the Tiger.*
Macaulay, David. 1995. *Shortcut.*
Polacco, Patricia. 1990. *Just Plain Fancy.*
Say, Allen. 1993. *Grandfather's Journey.*
Van Allsburg, Chris. 1986. *The Stranger.*
Yolen, Jane. 1992. *Encounter.*

Inference

Innocenti, Roberto. 1991. *Rose Blanche.*
Macaulay, David. 1997. *Rome Antics.*
McCully, Emily Arnold. 1992. *Mirette on the High Wire.*
Oppenheim, Shulamith. 1992. *The Lily Cupboard.*
Van Allsburg, Chris. 1979. *The Garden of Abdul Gasazi.*

Irony

Alexander, Lloyd. 1992. *The Fortune-Tellers.*
Berry, James. 1997. *First Palm Trees.*
de Maupassant, Guy. 1992. *The Necklace.*
Kasza, Keiko. 1997. *The Rat and the Tiger.*
Parnall, Peter. 1971. *Mountain.*
Rylant, Cynthia. 1992. *An Angel for Solomon Singer.*
Say, Allen. 1993. *Grandfather's Journey.*
Scieszka, Jon. 1991. *The Frog Prince, Continued.*
Snyder, Dianne. 1988. *The Boy of the Three-Year Nap.*
Trivizas, Eugenios. 1993. *The Three Little Wolves and the Big Bad Pig.*

Metaphor

Bang, Molly. 1998. *When Sophie Gets Angry—Really, Really Angry.*
Carlstrom, Nancy White. 1991. *Goodbye, Geese.*

Chall, Marsha Wilson. 1992. *Up North at the Cabin.*
Gregory, Valiska. 1992. *Through the Mickle Woods.*
Martin, Rafe. 1992. *The Rough-Face Girl.*
Mathews, Sally Schofer. 1994. *The Sad Night: The Story of an Aztec Victory and Spanish Loss.*
Paterson, Katherine. 1990. *The Tale of the Mandarin Ducks.*
Thomas, Joyce Carol. 1993. *Brown Honey in Broomwheat Tea.*
Van Allsburg, Chris. 1986. *The Stranger.*
Yolen, Jane. 1968. *Greyling.*
———. 1987. *Owl Moon.*
———. 1992. *Encounter.*

Onomatopoeia

Bond, Rebecca. 2000. *Bravo, Maurice.*
Bunting, Eve. 1994. *Smoky Night.*
Climo, Shirley. 1993. *The Korean Cinderella.*
Garland, Sherry. 1994. *I Never Knew Your Name.*
Moss, Lloyd. 1995. *Zin! Zin! Zin! A Violin.*
Schertle, Alice. 1996. *Keepers.*
Showers, Paul. 1961. *The Listening Walk.*
Yolen, Jane. 1990. *Sky Dogs.*
———. 1993. *Welcome to the Green House.*

Parody

Addams, Charles. 2002. *The Charles Addams Mother Goose.*
Briggs, Raymond. 1997. *Jim and the Beanstalk.*
Dewan, Ted. 1998. *The Sorcerer's Apprentice.*
Johnston, Tony. 1992. *The Cowboy and the Black-Eyed Pea.*
Miranda, Anne. 1997. *To Market to Market.*
Palatini, Margie. 1995. *Piggie Pie.*
Scieszka, Jon. 1994. *The Book That Jack Wrote.*
———. 1989. *The True Story of the Three Little Pigs.*
Seuss, Dr. 1984. *The Butter Battle Book.*
Smith, Lane. 1993. *The Happy Hocky Family.*
Stern, Robert. 1991. *The House That Bob Built.*
Tolhurst, Marilyn. 1991. *Somebody and the Three Blairs.*
Wilsdorf, Anne. 1993. *Princess.*
Zemach, Harve. 1973. *Duffy and the Devil.*

Personification

Begay, Shonto. 1995. *Navajo: Visions and Voices Across the Mesa.*
Browne, Anthony. 1985. *Gorilla.*
Burton, Virginia Lee. 1969. *The Little House.*
Day, Alexandra. 1994. *Frank and Ernest on the Road.*
Engel, Diana. 1999. *Josephina Hates Her Name.*
Fancher, Lou. 2002. *The Velveteen Rabbit.*
Highwater, Jamake. 1981. *Moonsong Lullaby.*
———. 1977. *Anpao: An American Indian Odyssey.*
Hughes, Langston. 1995. *The Block.*
Magsamen, Sandra. 2001. *The Story of the Heart.*
Pinkney, Andrea Davis. 1996. *Bill Pickett: Rodeo-Ridin' Cowboy.*
Siebert, Diane. 1991. *Sierra.*
Steig, William. 1969. *Sylvester and the Magic Pebble.*
Zemach, Harve. 1973. *Duffy and the Devil.*

Point of View

Bunting, Eve. 1990. *The Wall.*
Melmed, Laura K. 1993. *The First Song Ever Sung.*
Mochizuki, Ken. 1999. *Passage to Freedom: The Sugihara Story.*
Say, Allen. 1991. *Tree of Cranes.*
Scieszka, Jon. 1989. *The True Story of the Three Little Pigs.*
Seymour, Tres. 1996. *Gulls of the Edmund Fitzgerald.*
Yolen, Jane. 1992. *Letting Swift River Go.*

Satire

Alexander, Lloyd. 1992. *The Fortune-Tellers.*
Allard, Harry. 1977. *It's So Nice to Have a Wolf Around the House.*
Leaf, Munro. 1936. *The Story of Ferdinand.*
Parnell, Peter. 1971. *Mountain.*
Scieszka, Jon. 1989. *True Story of the Three Little Pigs.*
———. 1994. *The Book That Jack Wrote.*
Smith, Lane. 1993. *The Happy Hocky Family.*
Wilsdorf, Anne. 1993. *Princess.*

Simile

Goble, Paul. 1982. *The Girl Who Loved Wild Horses.*
Igus, Toyomi. 1996. *Two Mrs. Gibsons.*

Johnston, Tony. 1996. *The Wagon.*
Lorbiecki, Marybeth. 1996. *Just One Flick of a Finger.*
Sheldon, Dyan. 1991. *The Whales' Song.*
Turner, Ann Warren. 1987. *Nettie's Trip South.*
Yolen, Jane. 1987. *Owl Moon.*

Symbolism

Altman, Linda Jacobs. 1993. *Amelia's Road.*
Baylor, Byrd. 1994. *The Table Where Rich People Sit.*
Bunting, Eve. 1991. *Fly Away Home.*
Duvoisin, Robert. 1950. *Petunia.*
Garland, Sherry. 1993. *The Lotus Seed.*
Goble, Paul. 1982. *The Girl Who Loved Wild Horses.*
Gregory, Valiska. 1992. *Through the Mickle Woods.*
Grifalcone, Ann. 1993. *Kinda Blue.*
Mills, Lauren. 1991. *The Rag Coat.*
Polacco, Patricia. 1994. *Pink and Say.*
Ringgold, Faith. 1991. *Tar Beach.*
Rosen, Michael J. 1992. *Home.*
Rylant, Cynthia. 1992. *An Angel for Solomon Singer.*
Say, Allen. 1993. *Grandfather's Journey.*
Stanley, Diane. 1997. *Rumpelstiltskin's Daughter.*
Thompson, Colin. 1996. *How to Live Forever.*

Voice

Blood, Charles, and Martin Link. 1984. *The Goat in the Rug.*
Cameron, Ann. 1981. *The Stories Julian Tells.*
Choldenko, Gennifer. 1997. *Moonstruck: The True Story of the Cow That Jumped over the Moon.*
Grimes, Nikki. 1994. *Meet Danitra Brown.*
Hewitt, Kathryn. 1984. *Two by Two: The Untold Story.*
Hines, Anna. 1996. *When We Married Gary.*
Isaacs, Anne. 1994. *Swamp Angel.*
Joseph, Lynn. 1992. *An Island Christmas.*
Meddaugh, Susan. 1997. *Cinderella's Rat.*
Munsch, Robert. 1980. *The Paper Bag Princess.*
Willis, Jeanne. 1989. *Earthlets, as Explained by Professor Xargle.*
Yolen, Jane. 1992. *Encounter.*
———. 1987. *Piggins.*

Appendix F

Books for Shared Reading

Fiction

The following are some current favorites, mostly novels. The theme of each book is indicated after its title. Many of the books listed for lower grade levels are appreciated by older students as well.

Grades 4–6

Blackwood, Gary. 1998. *The Shakespeare Stealer*. Identity.

Couloumbis, Audrey. 1999. *Getting Near to Baby*. Family.

Curtis, Christopher Paul. 1999. *Bud, Not Buddy*. Family.

DiCamillo, Kate. 2000. *Because of Winn-Dixie*. Friendship.

———. 2001. *The Tiger Rising*. Friendship.

Draper, Sharon. 1997. *Forged by Fire*. Family.

Fleischman, Paul. 1997. *Seedfolks*. Responsibility.

Gantos, Jack. 2000. *Joey Pigza Loses Control*. Family.

———. 2001. *Joey Pigza Swallowed the Key*. School.

Griffin, Adele. 1997. *Sons of Liberty*. Survival.

Haddix, Margaret Peterson. 1998. *Among the Hidden*. Survival.

———. 1999. *Just Ella*. Identity.

———. 2001a. *Among the Imposters*. Survival.

———. 2001b. *The Girl with 500 Middle Names*. Identity.

Hansen, Joyce. 2001. *One True Friend*. Friendship.

Howe, James. 1997. *The Watcher*. Family.

———. 2001. *The Misfits*. Friendship.

Jimenez, Francisco. 1997. *The Circuit: Stories from the Life of a Migrant Child*. Survival.

Levine, Gail Carson. 1997. *Ella Enchanted*. Identity.

Neufeld, John. 1999. *Boys Lie*. Peer Pressure.

Peck, Richard. 1998. *A Long Way from Chicago: A Novel in Stories* [Short Stories]. Family.

———. 2000. *A Year Down Yonder* [Short Stories]. Family.

Philbrick, Rodman. 1993. *Freak the Mighty.* Friendship.

Rylant, Cynthia. 1995. *The Van Gogh Café* [Short Stories]. Hope.

Sachar, Louis. 1998. *Holes.* Responsibility.

Snicket, Lemony. 1999. *The Reptile Room: A Series of Unfortunate Events.* 2d ed. [Mystery].

Spinelli, Jerry. 1990. *Maniac Magee.* Identity.

Grades 6–9

Atkins, Catherine. 1999. *When Jeff Comes Home.* Identity.

Bennett, Cherie. 1998. *Life in the Fat Lane.* Identity.

Brooks, Bruce. 1999. *Vanishing.* Family.

Bunting, Eve. 1999. *Blackwater.* Family.

Cole, Brock. 1997. *The Facts Speak for Themselves.* Crime/Identity.

Cormier, Robert. 1999. *Frenchtown Summer* [Poetry]. Family.

Creech, Sharon. 1995. *Absolutely Normal Chaos.* Identity.

———. 2001. *Love That Dog* [Poetry]. School.

Fleischman, Paul. 2001. *Seek.* Family.

Fraustino, Lisa Rowe, ed. 1998. *Dirty Laundry: Stories About Family Secrets* [Short Stories]. Family.

Gilbert, Barbara Snow. 1996. *Stone Water.* Family.

Griffin, Adele. 2001. *Amandine.* Identity.

Haddix, Margaret Peterson. 1996. *Don't You Dare Read This, Mrs. Dunphrey.* Family.

Hesser, Terry Spencer. 1998. *Kissing Doorknobs.* Identity/Illness.

Holt, Kimberly Willis. 1998. *My Louisiana Sky.* Responsibility.

———. 1999. *When Zachary Beaver Came to Town.* Friendship.

———. 2002. *Dancing in Cadillac Light.* Death.

Konigsburg, E. L. 2000. *Silent to the Bone.* Friendship.

Korman, Gordon. 2000. *No More Dead Dogs.* School.

Levine, Gail Carson. 2000. *The Wish.* Friendship.

Mazer, Norma Fox. 1999. *Good Night, Maman.* Survival.

Naylor, Phyllis Reynolds. 1998. *Sang Spell.* Survival.

Nolan, Han. 1997. *Dancing on the Edge.* Family.

———. 1999. *A Face in Every Window.* Family.

Philbrick, Rodman. 2000. *The Last Book in the Universe.* Identity.

Spinelli, Jerry. 2000. *Stargirl.* Peer Pressure.

Woodson, Jacqueline. 2000. *Miracle's Boys.* Family.

Grades 9–12

Anderson, Laurie Halse. 1999. *Speak.* School.

Bennett, Jay. 1991. *Coverup.* Crime/Guilt.

Cormier, Robert. 2001. *Rag and Bone Shop*. Crime/Guilt.

Ferris, Jean. 1999. *Bad*. Crime/Guilt.

———. 2001. *Of Sound Mind*. Responsibility.

Flinn, Alex. 2001. *Breathing Underwater*. Responsibility.

Fleischman, Paul. 1998. *Whirligig* [Short Stories]. Responsibility.

Glenn, Mel. 1996. *Who Killed Mr. Chippendale?* [Poetry] Crime.

———. 1997. *The Taking of Room 114* [Poetry]. Crime.

———. 2000. *Split Image* [Poetry]. Identity.

Haddix, Margaret Peterson. 1997. *Leaving Fishers*. Peer Pressure.

Hawes, Louise. 1999. *Rosey in the Present Tense*. Death.

Klass, David. 2001. *You Don't Know Me*. Identity.

Lubar, David. 1999. *Hidden Talents*. School.

Lynch, Chris. 2001. *Freewill*. Crime/Identity.

Mazer, Norma Fox. 1993. *Out of Control*. Peer Pressure.

———. 2000. *When She Was Good*. Family.

McDonald, Joyce. 1997. *Swallowing Stones*. Responsibility.

Myers, Walter Dean. 1999. *Monster* [Multigenre]. Crime/Guilt.

Rapp, Adam. 1997. *The Buffalo Tree*. School.

Strasser, Todd. 2000. *Give a Boy a Gun*. Crime/Peer Pressure.

Thomas, Robb. 1996. *Rats Saw God*. School.

———. 1997a. *Doing Time: Notes from the Undergrad* [Short Stories]. School.

———. 1997b. *Slave Day* [Short Stories]. School.

Tomey, Ingrid. 1999. *Nobody Else Has to Know*. Crime/Guilt.

Trueman, Terry. 2000. *Stuck in Neutral*. Identity.

Wolff, Virginia Euwer. 2001. *True Believer* [Poetry]. Identity.

Nonfiction

High-interest informational books.

Feldman, David. 1987. *Why Do Clocks Run Clockwise and Other Imponderables*.
Answers questions such as what is the purpose of warning labels on mattresses?

———. 1989a. *When Do Fish Sleep and Other Imponderables of Everyday Life*.
Answers questions such as why don't birds tip over when they sleep on a telephone wire?

———. 1989b. *Who Put the Butter in Butterfly? And Other Fearless Investigations into Our Illogical Language*.
Uncovers mysteries about vocabulary.

———. 2000. *A World of Imponderables: The Answers to Life's Most Mystifying Questions.*
Answers questions such as why skyscrapers are never made out of bricks and why male birds tend to be more colorful than females.

Goldwyn, Martin M. 1979. *How a Fly Walks Upside Down and Other Curious Facts.*
Provides science facts such as why the ocean is salty and the sky is blue.

Lewis, Paul Owen. 1991. *Ever Wondered? For Explorers, Inventors and Artists of All Ages.*
Can be used to generate ideas for writing, drawing, classroom discussions, inventions, games, costumes, maps.

McLain, Bill. 1999. *Do Fish Drink Water?*
The official webmaster of Xerox provides answers to the questions he receives, such as whether people born blind can see in their dreams.

———. 2001. *What Makes Flamingoes Pink?*
Provides answers to everyday questions.

Myers, Jack. 1991. *What Makes Popcorn Pop?*
The science editor of Highlights magazine answers frequently asked questions about science.

Nash, Bruce, and Allan Zullo. 1992. *Believe It or Else.*
Bizarre stories about baseball that were told in locker rooms or printed in newspapers.

Simon and Schuster. 1984. *Why Things Are: A Guide to Understanding the World Around Us.*
Answers questions such as why do snakes dance for snake charmers and why does a balloon float in the air?

Strasser, Todd. 1998. *Kids' Book of Gross Facts and Feats.*
Book full of weird, wacky, and fascinating scientific facts.

Appendix G

High-Interest Leveled Books for Paired Shared Reading

Recorded Books, LLC
270 Skipjack Road
Prince Frederick, MD 20678
800-638-1304; fax 410-535-5499
www.recordedbooks.com

Recorded Books' SmartReader collection offers books on high-interest topics for middle and high school students, such as the following:

Close to Death
> What happens during a near-death experience? How does it affect a person's life?

Dark Hunger
> Who is the menacing figure stalking through her house? Once she thought of him as a friend; now she knows that she and her son are his prey.

Elisabeth and Mouse
> When her brother Harry returns from the New World with tales of adventure, seventeen-year-old Elisabeth is determined to see America for herself.

Danger in the Canyon
> When Joe and Steve set out to hike in Thunder Canyon, the weather changes suddenly, and they must remember the survival skills they have learned.

Montana Showdown
> With the help of a legendary character, one lonesome stranger learns to stand up to racism in the Old West.

Murder in Cabin A-13
> A honeymoon voyage turns into a nightmare when a groom is found stabbed in his cabin.

Nowhere to Hide
> Susie Lewis, who uses a wheelchair, feels helpless when a ruthless killer breaks into her apartment.

Sundance

P.O. Box 1326

Littleton, MA 01460

800-343-8204; fax 800-456-2419

www.sundancepub.com

Sundance offers packages of books in several of the following categories:

Sports Biographies (4–9)

Explores the paths sports stars traveled over the course of their careers.

Chapters in History (4–9)

Exciting historical fiction novels to entice reluctant readers.

Humor (4–9)

Popular humorous children's books, including favorites such as Clements's *Frindle,* Sachar's *There's a Boy in the Girls' Bathroom,* and Peck's *A Long Way from Chicago.*

Supa Doopers (4–9)

Slightly irreverent, light-hearted, fast-paced stories help students progress to fluent independent reading.

Thrillology (4–9)

Mini-anthologies packed with science fiction, horror, fantasy, adventure, and ghost stories.

Fact Meets Fiction (4–9)

Eight sets of paired fiction and nonfiction books featuring popular topics like disasters, daring feats, unbelievable odds, and amazing science.

Perfection Learning Corporation

1000 North Second Avenue

P.O. Box 500

Logan, IA 51546-0500

800-831-4190; fax 800-543-2745

www.perfectionlearning.com

Perfection offers collections of novels designed for struggling readers at different grade levels and on various topics:

Adventure (4–9)

Exciting plots and fully developed narratives to engage readers.

Historical Fiction (4–9)

Fast-paced, easy-to-read historical novels keep readers turning the pages.

Humor (4–9)

Outstanding and highly recommended stories in these Cover-to-Cover collections.

Suspense (6–12)

Timeless plots and books kids love.

Contemporary Issues (6–12)

Students provided with texts where they must decide about the choices characters make.

Steck-Vaughn

P.O. Box 690789

Orlando, FL 32819-0789

800-531-5015; fax 800-699-9459

www.steck-vaughn.com

Steck-Vaughn provides several collections of nonfiction and fiction content area books that will appeal to struggling readers:

True Tales (4–12)

Presents powerful real-life events with direct connections to geography and science. Gripping accounts of personal triumph over tragedy put geography and science in a very real context.

Steadwell Books (4–12)

Includes attention-getting photos and informative illustrations, maps, and time lines to communicate social studies and science concepts. Some of the collections are Prehistoric Creatures Then & Now; Our Universe; Explorers and Exploration; and American Government.

Unsolved Mysteries (4–12)

Provides accounts of puzzling events while legendary creatures examine the facts, offer rational explanations when possible, and leave the mystery an open-ended question. The collections include Alien Visitors and Abductions; The Bermuda Triangle; Mysterious Healing; and Powers of the Mind.

Rigby

P.O. Box 797

Crystal Lake, IL 60039-0797

800-822-8661; fax 800-427-4429

www.rigby.com

Rigby provides leveled, shared, content area resources for grades 4–6, including fiction and nonfiction selections in the areas of art, health, social studies, science, and technology as well as "action packs": That's a Laugh; Challenges and Choices; Friends and Friendship; and Action and Adventure.

Appendix H

Complete Texts

Ex Poser

Paul Jennings

There are two rich kids in our class. Sandra Morris and Ben Fox. They are both snobs. They think they are too good for the rest of us. Their parents have big cars and big houses. Both of them are quiet. They keep to themselves. I guess they don't want to mix with the ruffians like me.

Ben Fox always wears expensive gym shoes and the latest fashions. He thinks he is good-looking with his blue eyes and blond hair. He is a real poser.

Sandra Morris is the same. And she knows it. Blue eyes and blond hair too. Skin like silk. Why do some kids get the best of everything?

Me, I landed pimples. I've used everything I can on them. But still they bud and grow and burst. Just when you don't want them to. It's not fair.

Anyway, today I have the chance to even things up. Boffin is bringing along his latest invention—a lie detector. Sandra Morris is the victim. She agreed to try it out because everyone knows that she would never tell a lie. What she doesn't know is that Boffin and I are going to ask her some very embarrassing questions. Boffin is a brain. His inventions always work. He is smarter than the teachers. Everyone knows that. And now he has brought along his latest effort. A lie detector.

He tapes two wires to Sandra's arm. "It doesn't hurt," he says. "But it is deadly accurate." He switches on the machine, and a little needle swings into the middle of the dial. "Here's a trial question," he says. "Are you a girl?"

Sandra nods.

"You have to say yes or no," he says.

"Yes," replies Sandra. The needle swings over to TRUTH. Maybe this thing really works. Boffin gives a big grin.

"This time tell a lie," says Boffin. "Are you a girl?" he asks again.

Sandra smiles with that lovely smile of hers. "No," she says. A little laugh goes up, but then all the kids in the room gasp. The needle points to LIE. This lie detector is a terrific invention.

"Okay," says Boffin. "You only have seven questions, David. The batteries will go flat after another seven questions." He sits down behind his machine and twiddles the knobs.

This is going to be fun. I am going to find out a little bit about Sandra Morris and Ben Fox. It's going to be very interesting. Very interesting indeed.

I ask my first question. "Have you ever kissed Ben Fox?"

Sandra goes red. Ben Fox goes red. I have got them this time. I am sure they have something going between them. I will expose them.

"No," says Sandra. Everyone cranes his neck to see what the lie detector says. The needle points to TRUTH.

This is not what I expected. And I only have six questions left. I can't let her off the hook. I am going to expose them both.

"Have you ever held his hand?"

Again she says, "No." And the needle says TRUTH. I am starting to feel guilty. Why am I doing this?

I try another tack. "Are you in love?" I ask.

A red flush starts to crawl up her neck. I am feeling really mean now. Fox is blushing like a sunset.

"Yes," she says. The needle points to TRUTH.

"Does he have blue eyes?" I ask.

"No," she says.

"Brown?" I say.

"No," she says again.

I don't know what to say next. I look at each kid in the class very carefully. Ben Fox has blue eyes. I was sure that she loved him.

"This thing doesn't work," I say to Boffin. "I can't see one kid who doesn't have either blue eyes or brown eyes."

"We can," says Boffin. They are all looking at me.

I can feel my face turning red now. I wish I could sink through the floor, but I get on with my last question. "Is he an idiot?" I ask.

Sandra is very embarrassed. "Yes," she says in a voice that is softer than a whisper. "And he has green eyes."

Reptiles and Children Don't Mix: Agency Says Youngsters Risk Salmonella Infection from Snakes, Turtles and Lizards

Susan Okie

Got a baby or a toddler in the house? Get rid of that iguana.

Pet reptiles—including all types of lizards, snakes and turtles—can be a source of life-threatening infections and do not belong in households that have children younger than 5, according to a recommendation issued last week by the federal Centers for Disease Control and Prevention.

Reptiles also shouldn't be handled by small children or by anyone whose immune system doesn't work well, the agency cautioned. In addition, the animals should not be kept as pets in preschools and day-care centers.

With the growing popularity of snakes and lizards as pets, health officials are concerned about a recent increase in reptile-related salmonella infections. Although most cases of salmonella are caused by food contamination, reptiles account for about 93,000 cases of such illness each year, or about 7 percent of the total.

Many people are aware turtles can carry salmonella bacteria—in fact, the sale of small turtles as pets was banned for that reason in 1975—but most consumers and even many pet-store owners apparently don't know that lizards and snakes can be carriers, too.

Salmonella infections can cause fever, vomiting, bloody diarrhea and sometimes blood poisoning, meningitis or death.

People can become infected by handling the animal or objects contaminated with the reptile's feces. Touching the reptile isn't necessary. According to the CDC, some cases of reptile-associated illness have occurred in infants who never even touch the scaly family pet, presumably resulting from having been held by people whose hands were contaminated.

Reptiles carry salmonella in their digestive tracts and shed the bacteria in their feces. The microbes don't make them sick. There is no reliable test or treatment to ensure a pet reptile won't carry the bacteria. "You can test it one week and it will be negative, two weeks later and it will be positive," said Stephanie Wong, a veterinarian with the CDC's food-borne and diarrheal-diseases branch. "We feel there is no way to say that a reptile is salmonella-free."

Wong said CDC officials are so concerned about the risk to young children they decided last week to strengthen one of the new guidelines after it had been printed in the agency's weekly bulletin. Originally, the recommendation had said reptiles should not be kept in households with children less than 1 year old; this was revised to include households with children younger than 5.

About 3 percent of U.S. households have reptiles, according to a CDC estimate based in part on an industry survey. "They're becoming more common household pets," Wong said.

The symptoms of salmonella infection—typically abdominal cramps, diarrhea, fever and sometimes vomiting or headaches—begin 24 to 72 hours after exposure. Severe cases are treated with antibiotics. Drugs usually aren't necessary in mild cases of illness, Wong said, and their use is discouraged because they may promote the emergence of resistant strains.

Play It Safe

To help prevent the transmission of salmonella from reptiles to humans, the CDC recommends:

- Pet stores, veterinarians and pediatricians inform owners and potential owners of reptiles about the risk of salmonella infection.
- People always wash their hands thoroughly with soap and water after handling reptiles or reptile cages.
- Children, people with compromised immune systems and others at increased risk for infection or serious complications of a salmonella infection should avoid contact with reptiles.
- Pet reptiles be kept out of households with children younger than 5 and with anyone with a compromised immune system. Families expecting a new child should remove the pet reptile before the infant arrives.
- Pet reptiles not be kept in child-care centers.
- Pet reptiles not be allowed to roam freely throughout a home.
- Pet reptiles be kept out of kitchens and other food-preparation areas. Kitchen sinks should not be used to bathe reptiles or to wash their dishes, cages or aquariums. If bathtubs are used, they should be cleaned thoroughly and disinfected with bleach.

The Hangman

Maurice Ogden

Into our town the Hangman came
Smelling of gold and blood and flame
And he paced our bricks with a diffident air
And he built his frame on the courthouse square.

The scaffold stood by the courthouse side,
Only as wide as the door was wide,
A frame as tall, or little more,
Than the capping sill of the courthouse door.

And we wondered, whenever we had the time,
Who the criminal, what the crime,
The Hangman judged with the yellow twist
Of knotted hemp in his busy fist.

And innocent though we were, with dread
We passed those eyes of buckshot lead;

Till one cried, "Hangman, who is he
For whom you raised the gallows-tree?"

And a twinkle grew in the buckshot eye,
And he gave us a riddle instead of reply;
"He who serves me best," said he,
"Shall earn the rope of the gallows-tree."

And he stepped down, and laid his hand
On a man who came from another land
And we breathed again, for another's grief,
At the Hangman's hand was our relief.

And the gallows frame on the courthouse lawn
By tomorrow's sun would be struck and gone.
So we gave him way, and no one spoke,
Out of respect for his hangman's cloak.

The next day's sun looked down
On the roof and street in our quiet town
And, stark and black in the morning air,
The gallows-tree on the courthouse square.

And the Hangman stood at his usual stand
With the yellow hemp in his busy hand;
With his buckshot eye and his jaw like a pike
And his air so knowing and businesslike.

And we cried: "Hangman, have you not done,
Yesterday with the alien one?"
Then we fell silent, and stood amazed;
"Oh, not for him was the gallows raised . . ."

He laughed as he looked at us;
". . . Did you think I'd gone to all this fuss
To hang one man? That's a thing I do
To stretch the rope when the rope is new."

Then one cried "Murderer!" One cried, "Shame!"
And into our midst the Hangman came
To that man's place. "Do you hold," said he,
"With him that was meat for the gallows-tree?"

And he laid his hand on that one's arm,
And we shrank back in quick alarm
And we gave him way, and no one spoke,
Out of fear of his hangman's cloak.

That night we saw with dread surprise
The Hangman's scaffold had grown in size.
Fed by the blood beneath the chute
The gallows-tree had taken root.

Now as wide or a little more,
Than the steps that led to the courthouse door,
As tall as the writing, or nearly as tall,
Halfway up the courthouse wall.

The third he took—we had all heard tell—
Was a usurer and infidel,
And: "What," said the Hangman, "have you to do
With the gallows-bound, and he a Jew?"

And we cried out: "Is this the one he
Who has served you well and faithfully?"
The Hangman smiled: "It's a clever scheme
To try the strength of the gallows-beam."

The fourth man's dark, accusing song
Had scratched our comfort hard and long;
And: "What concern," he gave us back,
"Have you for the doomed—the doomed and Black?"

The fifth. The sixth. And we cried again:
"Hangman, Hangman, is this the man?"
"It's a trick," he said, "that we hangmen know
For easing the trap when the trap swings slow."

And so we ceased and asked no more,
As the Hangman tallied his bloody score;
And sun by sun, and night by night,
The gallows grew to monstrous height.

The wings of the scaffold opened wide
Till they covered the square from side to side;
And the monster crossbeam, looking down,
Cast its shadow across the town.

Then through the town the Hangman came
And he called in the empty streets MY NAME—
And I looked at the gallows soaring tall
And thought: "There is no one left at all,

For hanging, and so he calls to me
To help pull down the gallows-tree."
And I went out with right good hope
To the Hangman's tree and the Hangman's rope.

He smiled at me as I came down
To the courthouse square through the silent town,
And supple and stretched in his busy hand
Was the yellow twist of the hempen strand.

And he whistled his tune as he tried the trap
And it sprang down with a ready snap—
And then with a smile of awful command
He laid his hand upon my hand.

"You tricked me, Hangman!" I shouted then,
"That your scaffold was built for other men . . .
And I no henchman of yours," I cried.
"You lied to me, Hangman, foully lied!"

Then a twinkle grew in his buckshot eye:
"Lied to you?" "Tricked you?" he said, "Not I.
For I answered straight and I told you true:
The scaffold was raised for none but you."

"For who has served more faithfully
Than you with your coward's hope?" said he,
"And where are the others who might have stood
Side by side in the common good?"

"Dead," I whispered: and amiably
"Murdered," the Hangman corrected me:
"First the alien, then the Jew . . .
I did no more than you let me do."

Beneath the beam that blocked the sky,
None stood so alone as I—
And the Hangman strapped me and no voice there
Cried "STAY!" for me in the empty square.

On the Trail of the Komodo Dragon

Jack Myers

This lizard is big enough for a storybook.

Halfway around the world, on Komodo, an island of Indonesia, lives the world's largest lizard. It may grow to be as long as a dining table and as heavy as a grown man. It is sometimes called the Komodo dragon.

The ideas most of us have about dragons come from stories set in olden times. Dragons are pictured as scary animals, maybe shaped like big alligators, breathing fire through mouths full of big teeth. Thinking about those storybook dragons was enough to make me curious. If there is a real animal out there that someone would call a dragon, what is it like?

Fortunately, there's an answer to that question because a scientist named Walter Auffenberg led a team that spent more than a year studying it. But I should warn you that the Komodo dragon is not a very nice animal, even though it doesn't breathe fire. In some ways, it is completely yucky.

Komodo is a small island, not more than twenty miles across. Together with several neighboring islands, Komodo is home to about five thousand of the big lizards, which are locally called oras. Although a few people live in villages there, the whole island is now a national park, and the oras have been protected since 1915.

Big Babies

An ora begins life by cutting itself out of a grapefruit-sized egg. It comes out as a hatchling, almost two feet long. That's longer than most kinds of adult lizards.

By the time it is fully grown, at about twelve years old, it may be eight to ten feet long and weigh more than two hundred pounds. Then it gets to be called a dragon and is not an animal you would like to have in your back-yard.

To study oras, scientists set out big funnel-shaped traps made of bamboo and then baited with dead animals. The lizards' noses led them to the traps. (Oras are scavengers, which means that they eat dead animals. Also, they have a keen sense of smell, which they use in finding food.)

The captured oras were weighed and measured. The biggest was more than eight feet long. Some were fitted with a harness holding a little radio. Then the scientists could track the lizards by radio to see where and how they spent their time. And some oras were fitted with electrical thermometers and radios that broadcasted their body temperatures. Finally, 117 of them were marked with a little spray paint and given names or numbers.

Big Appetites

Although oras eat dead animals when they can, they are also predators. That's no surprise. Most lizards are predators. We don't always think of them that way since they eat little animals, such as insects.

That's what little oras eat, too. But as they grow up, they go for larger animals, like rats and birds. And as adults they often attack large animals, including deer, horses, and water buffalo. Some have even attacked humans.

By watching some of the large oras day after day, the scientists learned that the most common prey were deer. An ora can't catch a deer in a race. Instead it waits in ambush near a trail. Then it rushes out and makes a surprise attack. An ora has big, scary-looking teeth with sawtooth edges. So it can give a very bad bite.

From the way oras hunt live animals and find dead ones, the scientists have no doubt that these lizards depend on their keen sense of smell. They also have long tongues, forked like the tongues of snakes. Like snakes, oras flick out their tongues to touch things. When they find something that might be good to eat, they always check it out by touching it with the tongue.

A Tropical Home

Most big-time predators, like wolves and lions, are "warm-blooded" and have an automatic temperature control like a human's. Their body machinery is always revved up and ready to go. But lizards are "cold-blooded." They need to find ways to manage their body temperature. Before they can go hunting in the morning, oras need to lie in the sun until their bodies warm up.

On most days an ora spends an hour or more basking in the early morning sun. Then it carefully stays in the shade during the afternoon, when it is in danger of getting too warm.

The scientists' records showed that oras are able to keep their body temperature between 95 and 104 degrees Fahrenheit. At night the temperature often dropped to 80 degrees and sometimes to 76 degrees. Then the lizards found cover in hollow logs, burrows, or other snug places to stay warm.

You can see why the Komodo dragon lives only on Komodo and a few nearby islands. These islands have no other big predators that might compete with oras, and that small part of the world has a steady and cozy temperature. You're not likely to find a Komodo dragon in your backyard.

Appendix I

Forms

I.1 Words in Context

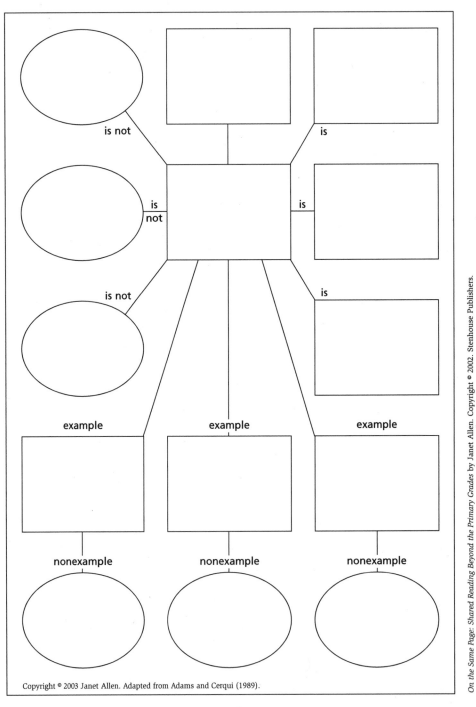

is not

is

is
not

is

is not

is

example

example

example

nonexample

nonexample

nonexample

On the Same Page: Shared Reading Beyond the Primary Grades by Janet Allen. Copyright © 2002. Stenhouse Publishers.

I.2 Character Chart

Character	Physical Characteristics	Outstanding Features	Personality Traits	Quote Worth Remembering

1.3 Guiding Readers Through the Text

Title:		
Page Nos.	Possibilities to Explore	Additional Ideas

On the Same Page: Shared Reading Beyond the Primary Grades by Janet Allen. Copyright © 2002. Stenhouse Publishers.

I.4 Reading . . . Thinking . . . **Responding . . .**

Title:

Reading	Thinking	Responding

1.5 Fleshing Out a Character

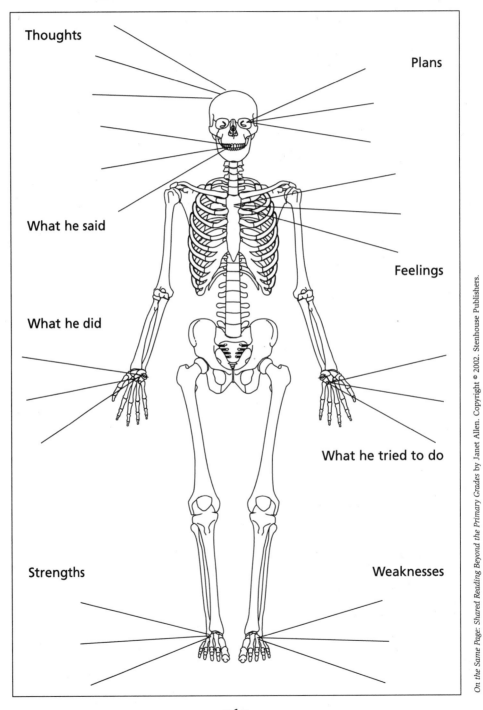

Thoughts

Plans

What he said

Feelings

What he did

What he tried to do

Strengths

Weaknesses

On the Same Page: Shared Reading Beyond the Primary Grades by Janet Allen. Copyright © 2002. Stenhouse Publishers.

I.6 It's a Matter of Perspective

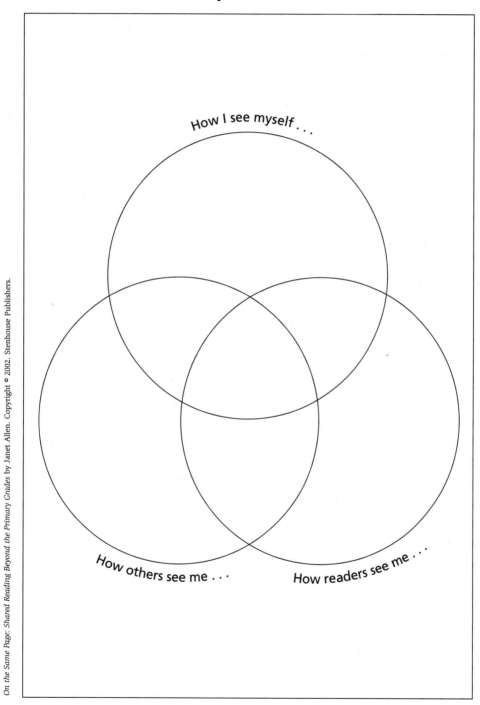

I.7 Language Collection I

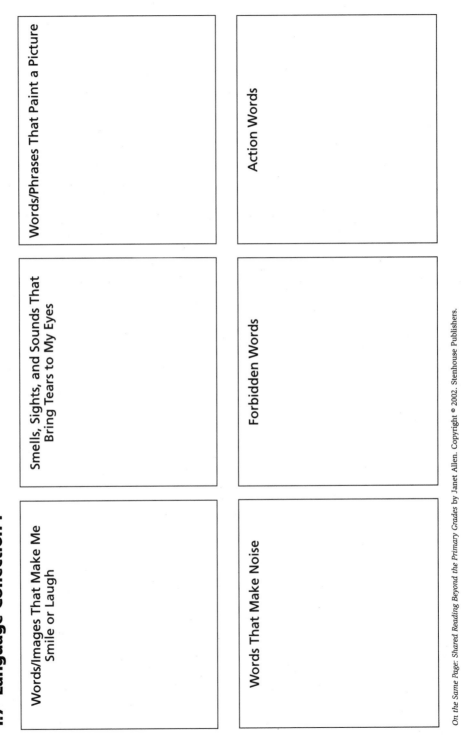

Words/Phrases That Paint a Picture

Action Words

Smells, Sights, and Sounds That Bring Tears to My Eyes

Forbidden Words

Words/Images That Make Me Smile or Laugh

Words That Make Noise

On the Same Page: Shared Reading Beyond the Primary Grades by Janet Allen. Copyright © 2002. Stenhouse Publishers.

On the Same Page: Shared Reading Beyond the Primary Grades by Janet Allen. Copyright © 2002. Stenhouse Publishers.

I.8 Language Collection II

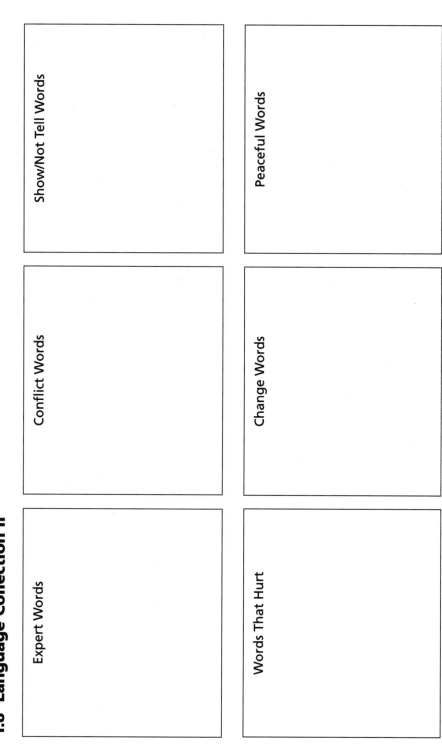

Expert Words

Conflict Words

Show/Not Tell Words

Words That Hurt

Change Words

Peaceful Words

1.9 Words We Can Read, A–Z

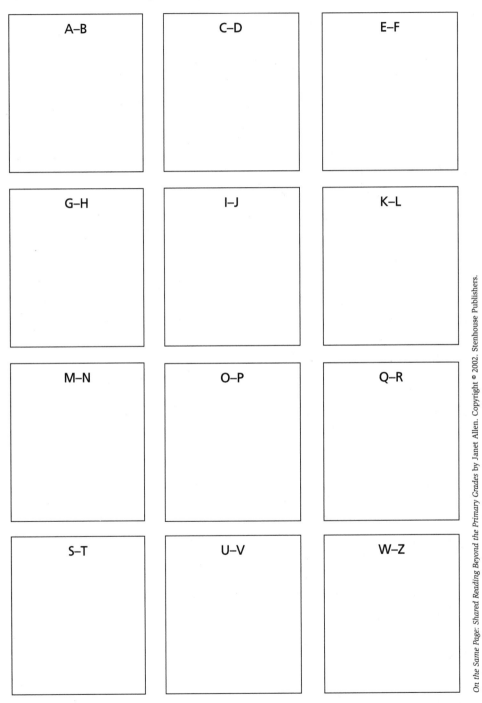

A–B	C–D	E–F
G–H	I–J	K–L
M–N	O–P	Q–R
S–T	U–V	W–Z

On the Same Page: Shared Reading Beyond the Primary Grades by Janet Allen. Copyright © 2002. Stenhouse Publishers.

I.10 Word in My Context

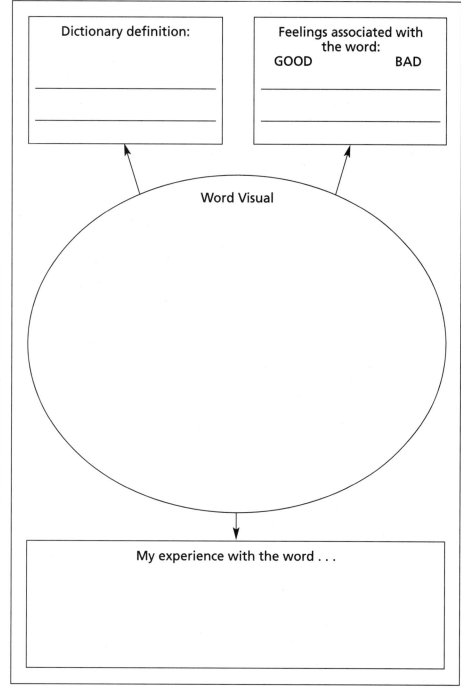

| Dictionary definition: | Feelings associated with the word:
GOOD   BAD |

Word Visual

My experience with the word . . .

I.11 Alike but Different

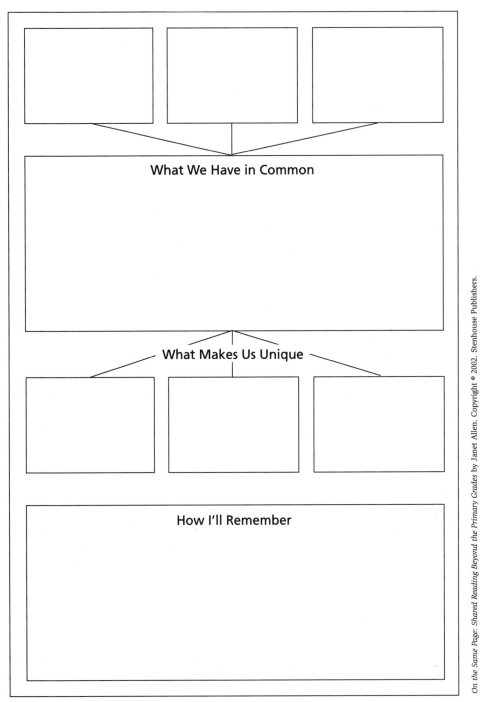

What We Have in Common

What Makes Us Unique

How I'll Remember

On the Same Page: Shared Reading Beyond the Primary Grades by Janet Allen. Copyright © 2002. Stenhouse Publishers.

I.12 Information Quest

Source:	Source:	Source:
_____	_____	_____
Facts:	Connections to existing background knowledge: (personal and previous source)	Compare: (new info to previous discoveries)
_____	_____	_____
_____	_____	_____
_____	_____	_____
_____	_____	_____
_____	_____	Contrast: (new info not encountered before)
_____	_____	_____
_____	_____	_____
Questions:	Patterns of discovered information:	_____
_____	_____	_____
_____	_____	Questions I still have:
_____	_____	_____
_____	_____	_____
_____	_____	_____
_____	_____	_____
_____	_____	_____

I.13 Multiple Sources, Multiple Perspectives

Sources	Factual Information	Reading Between the Lines Information	Questions

I.14 Cause and Effect in Science

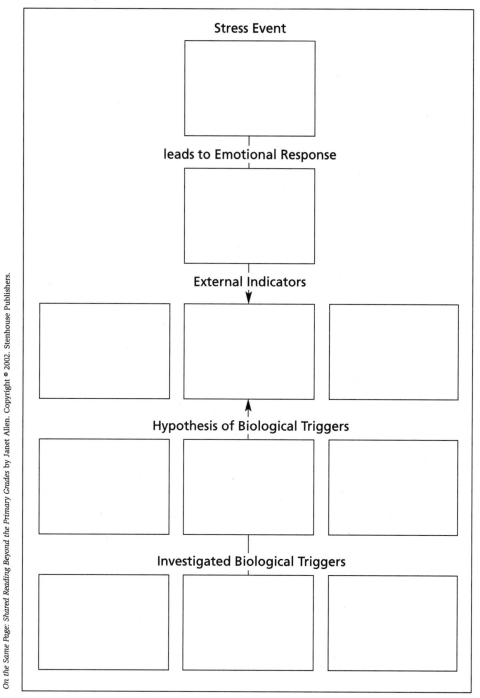

Stress Event

leads to Emotional Response

External Indicators

Hypothesis of Biological Triggers

Investigated Biological Triggers

1.15 Text to Text

Compare and Contrast: _____ ⟷ _____		

On the Same Page: Shared Reading Beyond the Primary Grades by Janet Allen. Copyright © 2002. Stenhouse Publishers.

I.16 Student Self-Assessment of Strategic Reading

Before Reading

Yes   No

_____ _____   1.   I asked myself why I was reading this text.

_____ _____   2.   I looked at the title/subtitles to predict content.

_____ _____   3.   I asked myself what I already knew about the topic/content.

_____ _____   4.   I looked at any pictures or visuals to build background knowledge for the content.

_____ _____   5.   I made a plan for monitoring my reading.

During Reading

Yes   No

_____ _____   1.   I used text supports to help me read.

_____ _____   2.   I asked myself questions I thought might be answered in further reading.

_____ _____   3.   I tried to make connections to what I was reading.

_____ _____   4.   I tried to determine the author's purpose for writing.

_____ _____   5.   I asked myself what I was supposed to be learning.

_____ _____   6.   I stopped when I got confused and tried to figure out how to make the text make sense (used fix-up strategies).

After Reading

Yes   No

_____ _____   1.   I was able to list, talk about, or highlight main points of what I read.

_____ _____   2.   I was able to organize my ideas so that I could demonstrate learning.

_____ _____   3.   I was able to demonstrate comprehension by completing reading-related tasks (academic journals, questions).

_____ _____   4.   I used a system to keep track of important information from my reading.

I.17 Understanding a Concept ABC x 2

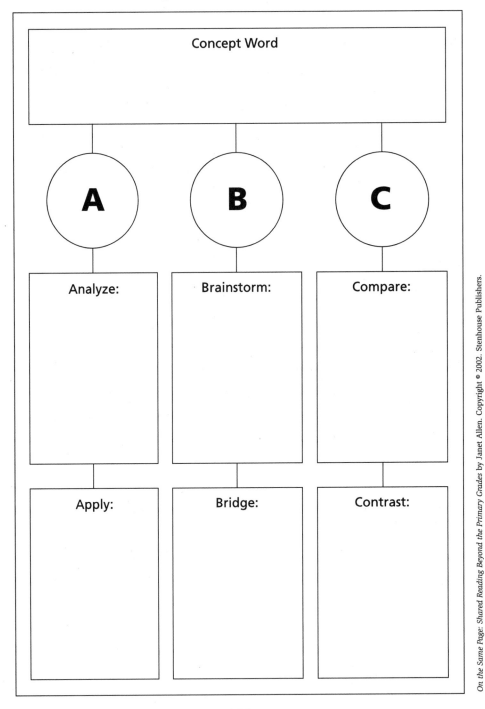

Concept Word

A   B   C

Analyze: Brainstorm: Compare:

Apply: Bridge: Contrast:

I.18 Triple Entry Journal

Noting and Worth Remembering	Making Connections	Questioning

I.19 Who Is My Audience?

Text	Audience	Language That Indicates Author Awareness of Audience	Elements (Character, Setting, Tone) Indicating Awareness of Audience	Changes Necessary if Audience Changed

On the Same Page: Shared Reading Beyond the Primary Grades by Janet Allen. Copyright © 2002. Stenhouse Publishers.

On the Same Page: Shared Reading Beyond the Primary Grades by Janet Allen. Copyright © 2002. Stenhouse Publishers.

I.20 Guided Response

What I know so far about the story is . . .	What I've learned so far about the main character is . . .	What I've learned about myself by reading this is . . .	What I've learned about my reading is . . .

So, I think . . . .

I.21 Historical Event Guided Response

What I know so far about this event is . . .	What I've learned so far about the cause of the event is . . .	How I think I would have responded if I had been living during this event is . . .	I think the real problem is . . .

So, I think the outcome will be . . .

On the Same Page: Shared Reading Beyond the Primary Grades by Janet Allen. Copyright © 2002. Stenhouse Publishers.

I.22 **Scientific Guided Response**

What I already knew about this phenomenon was . . .	What I've learned so far from my observations is . . .	What I've learned from my reading is . . .	What I now know is . . .

I think this process is similar to _____ because . . .

I.23 Mathematical Guided Response

What I think the problem is asking me to do is . . .	The steps I had to take to solve the problem were . . .	The difficulties I encountered were . . .	This type of problem solving is easy/hard for me because . . .

So, I've learned . . .

On the Same Page: Shared Reading Beyond the Primary Grades by Janet Allen. Copyright © 2002. Stenhouse Publishers.

I.24 Becoming a Better Writer: Using Writers' Tools

Conventions of print	I use this when . . .	This convention helps communication because . . .	An example from my reading is . . .
Conventions of text	I use this when . . .	This convention helps communication because . . .	An example from my reading is . . .
Conventions of genre	I use this when . . .	This convention helps communication because . . .	An example from my reading is . . .

1.25 Effective Description

Text Sample	Characteristics of This Writer's Description	What Makes These Descriptive Passages Effective/Ineffective

Patterns of effective descriptive writing I will transfer to my writing:

_____

_____

On the Same Page: Shared Reading Beyond the Primary Grades by Janet Allen. Copyright © 2002. Stenhouse Publishers.

I.26 Book Pass

Title	Author	Comment

I.27 Concept Ladder

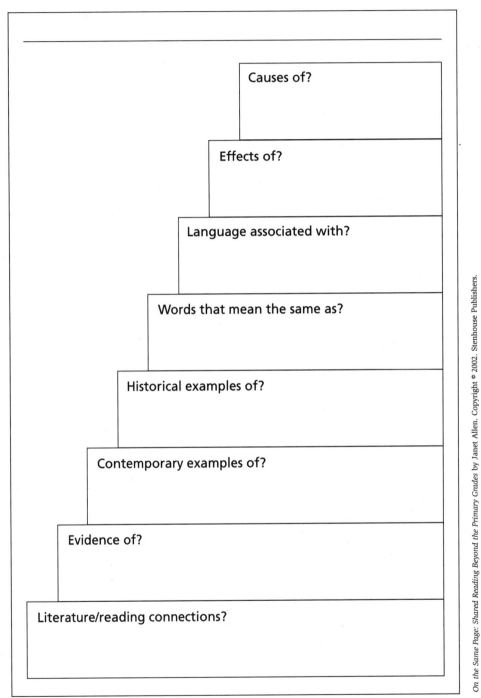

Causes of?

Effects of?

Language associated with?

Words that mean the same as?

Historical examples of?

Contemporary examples of?

Evidence of?

Literature/reading connections?

I.28 **Content Brainstorming**

Chapter Title _____

Key Words

Headings

Subheadings

_____

Picture Walk: What predictions can you make about content based on visuals?

Caption:

Caption:

Caption:

Connections and Questions

What predictions and connections could you make about what you will learn in the chapter based on above text supports?

What questions could you ask that would focus and guide your reading?

I.29 Assessment Tool

Critical Indicators for Developmental Reading Process

Student: Literacy Teacher: Grade: School Year:

A. Foundation Reading
Students learn to . . .

A1. Enjoyment
— A1.1 like words and word play
— A1.2 see humor and emotion in events or characters
— A1.3 mimic interesting words or rhyming patterns
— A1.4 express choices for texts
— A1.5 find favorite authors

A2. Text has meaning
— A2.1 know that oral language can be written down for reading by self or others
— A2.2 understand that letters form words, and words form phrases or sentences
— A2.3 see connection between background knowledge and understanding of language
— A2.4 discover or infer author intentions or purpose of text
— A2.5 know that writers use predictable patterns or support to help readers

---

B. Structural Support
Students develop ability to . . .

B1. Visualization
— B1.1 identify language in a text that would help create images in the mind
— B1.2 uses descriptive language to describe connections to the text
— B1.3 use sensory language (five senses) in a text to create images
— B1.4 describe oneself as if in the context of the text
— B1.5 use mental images to infer, make connections, and predict

B2. Questioning
— B2.1 create questions prompted by the text (title, cover, pictures, events, author)
— B2.2 create literal questions to help with recall, sequencing, and summarizing
— B2.3 create complex inferential questions that lead to deeper understanding of the text

---

C. Experienced and Knowledgeable Reading
Students have internalized . . .

— C1. reading strategies to understand diverse genres
— C2. ways to use texts as resources for writing
— C3. an ability to monitor and adjust reading for audience and purpose
— C4. strategies that are automatic—skills
— C5. multiple ways to determine word meaning for unknown or specialized vocabulary
— C6. a method for adjusting reading rate for purpose and audience

---

On the Same Page: Shared Reading Beyond the Primary Grades by Janet Allen. Copyright © 2002. Stenhouse Publishers.

On the Same Page: Shared Reading Beyond the Primary Grades by Janet Allen. Copyright © 2002. Stenhouse Publishers.

I.29 Assessment Tool (continued)

Critical Indicators for Developmental Reading Process

Student: Literacy Teacher: Grade: School Year:

A. Foundation Reading Students learn to . . .	B. Structural Support Students develop ability to . . .	C. Experienced and Knowledgeable Reading Students have internalized . . .
A3. Conventions of text/print ___ A3.1 recognize predictable patterns of language (syntax) in text ___ A3.2 recognize predictable characteristics of genre ___ A3.3 punctuate to support readers ___ A3.4 use surface features of text (boldface, italics, highlights, underlines) to support readers ___ A3.5 use pictures, graphs, headings, paragraphs to support readers **A4. Decoding** ___ A4.1 use sight words to increase fluency ___ A4.2 build bank of sight words by connecting words with similar meanings and patterns ___ A4.3 use phonetic knowledge to support word predictions ___ A4.4 use known prefixes, root words, suffixes to analyze unknown words (structural analysis)	**B3. Inferring** ___ B3.1 identify text clues (words, illustrations, title, cover, pictures, etc.) that help him/her infer ___ B3.2 identify background knowledge that helps him/her infer ___ B3.3 articulate how he/she combines text clues and background knowledge to infer ___ B3.4 use inferences to make predictions ___ B3.5 modify inference as new text clues are presented ___ B3.6 use inferences to draw conclusions or make a judgment	C7. independent reading pursuits _____

285

I.29 Assessment Tool (continued)

Critical Indicators for Developmental Reading Process

Student: Literacy Teacher: Grade: School Year:

A. Foundation Reading Students learn to . . .	B. Structural Support Students develop ability to . . .	C. Experienced and Knowledgeable Reading Students have internalized . . .

A5. Connections

___ A5.1 make personal connections to text

___ A5.2 see connections between and among texts (genre, author, style, topic)

___ A5.3 discover similarities and differences between and among texts

___ A5.4 see connections between world events and text

A6. Responses

___ A6.1 move from "seeing" the words to "living" the words on the page

___ A6.2 understand that language can produce emotional or physical responses while reading

___ A6.3 see their spoken responses as support for written responses

___ A6.4 imagine themselves in the book (character, events)

___ A6.5 find comfort, enjoyment, and new ways of thinking through reading

B4. Analysis/Synthesis

___ B4.1 differentiate between essential ideas and nonessential ideas based on a specific purpose

___ B4.2 combine related ideas to formulate an original idea, a new line of thinking, or a new creation

___ B4.3 recognize the relationship between the author's intention and the author's words

___ B4.4 determine the author's purpose

___ B4.5 understand that each "part" of the text works together to create the total effect of the author's intentions

___ B4.6 use the text to support his/her response to the text

I.29 Assessment Tool *(continued)*

Critical Indicators for Developmental Reading Process

Student:	Literacy Teacher:	Grade:	School Year:

A. Foundation Reading
Students learn to . . .

A7. Purpose of Text

___ A7.1 establish purpose for reading a text (information, enjoyment)

___ A7.2 infer the author's purpose for writing the text

___ A7.3 use text supports to help obtain information from the text (table of contents, glossary, index, references, footnotes, visuals)

___ A7.4 understand patterns of informational text organization (sequence/directions, cause/effect, problem/solution, listing/description, comparison/contrast)

___ A7.5 discover cue words that indicate type of informational text structures (sequence: first, then, next, finally)

___ A7.6 use cue words as a support for reading, remembering, and recounting information from text

I.29 Assessment Tool *(continued)*

Critical Indicators for Developmental Reading Process

Student: Literacy Teacher: Grade: School Year:

A. Foundation Reading
Students learn to . . .

A8. Monitor Reading

___ A8.1 recognize when text stops making sense and loses meaning

___ A8.2 develop strategies for maintaining focus during reading

___ A8.3 make notes or use aids (Post-its, markers, charts) to keep track of information

___ A8.4 establish self-questioning strategies in order to support, anticipate, and remember significant ideas from the text (What should I remember from this paragraph? How will I remember it? What is the connection between this chapter and the last one I read?)

___ A8.5 identify areas in text causing confusion (word meaning, sentence structures, insufficient/ inappropriate background knowledge, readability, literary devices, plot-character confusion)

___ A8.6 see that readers use a repertoire of strategies for overcoming text confusion and maintaining reading focus

288

On the Same Page: Shared Reading Beyond the Primary Grades by Janet Allen. Copyright © 2002. Stenhouse Publishers.

Appendix J

Guiding Readers Through
the Text

1.3 Guiding Readers Through the Text

Title: *Freak the Mighty*		
Page Nos.	Possibilities to Explore	Additional Ideas
1–20	(1) I never had a brain until Freak came along and let me borrow his for a while, and that's the truth . . ." (discuss self-image) (1) Begin Methods of Communication graphic as a way of discussion how we let people know what we're feeling and thinking. (2) Discuss memories: "remembering is a great invention of the mind" (2) Names we give ourselves: "I'm Robot Man" (3) Names "Mad Max they were calling me, or Max Factor . . ." (4) Read 1st paragraph for writing: Places we find to get comfort/hide. (5) Stop and discuss how Max sees himself and what he's used to. Make those opinions. (15) use "sobriquet" and "demeanor" to discuss context as word attack. (16) Revisit context with "quest." Use Making Connections graphic. (17) Revisit context with "robotics." (18) Opiate (19) OH: "I also read tons of books so I can figure out what's true and what's fake, which isn't always easy. Books are like truth serum—if you don't read, you can't figure out what's real." Do a class chart: "Books are like . . ." (20) Use "Jumping to Conclusions" as a way to pull together understanding of the characters.	
21–40	(21) Writing: Description of place to hide/escape/feel comfortable. (27) Crying because of happiness (something new for Max) (31) Language play: "Close encounters of the turd kind" (39) Discuss Max's fears at this point.	

On the Same Page: Shared Reading Beyond the Primary Grades by Janet Allen. Copyright © 2002. Stenhouse Publishers.

I.3 Guiding Readers Through the Text *(cont.)*

Title: *Freak the Mighty*		
Page Nos.	Possibilities to Explore	Additional Ideas
21–40 (cont.) 41–62	(40) Origin of name Freak the Mighty (41) Do prediction here using Learning to Read Between the Lines—Prediction (43) "He's taking evasive action." Begin Looking at Our Options (49) "Castle of Avarice" "Bloated Moat" What are these? (60) Using adages: "Necessity is the mother of invention." Give students a piece of string and paper clip and have groups brainstorm as many things as possible they could create or use these items for. (61) "She's a damsel who causes distress." Prediction/discuss convention of italics as a reading clue.	
21–40	(63) Gram is really adamant about the "new Testaments." Why? (64) Mutual benefit of friendship (71) How does Loretta Lee compare/contrast with Kevin's image of a fair damsel? (81) Discuss what makes reading memorable: OH: "Freak has been showing me how to read a whole book and for some reason it all makes sense, where before it was just a bunch of words I didn't care about." (86) "The worst thing happens later, in the cafeteria." What could be worse than what Max has just learned? (87) Mrs. Addison: "You're going to be okay, Maxwell Kane. I'm sure of it now." What has made her form this opinion?	
88–114	(89) Highlight "white space" as a reading clue (90) Why does Grim want a gun all of a sudden? (94–95) Write family stories that have become "tall tales." Use something from Big Fish as a demonstration. "I'm telling tales, my dear, not lies. Lies are mean things, and tales are meant to entertain."	

I.3 Guiding Readers Through the Text *(cont.)*

Title: *Freak the Mighty*

Page Nos.	Possibilities to Explore	Additional Ideas
88–114 (cont.)	(98–99) Writer's craft lesson: Building Suspense in Writing (103) Symbolism: fresh start at Christmas (104) Foreshadowing: "Once a car goes by real slow around the point and I've got this strange feeling there's no one at the wheel." (114) ". . . trying not to think of things I don't want to remember." I wonder why this chapter ends with these words.	
115–134	(127) Flashback: ". . . he's squeezing her dead with his bare hands, and no one can stopo him, no one, no one." (134) Story structure: If the book ended here, what part of the stroy would be left unfinished?	
135–160	(136) "You can't judge a book by its cover." Max, Iggy, Loretta (142) "Which is something I'll always remember, him saying that and me trying to figure it out." (160) Writing: Create a class dictionary with words that are important to the class.	

On the Same Page: Shared Reading Beyond the Primary Grades by Janet Allen. Copyright © 2002. Stenhouse Publishers.

I.3 Guiding Readers Through the Text *(cont.)*

Title: *Holes*		
Page Nos.	**Possibilities to Explore**	**Additional Ideas**
1–20	(4) Foreshadowing (3, 11) Setting (5) Prediction (7) Writing prompt: "He'd just been in the wrong place at the wrong time." (8) Family stories (9) Palindromes: Stanley Yelnats (10) Famous outlaws: claim to fame, roots of crime (13) School rules (19) Character analysis: Zero nicknames; adjusting to new environments	
21–40	(21–22) Scarcity, prospect rich vs. lean content (28, 32, 33) White space (31) Curses (35) Health advantages of sweating Elya's journey compared with Stanley's family pride	
41–68	(41) Yellow-spotted lizards: real or created? I wonder: "They eat small animals, insects, certain cactus thorns, and the shells of sunflower seeds." (Why sunflower seeds? Is this a clue?) (47) Stanley's nickname: Caveman—source? (49) Fossils (57) Writing prompt: "But it's not my fault . . ." (58) Zero's response: "I like to dig holes." (63) Stanley moved up one place in line. Significance? (64) X'ray's refusal to discuss gold tube—what's up? (68) What is the Warden up to? What inferences can be made about here?	
69–91	(76, 81, 82) Revisit character analysis of Zero (84) Racial issues: "On the lake they were all the same reddish brown color—the color of dirt."	

On the Same Page: Shared Reading Beyond the Primary Grades by Janet Allen. Copyright © 2002. Stenhouse Publishers.

I.3 Guiding Readers Through the Text (cont.)

Title: *Holes*		
Page Nos.	**Possibilities to Explore**	**Additional Ideas**
69–91 (cont.)	(85) Writing prompt: the wrong place at the wrong time (91) Foreshadowing	
92–115	(93) Author's clues: "Found refuge on God's thumb." Possible meanings? (93) Writing prompt: "The rattlesnake would be a lot more dangerous if it didn't have a rattle." (99) Making and confirming predictions: what does Stanley know and what good does it do him? (100) Foreshadowing (108) Folk cures (110) Reading between the lines: "That's our schoolhouse. It shows how much we value education in Green Lake." What do we know about these people? (114) Active reading: "You make the decision."	
116–144	(119) Writing: "He couldn't help but think that a hundred times zero was still nothing." (119) Significance of Zero telling Stanley his real name (125) Part 2 is entitled "The Last Hole." Predictions? (138–139) In what ways did Mr. Pendanski's actions bring on Zero's attack (cause and effect). What makes Zero snap? (144) What is the Warden up to now? Why does she want Zero erased from the files? (145) Writing: "He has nobody," said Mr. Pendanski. "He was nobody."	
145–172	(148) Use Looking at Our Options to discuss what Stanley might have done differently (154) In discovering the boat wreckage, what has Stanley really discovered?	

On the Same Page: Shared Reading Beyond the Primary Grades by Janet Allen. Copyright © 2002. Stenhouse Publishers.

I.3 Guiding Readers Through the Text *(cont.)*

Title: *Holes*		
Page Nos.	**Possibilities to Explore**	**Additional Ideas**
145–172 (cont.)	((155) Sploosh? Where does Zero come up with this? What would you have named this? (160) Writing: "When you spend your whole life living in a hole," he said, "the only way you can go is up." (166) Friendship: Zero's sacrifice—what creates a friendship where that kind of sacrifice is possible? (169) Good opportunity to teach inference: "Weeds and bugs," he said. "There's got to be water around somewhere." (170) Goal setting (see overhead) (172) What has Stanley discovered at the end of this sectioin? Predictions for how this might help them based on prior knowledge from the book?	
173–203	(203) Inference: "Stanley awoke in a meadow . . ." (177) Stop at white space and predict what we think the author will tell us next. (184) Discuss fate: "If I had just kept those old smelly sneakers, then neither of us would be here right now." (185) Discuss learning to like ourselves (last three paragraphs) (188) "You want to dig one more hole?" Stanley asked him. What is going on inside Stanley's head here? (188) Writing/Discussion: If you were the author, what options would you have for finishing the story at this point? (203) How did this happen? "Thank you," said the Warden. "You boys have been a great help." Predictions: If I were Stanley and Zero at this point, I would . . .	
204–233	(204–215) Use the Creating a Mental Image chart to record words, phrases, and inferences that would indicate what is going on inside Stanley and Zero's heads during this time.	

On the Same Page: Shared Reading Beyond the Primary Grades by Janet Allen. Copyright © 2002. Stenhouse Publishers.

1.3 Guiding Readers Through the Text *(cont.)*

Title: *Holes*		
Page Nos.	**Possibilities to Explore**	**Additional Ideas**
204–233 (cont.)	(225) How does the adage, "What goes around comes around" fit here? (226) Part 3 is entitled "Filling in the Holes." Predictions? (233) What holes were filled in for us (literally and figuratively)?	

Literature References

Allen, Roger, and Stephan D. Allen. 1995. *Winnie-the-Pooh on Problem Solving: In Which Pooh, Piglet and Friends Explore How to Solve Problems, So You Can Too.* New York: Dutton.

Amato, Mary. 2000. *The Word Eater.* New York: Holiday House.

Anderson, Laurie Halse. 1999. *Speak.* New York: Farrar, Straus and Giroux.

Angelou, Maya. 1986a. "Alone." In *Poems.* New York: Bantam Books.

———. 1986b. "No Losers No Weepers." In *Poems.* New York: Bantam Books.

———. 1993 [1969]. *I Know Why the Caged Bird Sings.* New York: Bantam Books.

Atkin, S. Beth, ed. 1996. *Voices from the Streets: Young Former Gang Members Tell Their Stories.* Boston: Little, Brown.

Avi. 1991. *Nothing but the Truth.* New York: Orchard Books.

The Beatles. 1967. "With a Little Help from My Friends." Recorded on *Sgt. Pepper's Lonely Hearts Club Band.* Capitol Records.

Berg, Elizabeth. 1993. *Durable Goods.* New York: Random House.

Bertrand, Diane Gonzales. 1999. *Trino's Choice.* Houston, TX: Pinata Books.

Bode, Janet, and Stan Mack. 1996. *Hard Time: A Real Look at Juvenile Crime and Violence.* New York: Delacorte.

Bridgers, Sue Ellen. 1996. *All We Know of Heaven.* Wilmington, NC: Banks Channel Books.

Brooks, Martha. 1994. "Moonlight Sonata." In *Traveling on into the Light and Other Stories.* New York: Penguin.

Brown, Marcia. 1998 [1954]. *Cinderella, or, The Little Glass Slipper: A Free Translation from the French of Charles Perrault.* 2d ed. New York: Aladdin Books.

Browning, Colleen. 1997. "Union Mixer." Artwork included in *Elements of Literature, Third Course.* New York: Holt, Rinehart and Winston.

Bullard, Sarah. 1993. "Schoolgirls Killed in Bombing of 16th Street Baptist Church, Birmingham, Alabama." In *Free at Last: A History of the Civil Rights Movement and Those Who Died in the Struggle.* Montgomery, AL: Southern Poverty Law Center.

Bunting, Eve. 1988. *A Sudden Silence.* San Diego: Harcourt.

———. 1996. *Going Home.* New York: HarperCollins.

———. 1999. *Blackwater.* New York: HarperCollins.

Burgess, Melvin. 1998. *Smack.* New York: Henry Holt.

Butler, Daniel, and Alan Ray. 1997. "That's a Spiceeeeeey 'Meatball'!" In *The World's Dumbest Criminals.* New York: Scholastic.

Canada, Geoffrey. 1995. *fist stick knife gun.* Boston: Beacon Press.

Carnes, Jim. 1996. "Home Was a Horse Stall." In *Us & Them.* New York: Oxford University Press.

Carroll, Lewis. 1999 [1960]. *The Annotated Alice: Alice's Adventures in Wonderland and Through the Looking Glass.* Introduction and notes by Martin Gardner. Definitive ed. New York: Norton.

Cheripko, Jan. 1996. *Imitate the Tiger.* Honesdale, PA: Boyds Mills Press.

Cisneros, Sandra. 1984. *The House on Mango Street*. Houston, TX: Arte Publico Press.

Climo, Shirley. 1989. *The Egyptian Cinderella*. New York: HarperCollins.

Collins, Billy. 1988. "The History Teacher." In *The Apple That Astonished Paris*. Little Rock: University of Arkansas Press.

Collins, Sheila Hebert. 1998. *Cendrillon: A Cajun Cinderella*. Gretna, LA: Pelican Publishing Co.

Cooney, Caroline. 1990. *The Face on the Milk Carton*. New York: Bantam Books.

Cooper, James Fenimore. 1841. *The Deerslayer*. Philadelphia: Lea and Blanchard.

Cormier, Robert. 1974. *The Chocolate War*. New York: Dell.

———. 1991. *We All Fall Down*. New York: Delacorte.

———. 1997. *Tenderness*. New York: Delacorte.

———. 1998. *Heroes*. New York: Delacorte.

Covington, Dennis. 1991. *Lizard*. New York: Delacorte.

Crew, Linda. 1989. *Children of the River*. New York: Bantam Books.

Crutcher, Chris. 1992. *Athletic Shorts: Six Short Stories*. Thorndike, ME: Thorndike Press.

———. 1993. *Staying Fat for Sarah Byrnes*. New York: Greenwillow Books.

———. 1995. *Ironman*. New York: Greenwillow Books.

Curtis, Christopher Paul. 1995. *The Watsons Go to Birmingham—1963*. New York: Delacorte.

Dahl, Roald. 1988. "The Song of the Centipede." In *James and the Giant Peach*. New York: Puffin.

Destiny's Child. 2001. "Survivor." Recorded on *Survivor*. Columbia Records.

Dickens, Charles. 1844. *A Christmas Carol*. London: Chapman and Hall.

Dixon, Ann. 1994. *The Sleeping Lady*. Anchorage: Alaska Northwest Books.

Draper, Sharon. 1994. *Tears of a Tiger*. New York: Atheneum.

Duncan, Lois. 1978. *Killing Mr. Griffin*. Boston: Little, Brown.

Edwards, Pamela Duncan. 1997. *Dinorella, A Prehistoric Fairy Tale*. New York: Hyperion.

Elias, Marilyn. 2001a. "Beaten Unconsciously: Violent Images May Alter Kids' Brain Activity, Spark Hostility." *USA Today*, April 19.

———. 2001b. "Kids Drink Too Much Juice, Doctors Say." *USA Today*, May 8.

Enzensberger, Hans Magnus. 1998. *The Number Devil: A Mathematical Adventure*. New York: Henry Holt.

Evans, Richard Paul. 2001. *The Tower: A Story of Humility*. New York: Simon and Schuster.

Ewing, Lynne. 1998. *Party Girl*. New York: Knopf.

Farley, Christopher John. 2000. "The Ghosts of Alabama." *Time*, May 29.

Ferris, Jean. 1999. *Bad*. New York: Farrar, Straus and Giroux.

Flake, Sharon. 1998. *The Skin I'm In*. New York: Hyperion.

Fleischman, Paul. 1997. *Seedfolks*. New York: HarperCollins.

———. 1998. *Whirligig*. New York: Henry Holt.

Florian, Douglas. 1994. "Mr. Backward." In *Bing, Bang, Boing*. New York: Harcourt.

Fox, Mem. 1985. *Wilfrid Gordon McDonald Partridge*. La Jolla, CA: Kane Miller.

Frank, Anne. 1958. *The Diary of Anne Frank*. New York: Dramatists Play Service.

Frank, David V., et al. 2001. *Focus on Physical Science*. California ed. Science Explorer Ser. Needham, MA: Prentice Hall.

Frasier, Debra. 2000. *Miss Alaineus: A Vocabulary Disaster*. San Diego: Harcourt.

Gallo, Donald R., ed. 1997. *No Easy Answers: Short Stories About Teenagers Making Tough Choices*. New York: Delacorte.

Gantos, Jack. 2000a. *Joey Pigza Loses Control.* New York: Farrar, Straus and Giroux.

———. 2002b. *Hole in My Life.* New York: Farrar, Straus and Giroux.

Garland, Sherry. 1994. *I Never Knew Your Name.* Boston: Houghton Mifflin.

Gaynor, Gloria. 1978. "I Will Survive." Recorded on *Love Tracks.* Polydor.

Gilbert, Barbara Snow. 1996. *Stone Water.* Asheville, NC: Front Street.

Glenn, Mel. 1988. "Belinda Enriquez, Period 3, Room 122." In *Back to Class.* Boston: Houghton Mifflin.

———. 1996. *Who Killed Mr. Chippendale?* New York: NAL.

———. 1997. *The Taking of Room 114.* New York: NAL.

Gordon, Karen Elizabeth. 1993. *The Deluxe Transitive Vampire: The Ultimate Handbook of Grammar for the Innocent, the Eager, and the Doomed.* New York: Pantheon.

———. 1997. *Torn Wings and Faux Pas: A Flashbook of Style, a Beastly Guide Through the Writer's Labyrinth.* New York: Pantheon.

Gorog, Judith. 1994. *When Nobody's Home: Fifteen Baby-sitting Tales of Terror.* New York: Scholastic.

Greene, Bette. 1991. *The Drowning of Stephan Jones.* New York: Bantam Books.

Griffin, Adele. 2001. *Amandine.* New York: Hyperion.

Haddix, Margaret Peterson. 2000. *Turnabout.* New York: Simon and Schuster.

Hakim, Joy. 1995. "Forgetting the Constitution." In *A History of US.* New York: Oxford University Press.

Harper, Michael. 2000. "American History." In *Songlines in Michaeltree: New and Collected Poems.* Urbana: University of Illinois Press.

Hautman, Pete. 1996. *Mr. Was.* New York: Simon and Schuster.

Head, Ann. 1967. *Mr. and Mrs. Bo Jo Jones.* New York: New American Library.

Hearne, Betsy. 1998. *Listening for Leroy.* New York: Margaret K. McElderry.

Herek, Stephen, dir. 1992. *The Mighty Ducks.* Walt Disney Video.

Herrera, Juan Felipe. 1999. *CrashBoomLove: A Novel in Verse.* Albuquerque: University of New Mexico Press.

Hickox, Rebecca. 1998. *The Golden Sandal: A Middle Eastern Cinderella Story.* New York: Holiday House.

Hinton, S. E. 1967. *The Outsiders.* New York: Dell.

Hobbs, Will. 1998. *The Maze.* New York: Avon Books.

Hoffman, Alice. 2000. *The River King.* New York: Penguin Putnam.

Holbrook, Sara. 1996a. "Labels." In *Am I Naturally This Crazy?* Honesdale, PA: Boyds Mills Press.

———. 1996b. "Mistrust." In *The Dog Ate My Homework.* Honesdale, PA: Boyds Mills Press.

———. 1996c. "You Promised." In *The Dog Ate My Homework.* Honesdale, PA: Boyds Mills Press.

———. 1998. "Bang, I Gotcha." In *Walking on the Boundaries of Change: Poems of Transition.* Honesdale, PA: Boyds Mills Press.

Jennings, Paul. 1993. "Ex Poser." In *Unmentionable! More Amazing Stories.* New York: Viking Penguin.

———. 1996. "A Mouthful." In *Uncovered! Weird, Weird Stories.* New York: Viking Penguin.

———. 1998. "Licked." In *Covered with Nails and Other Stories to Shock Your Socks Off.* New York: Viking Penguin.

Juster, Norton. 1989. [1961]. *The Phantom Tollbooth.* New York: Random House.

Karlin, Barbara. 1989. *Cinderella.* Boston: Little, Brown.

Keb' Mo'. 1998. "Everything I Need." Recorded on *Slow Down.* Sony.

King, Stephen. 1999. *Hearts in Atlantis.* New York: Simon and Schuster.

Klass, David. 1995. *Danger Zone.* New York: Scholastic.

Kohut, John J., and Roland Sweet, comp. 1993. *News from the Fringe: True Stories of Weird People and Weirder Times.* New York: Penguin.

Korman, Gordon. 2000. *No More Dead Dogs.* New York: Hyperion.

Korman, Gordon, and Bernice Korman. 1992. "Vocabulary." In *The D- Poems of Jeremy Bloom.* New York: Scholastic.

Lanse, Hal W. 2001. *Penelope Quagmire and the Lizard Men from Outer Space.* Hickory Corners, MI: ImaJinn Books.

Lasky, Kathryn. 1994. *Memoirs of a Bookbat.* San Diego: Harcourt.

Lee, Spike, dir. 1997. *Four Little Girls: An HBO Documentary Film.* In Association with 40 Acres and a Mule Filmworks, Inc. United States: HBO Documentary.

Limp Bizkit. 2000. "Break Stuff." Recorded on *Chocolate Starfish and the Hot Dog Flavored Water.* Flip/Interscope Records.

Loewen, James W. 1995. *Lies My Teacher Told Me: Everything Your American History Textbook Got Wrong.* New York: New Press.

Lorbiecki, Marybeth. 1996. *Just One Flick of a Finger.* New York: Penguin Putnam.

Louie, Ai-Ling. 1982. *Yeh-Shen: A Cinderella Story from China.* New York: Philomel Books.

Lovering, Jim. 1984. *It Was a Dark and Stormy Night,* ed. Scott Rice. New York: Viking Penguin.

Mahy, Margaret. 1990. *Seven Chinese Brothers.* New York: Scholastic.

Many, Paul. 1997. *These Are the Rules.* New York: Walker.

Marquis, Don. 1970 [1927]. "mehitabel was once cleopatra." In *archy and mehitabel.* New York: Anchor.

Marsden, John. 1998. *Prayer for the Twenty-First Century.* New York: Star Bright Books.

Martin, Rafe. 1992. *The Rough-Face Girl.* New York: Philomel.

Maruki, Toshi. 1980. *Hiroshima No Pika.* New York: Lothrop, Lee and Shepard.

Masoff, Joy. 2000. *Oh, Yuck! The Encyclopedia of Everything Nasty.* New York: Workman.

Mazer, Harry, ed. 1997. *Twelve Shots: Outstanding Short Stories About Guns.* New York: Delacorte.

McCammon, Robert. 1991. *Boy's Life.* Thorndike, ME: Thorndike Press.

McDonald, Joyce. 1997. *Swallowing Stones.* New York: Delacorte.

Medearis, Angela Shelf. 1995. *Skin Deep and Other Teenage Reflections.* New York: Macmillan.

Miklowitz, Gloria. 1997. "Confession." In *No Easy Answers,* ed. Donald R. Gallo. New York: Delacorte.

Mooney, Bel. 1997. *The Voices of Silence.* New York: Bantam.

Morley, Christopher. 1994. "Nursery Rhymes for the Tender-Hearted (Dedicated to Don Marquis)." In *Insectasides,* ed. Martha Paulos. New York: Viking. Poem originally published in 1921.

Mueller, Marnie. 1990a. "First Week at Tule Lake." In *Words on the Page, the World in Your Hand Volume 2,* ed. Catherine Lipkin and Virginia Solotaroff. New York: Harper and Row.

———. 1990b. "Issei Bachelor at Tule Lake." In *Words on the Page, the World in Your Hand Volume 2,* ed. Catherine Lipkin and Virginia Solotaroff. New York: Harper and Row.

———. 1990c. "Santa Anita Racetrack Assembly Center—March 1942." In *Words on the Page, the World in Your Hand Volume 2,* ed. Catherine Lipkin and Virginia Solotaroff. New York: Harper and Row.

———. 1990d. "Teenage Boy at Tule Lake." In *Words on the Page, the World in Your Hand Volume 2*, ed. Catherine Lipkin and Virginia Solotaroff. New York: Harper and Row.

———. 1990e. "Train Ride to Tule Lake Internment Camp—May 1942." In *Words on the Page, the World in Your Hand Volume 2*, ed. Catherine Lipkin and Virginia Solotaroff. New York: Harper and Row.

Myers, Jack. 1999. *On the Trail of the Komodo Dragon, and Other Explorations of Science in Action*. Honesdale, PA: Boyds Mills Press.

Myers, Walter Dean. 1988. *Scorpions*. New York: HarperCollins.

———. 1999. *Monster*. New York: HarperCollins.

Nash, Johnny. 1977. "I Can See Clearly Now." Recorded on *Johnny Nash Collection: 20 of My Favorite Songs*. Epic.

Nelson, Portia. 1993. "Autobiography in 5 Short Chapters." In *There's a Hole in My Sidewalk*. Hillsboro, OR: Beyond Words Publishers.

"The Nervous System." 1985. Silver Burdett, *Science*. Centennial ed. Morristown, NJ: Scott Foresman.

Newton, David E. 1995. *Teen Violence: Out of Control*. New York: Enslow.

Ogden, Maurice. 1959. *The Hangman*. Garden Grove, CA: n.p.

Okie, Susan. 1999. "Reptiles and Children Don't Mix." *Washington Post*, November 16, p. Z12.

Olson, Gretchen. 1998. *Joyride*. Honesdale, PA: Boyds Mills Press.

Pastan, Linda. 1985. "Whom Do You Visualize as Your Reader?" In *Pocket Poems*, ed. Paul Janeczko. New York: Simon and Schuster.

Paulsen, Gary. 1995. *The Rifle*. San Diego: Harcourt.

———. 1989. *The Winter Room*. New York: Scholastic.

Peck, Richard. 1984. "Priscilla and the Wimps." In *Sixteen*, ed. Donald R. Gallo. New York: Bantam Doubleday Dell.

———. 1985. *Remembering the Good Times*. New York: Bantam Doubleday Dell.

Philbrick, Rodman. 1993. *Freak the Mighty*. New York: Scholastic.

Plummer, Louise. 2000. *A Dance for Three*. New York: Delacorte.

Queen. 1979. "We Are the Champions." Recorded on *Queen Live Killers*. Elektra.

Randall, Dudley, ed. 1971. "Ballad of Birmingham." In *The Black Poets*. New York: Bantam Books.

Randle, Kristen D. 1998. *Breaking Rank*. New York: Morrow/Avon.

Rapp, Adam. 1997. *The Buffalo Tree*. Asheville, NC: Front Street.

Robinson, Edwin Arlington. 1989 [1897]. "Richard Cory." In *Maine Speaks: An Anthology of Maine Literature*. Brunswick, ME: Maine Writers and Publishers Alliance.

Rodriguez, Luis J. 1999. *It Doesn't Have to Be This Way: A Barrio Story*. San Francisco: Children's Book Press.

Rowling, J. K. 1998. *Harry Potter and the Sorcerer's Stone*. New York: Scholastic.

Ruiz, Miguel Angel. 1997. *The Four Agreements: A Practical Guide to Personal Freedom*. San Rafael, CA: Amber-Allen Publishing.

Sachar, Louis. 1998. *Holes*. New York: Farrar, Straus and Giroux.

San Souci, Robert D. 1998. *Cendrillon: A Caribbean Cinderella*. New York: Simon and Schuster.

Schroeder, Alan. 1997. *Smoky Mountain Rose: An Appalachian Cinderella*. New York: Penguin Putnam.

Scieszka, Jon. 2001. *Baloney*. New York: Penguin Putnam.

Sendak, Maurice. 1991. *Chicken Soup with Rice: A Book of Months*. New York: Scott Foresman.

Silverstein, Shel. 1981. *A Light in the Attic*. New York: Harper and Row.

Sloane, Paul. 1994. *Test Your Lateral Thinking IQ*. New York: Sterling Publishing.

Sloat, Teri. 1990. *The Eye of the Needle*. New York: Penguin Putnam.

Smith, Glenna Johnson. 1989. "Summer Person." In *Maine Speaks: An Anthology of Maine Literature*. Brunswick, ME: Maine Writers and Publishers Alliance.

Smith, Julie Dean. 1988. *Bride of Dark and Stormy*, ed. Scott Rice. New York: Penguin Books.

Sparks, Beatrice, ed. 1971. *Go Ask Alice*. New York: Avon Books.

———. 1979. *Jay's Journal*. New York: Simon and Schuster.

———. 1994. *It Happened to Nancy*. New York: Avon Books.

———. 1998. *Annie's Baby*. New York: Simon and Schuster.

———. 2000. *Treacherous Love*. New York: Avon Books.

Staples, Suzanne Fisher. 1989. *Shabanu: Daughter of the Wind*. New York: Knopf.

Steinbeck, John. 1937. *Of Mice and Men*. New York: Viking.

Stone, Ken. 1999. "Wilt's 100-Point Ball Was a Steal—and Fans' Cross to Bear for Decades." *San Diego Union Tribune*, October 14.

Strasser, Todd. 2000. *Give a Boy a Gun*. New York: Simon and Schuster.

"Sunday School Bombing." 1994. In *Bridges and Borders: Diversity in America*, by the editors of *Time* Magazine. New York: Warner Books.

Swarthout, Glendon. 1970. *Bless the Beasts and Children*. New York: Doubleday.

System of a Down. 2001. "Chop Suey." Recorded on *Toxicity*. American.

Taylor, Mildred. 1995. *The Well: David's Story*. New York: Penguin Putnam.

Teaching Tolerance. 1992. *A Time for Justice: America's Civil Rights Movement*. Montgomery, AL: Southern Poverty Law Center.

———. 1995. *The Shadow of Hate*. Montgomery, AL: Southern Poverty Law Center.

Thomas, Robb. 1997. *Doing Time: Notes from the Undergrad*. New York: Simon and Schuster.

Trudeau, Kevin. 1995. *Kevin Trudeau's Mega Memory: How to Release Your Superpower Memory in 30 Minutes or Less a Day*. New York: Morrow/Avon.

Tsuchiya, Yukio. 1988 [1951]. *Faithful Elephants: A True Story of Animals, People, and War*. Boston: Houghton Mifflin.

Twomey, Cathleen. 2001. *Charlotte's Choice*. Honesdale, PA: Boyds Mills Press.

Van Allsburg, Chris. 1990. *Just a Dream*. Boston: Houghton Mifflin.

VanOosting, James. 1997. *The Last Payback*. New York: HarperCollins.

Walter, Virginia. 1998. *Making up Megaboy*. New York: Delacorte.

Wiesel, Elie. 1960. *Night*. New York: Hill and Wang.

Wolff, Virginia Euwer. 1993. *Make Lemonade*. New York: Henry Holt.

Wynne-Jones, Tim. 1993. "Night of the Pomegranate." In *Some of the Kinder Planets*. New York: Orchard Books.

Yep, Laurence. 1977. *Child of the Owl*. New York: HarperCollins.

Professional References

Adams, D., and C. Cerqui. 1989. *Effective Vocabulary Instruction.* Kirkland, WA: Reading Resources.

Alexander, Patricia A., and Tamara L. Jetton. 2000. "Learning from Text: A Multidimensional and Developmental Perspective." In *Handbook of Reading Research Volume III,* ed. M. L. Kamil, P. B. Mosenthal, P. D. Pearson, and R. Barr. Mahwah, NJ: Erlbaum.

Allen, Janet. 1999. *Words, Words, Words: Teaching Vocabulary in Grades 4–12.* Portland, ME: Stenhouse.

———. 2000. *Yellow Brick Roads: Shared and Guided Paths to Independent Reading 4–12.* Portland, ME: Stenhouse.

Allington, Richard L. 2000. *What Really Matters for Struggling Readers: Designing Research-Based Programs.* New York: Addison Wesley Longman.

Baker, Scott, Deborah C. Simmons, and Edward Kameenui. 1995. *Vocabulary Acquisition: Curricular and Instructional Implications for Diverse Learners.* Technical Report No. 13. Eugene: University of Oregon, National Center to Improve the Tools of Educators.

Baumann, J. F., and E. J. Kameenui. 1991. "Research on Vocabulary Instruction: Ode to Voltaire." In *Handbook of Research on Teaching the English Language Arts,* ed. J. Flood, J. M. Jensen, D. Lapp, and J. R. Squire. New York: Macmillan.

Bean, Thomas. 2000. "Reading in the Content Areas: Social Constructivist Dimensions." In *Handbook of Reading Research Volume III,* ed. M. L. Kamil, P. B. Mosenthal, P. D. Pearson, and R. Barr. Mahwah, NJ: Erlbaum.

Beane, James. 1996. "Re-Entry Blues." In *Oops: What We Learn When Our Teaching Fails,* ed. Brenda Miller Power and Ruth Shagoury Hubbard. Portland, ME: Stenhouse.

Bettelheim, Bruno, and Karen Zelan. 1981. *On Learning to Read: The Child's Fascination with Meaning.* New York: Knopf.

Blachowicz, Camille, and Peter Fisher. 2000. "Vocabulary Instruction." In *Handbook of Reading Research Volume III,* ed. M. L. Kamil, P. B. Mosenthal, P. D. Pearson, and R. Barr. Mahwah, NJ: Erlbaum.

Brancato, Robin. 1992. "Lit-Lib: Using Literature to Teach Writing." In *Authors' Insights: Turning Teenagers into Readers and Writers,* ed. Donald R. Gallo. Portsmouth, NH: Heinemann-Boynton/Cook.

Bridges and Borders: Diversity in America. 1994. By the editors of *Time* Magazine. New York: Warner Books.

Caine, Renate, and Geoffrey Caine. 1994. *Making Connections: Teaching and the Human Brain.* Menlo Park, CA: Addison-Wesley.

Carroll, Lewis. 1999 [1960]. *The Annotated Alice: Alice's Adventures in Wonderland and Through the Looking Glass,* ed. Martin Gardner. Definitive ed. New York: Norton.

Chambers, Aidan. 1996. *Tell Me: Children, Reading and Talk.* Portland, ME: Stenhouse.

Costa, Arthur L., and Bena Kallick, eds. 2000. *Assessing and Reporting on Habits of Mind*. Alexandria, VA: Association for Supervision and Curriculum Development.

Davey, B. 1986. "Using Textbook Activity Guides to Help Students Learn from Textbooks." *Journal of Reading* 29: 489–494.

Davies, Robertson. 1990. *A Voice from the Attic: Essays on the Art of Reading*. Rev. ed. New York: Penguin Books.

Dorris, Michael, and Emilie Buchwald, eds. 1997. *The Most Wonderful Books: Writers on the Pleasures of Reading*. Minneapolis, MN: Milkweed Editions.

Duckworth, Eleanor. 1996. *"The Having of Wonderful Ideas" and Other Essays on Teaching and Learning*. 2d ed. New York: Teachers College Press.

Fletcher, Ralph, and JoAnn Portalupi. 1998. *Craft Lessons: Teaching Writing K–8*. Portland, ME: Stenhouse.

Fountas, Irene C., and Gay Su Pinnell. 2001. *Guiding Readers and Writers Grades 3–6: Teaching Comprehension, Genre, and Content Literacy*. Portsmouth, NH: Heinemann.

Fox, Mem. 2001. *Reading Magic: Why Reading Aloud to Our Children Will Change Their Lives Forever*. New York: Harcourt.

Gallo, Donald R. 1992. *Authors' Insights: Turning Teenagers into Readers and Writers*. Portsmouth, NH: Heinemann-Boynton/Cook.

Gladwell, Malcolm. 2000. *The Tipping Point: How Little Things Can Make a Big Difference*. Boston: Little, Brown.

Guthrie, John T., Solomon Alao, and Jennifer M. Rinehart. 1997. "Engagement in Reading for Young Adolescents." *Journal of Adolescent and Adult Literacy* 40: 6, 438–445.

Harvey, Stephanie, and Anne Goudvis. 2000. *Strategies That Work: Teaching Comprehension to Enhance Understanding*. Portland, ME: Stenhouse.

Hawkins, David. 1978. "Critical Barriers to Science Learning." *Outlook* 29: 3–23.

Hillocks, George, Jr. 1995. *Teaching Writing as Reflective Practice*. New York: Teachers College Press.

———. 1999. *Ways of Thinking, Ways of Teaching*. New York: Teachers College Press.

Holdaway, Don. 1979. *The Foundations of Literacy*. Portsmouth, NH: Heinemann.

Holt, John. 1969. "How Teachers Make Children Hate Reading." In *The Underachieving School*. New York: Pitman Publishing.

Keene, Ellin Oliver, and Susan Zimmerman. 1997. *Mosaic of Thought: Teaching Comprehension in a Reader's Workshop*. Portsmouth, NH: Heinemann.

King, Stephen. 2000. *On Writing: A Memoir of the Craft*. New York: Pocket Books.

Kirby, Dan, Tom Liner, and Ruth Vinz. 1988. *Inside Out: Developmental Strategies for Teaching Writing*. 2d ed. Portsmouth, NH: Heinemann-Boynton/Cook.

Kohn, Alfie. 1993. "Choices for Children: Why and How to Let Students Decide." *Phi Delta Kappan* 75 (1): 8–21.

Krashen, Stephen D. 1999. *Three Arguments Against Whole Language and Why They Are Wrong*. Portsmouth, NH: Heinemann.

Langer, Judith. 2000. *Beating the Odds: Teaching Middle and High School Students to Read and Write Well*. CELA Research Report Number 12014. 2d ed. Albany: National Research Center on English Learning and Achievement.

Levy, Steven. 1996. *Starting from Scratch: One Classroom Builds Its Own Curriculum*. Portsmouth, NH: Heinemann.

Marzano, Robert J., Debra J. Pickering, and Jane E. Pollock. 2001. *Classroom Instruction That Works*. Alexandria, VA: Association for Supervision and Curriculum Development.

McGinley, William J., and Peter R. Denner. 1987. "Story Impressions: A Prereading/Writing Activity." *Journal of Reading* 31 (3): 248–253.

Meek, Margaret. 1982. *Learning to Read.* Portsmouth, NH: Heinemann.

Moffett, James, and Betty Jane Wagner. 1991. *Student-Centered Language Arts, K–12.* 4th ed. Portsmouth, NH: Heinemann-Boynton/Cook.

Mooney, Margaret E. 1988. *Developing Life-Long Readers.* Wellington, NZ: Learning Media, Ministry of Education.

———. 1990. *Reading To, With, and By Children.* Katonah, NY: Richard C. Owen.

Nagy, William E. 1988. *Teaching Vocabulary to Improve Reading Comprehension.* Newark, DE: International Reading Association.

New Zealand Ministry of Education. 1985. *Reading in Junior Classes.* Katonah, NY: Richard C. Owen.

Ogle, D. M. 1986. "K-W-L: A Teaching Model That Develops Active Reading of Expository Text." *Reading Teacher* 39: 564–570.

Paris, Scott, Barbara Wasik, and Julianne Turner. 1991. "The Development of Strategic Readers." In *Handbook of Reading Research Volume II,* ed. R. Barr, M. L. Kamil, P. B. Mosenthal, and P. D. Pearson. New York: Longman.

Portalupi, JoAnn, and Ralph Fletcher. 2001. *Nonfiction Craft Lessons: Teaching Information Writing K–8.* Portland, ME: Stenhouse.

Raphael, T. E., and J. McKinney. 1983. "An Examination of Fifth- and Eighth-Grade Children's Question-Answering Behavior: An Instructional Study in Metacognition." *Journal of Reading Behavior* 14: 67–86.

Readence, J. E., T. W. Bean, and R. S. Baldwin. 1985. *Content Area Reading: An Integrated Approach,* 2d ed. Dubuque, IA: Kendall/Hunt.

Resnick, Lauren B. 1999. "Making America Smarter." In *Education Week* on the Web, June 16. < http://www.edweek.org/ew/vol-18/40thiswk.htm >.

Romano, Tom. 2000. *Blending Genre, Altering Style: Writing Multigenre Papers.* Portsmouth, NH: Heinemann-Boynton/Cook.

Schwartz, Lynne Sharon. 1996. *Ruined by Reading.* Boston: Beacon Press.

Seligman, M. E. P. 1975. *Helpless: On Depression, Development, and Death.* San Francisco: Freeman.

Smith, Frank. 1988. *Joining the Literacy Club.* Portsmouth, NH: Heinemann.

———. 1998. *The Book of Learning and Forgetting.* New York: Teachers College Press.

Smith, John W. A., and Warwick B. Elley. 1994. *Learning to Read in New Zealand.* Katonah, NY: Richard C. Owen.

Spinelli, Jerry. 2002. *Loser.* New York: HarperCollins.

Tovani, Cris. 2000. *I Read It, but I Don't Get It: Comprehension Strategies for Adolescent Readers.* Portland, ME: Stenhouse.

van den Broek, Paul, and Kathleen Kremer. 2000. "The Mind in Action: What It Means to Comprehend During Reading." In *Reading for Meaning: Fostering Comprehension in the Middle Grades,* ed. B. M. Taylor, M. F. Graves, and P. van den Broek. New York: Teachers College Press.

Vygotsky, Lev. 1978. *Mind in Society,* ed. M. Cole, V. John-Steiner, S. Scribner, and E. Souberman. Cambridge, MA: Harvard University Press.

Wigfield, Allan. 1997. "Children's Reading Motivations." In *NRRC News.* College Park: University of Maryland, National Reading Research Center.

Credits

Index

academic writing
  characteristics of, 123–24
  purposes of, 123
  support for, 127–28
accountable talk
  defined, 47
  environment for, 48–49
  fostering, 47–50
  modeling, 49
action verbs, 85
active learning, 48–49
Alao, Solomon, 54
Alexander, Patricia A., 74
Alike but Different form, 92, 93, 266
Allen, Janet, 20
Allington, Richard, 25, 31–32, 68, 104
alliteration, picture books for teaching, 233
"Alone" (Angelou), 162
Amandine (Griffin), 121
Amato, Mary, 94
"American History" (Harper), 97–98
analysis, assessment of, 74
Anderson, Laurie Halse, 2, 119
Angelou, Maya, 33, 130, 162, 191
Annotated Alice, The (Carroll), 4–5, 167
anticipation guides, 26
archy and mehitabel (Marquis), 133–34
art, shared reading resources, 207–8
assessment, 167–98. *See also* evaluation
  of analysis, 74
  of background knowledge, 159
  comprehension and, 180
  concerns about, 167–69
  of content literacy, 181–89

deadlines and, 169
defined, 169
evaluation *vs.*, 169, 171
of fluency and foundations, 171–75
generic exams on books, 163
guidelines for, 169–70
of language acquisition, 175
limiting, 169
multiple opportunities for, 169
ongoing, 169
scoring guides/rubrics, 170
specific, 170
of strategic reading skills, 72–74
test preparation, 194–97
of textbooks, 181–82
of word learning, 175–80
Assessment Tool form, 284–88
attention to reading, 55–56
audience, 120–23
audiobooks, 32
Authors' Insights (Gallo), 143
"Autobiography in 5 Short Chapters" (Nelson), 152–53
Avi, 123

background knowledge
  assessment of, 159
  building, for content inquiry, 97–101
  building, with Words in Context form, 26–27
  connecting to content from, 101–4
  content literacy and, 185
  free-writing about, 159
  supporting through multiple texts, 101
  word study and, 80–81, 91, 176
Bad (Ferris), 32–33, 191

Bailey, Ann, x, 11–12, 177–79
Bailey, John, x, 189–90
Baker, Scott, 77, 87, 109–10
"Ballad of Birmingham" (Randall), 162
"Bang, I Gotcha" (Holbrook), 41
Bauer, Marion Dane, 14
Bean, Thomas, 97
Beane, James, 165–66
"Beaten unconsciously: Violent images may alter kids' brain activity, spark hostility" (*USA Today*), 90–91
Beating the Odds: Teaching Middle and High School Students to Read and Write Well (Langer), 33–34
Becoming a Better Writer: Using Writers' Tools form, 279
Benitiz, Lori, x, 179–80
Berg, Elizabeth, 58–59
Bettlehein, Bruno, 22
Bible, 43
Big Books, 3
Bing, Bang, Boing (Florian), 88–89
Blachowicz, Camille, 110
Bless the Beasts and the Children (Swarthout), 2
book advertisements, student-created, 190
book choice. *See also* shared reading texts
  for accountable talk, 49
  critical characteristics, 11–23
  emotional experiences and, 14
  engagement and, 24–25
  expanding students' worlds through, 20–23